# The Politics of Pension Reform
*Institutions and Policy Change in Western Europe*

European pension systems are increasingly under pressure. In this book Giuliano Bonoli examines policy-makers' efforts to cope in a context where they are caught between public support for existing pension schemes and the expected inability to sustain current arrangements in the long run. The book explores the impact of formal institutions and decision-making procedures on welfare retrenchment and modernisation. It compares and assesses the process of pension policy-making in the UK, France and Switzerland, examining the factors that influence pension reform, and the relative impact upon the decision-making process of political parties and interest groups. The book provides a detailed description of new pension legislation and looks at the issues of demographic change, pension financing and likely developments on the wider European level. This analysis of pension reform will be of interest to policy-makers as well as students of the politics of the welfare state.

GIULIANO BONOLI is a Lecturer in Social Policy at the University of Fribourg, Switzerland.

# The Politics of Pension Reform
*Institutions and Policy Change in Western Europe*

Giuliano Bonoli
*University of Fribourg*

CAMBRIDGE
UNIVERSITY PRESS

PUBLISHED BY THE PRESS SYNDICATE OF THE UNIVERSITY OF CAMBRIDGE
The Pitt Building, Trumpington Street, Cambridge, United Kingdom

CAMBRIDGE UNIVERSITY PRESS
The Edinburgh Building, Cambridge CB2 2RU, UK    http://www.cup.cam.ac.uk
40 West 20th Street, New York, NY 10011–4211, USA    http://www.cup.org
10 Stamford Road, Oakleigh, Melbourne 3166, Australia
Ruiz de Alarcón 13, 28014 Madrid, Spain

First published 2000

Printed in the United Kingdom at the University Press, Cambridge

*Typeface* Plantin 10/12pt    *System* QuarkXPress™    [SE]

*A catalogue record for this book is available from the British Library*

*Library of Congress Cataloguing in Publication data*

Bonoli, Giuliano
    The politics of pension reform : institutions and policy change in Western
Europe / Giuliano Bonoli
        p.  cm.
    Includes bibliographical references and index.
    ISBN 0 521 77232 X (HB)    0 521 77606 6 (PB)
    1. Old age pensions – Government policy – Europe, Western – Case
studies.   2. Social security – Europe, Western – Case studies.   I. Title.

HD7105.35.E85  B66  2000
331.25′2′094 – dc21    99-087065

ISBN 0 521 77232 X hardback
ISBN 0 521 77606 6 paperback

# Contents

# Tables

# Acknowledgements

The research work on which this book is based has taken several years and has been carried out in various places, where I was lucky enough to benefit from the assistance of many friends and colleagues. This project started as a doctoral dissertation funded by the Department of Education of the Swiss canton of Ticino at the University of Kent at Canterbury. There I received much-appreciated guidance and encouragement from Vic George, who acted as supervisor for the study, and from Peter Taylor-Gooby, whose enthusiasm for academic research provided a constant source of inspiration. As external examiner, Roger Lawson helped transform what is usually a painful exercise into a pleasant and stimulating discussion.

The dissertation was finalised at the Institut des sciences sociales et pédagogiques, Unversity of Lausanne. There too I was able to count on the help of friends and colleagues for discussions, advice and diversion. I am particularly grateful to Sandro Cattacin, Olivier Giraud, Jean-Philippe Leresche, André Mach, François-Xavier Merrien, Yannis Papadopoulos and Juan-Francisco Perellon. I am also much indebted to my colleagues at the University of Bath, where I eventually completed this book: Ian Gough, Jane Millar, Theo Papadopoulos, Martin Powell and Graham Room. Throughout this project, I benefited from the advice and the encouragement of Jens Alber, Jochen Clasen, Maurizio Ferrera, John Myles, Paul Pierson and, especially, Bruno Palier. I hope that their influence on my thinking is visible in the pages that follow. Susi Pesko was there for most of the time, and her presence and support certainly made a difference.

Finally, at Cambridge University Press I am grateful to John Haslam for his encouragement, and to an anonymous reviewer for helpful comments and constructive criticism.

# Abbreviations

All Swiss abbreviations refer to the French version of the name. The English translations, as well as all translated text throughout the book, are by the author.

AVS          Assurance Vieillesse et Survivants (Swiss basic old age pension scheme)

CBI          Confederation of British Industry

CFDT          Confédération Française Démocratique des Travailleurs (French federation of trade unions)

CFE–CGC          Confédération Française de l'Encadrement–Confédération Générale des Cadres (French managers' association)

CFQF          Commission Fédérale pour les Questions Féminines (Swiss federal commission on women's issues)

CFTC          Confédération Française des Travailleurs Chrétiens (French federation of Catholic unions)

CGP          Commissariat Général au Plan (French planning commission)

CGPME          Confédération Générale des Petites et Moyennes Entreprises (French association of small and medium-sized businesses)

CGT          Confédération Générale du Travail (French federation of trade unions, close to the Communist Party)

CNAV          Caisse Nationale d'Assurance Vieillesse (French old age insurance fund)

CNPF          Conseil National du Patronnat Français (French association of employers)

CPAG          Child Poverty Action Group

CPS          Centre for Policy Studies

CSC          Confédération des Syndicats Chrétiens (Swiss federation of Christian unions)

CSG          Contribution Sociale Généralisée (French tax earmarked for social security)

| | |
|---|---|
| DHSS | Department of Health and Social Security (now Department of Social Security, DSS) |
| DTI | Department of Trade and Industry |
| EMU | European monetary union |
| FO | Force Ouvrière (French federation of trade unions) |
| FPTP | first-past-the-post (British electoral system) |
| FSV | Fonds de Solidarité Vieillesse (French old age solidarity fund) |
| GMP | guaranteed minimum pension |
| IEA | Institute of Economic Affairs |
| IoD | Institute of Directors |
| LFPR | labour force participation rates |
| NAPF | National Association of Pension Funds |
| OFAS | Office Fédéral des Assurances Sociales (Swiss federal office of social insurance) |
| OPB | Occupational Pension Board |
| PDC | Parti Democrate-Chrétien (Swiss Christian democratic party) |
| PRD | Parti Radical Démocratique (Swiss liberal democratic party) |
| PSS | Parti Socialiste Suisse (Swiss socialist party) |
| RATP | Régie Autonome des Transports Parisiens (Paris underground) |
| SERPS | State Earnings Related Pension Scheme |
| SNCF | Société Nationale des Chemins de Fer (French national railway company) |
| SSA | Social Security Act |
| TUC | Trades Union Congress |
| UDC | Union Démocratique du Centre (Swiss ex-farmers' party) |
| USS | Union Syndicale Suisse (Swiss federation of trade unions) |

# Introduction

The 1990s have been a decade of big changes for welfare states. The adaptation process which in the United States and in Britain started in the 1980s has become part of policy-making also in continental European countries. The main objective of reform is to restore the compatibility of social policies with the changing economic and demographic contexts. In most cases, this objective is pursued by retrenching existing social programmes. Welfare retrenchment, thus, is not any longer an Anglo-Saxon idiosyncrasy. Countries such as Sweden, France and Germany, in which social policies are widely praised and contribute to the structure of national identities, have all curtailed their welfare states in the last few years.

In both waves of retrenchment, pension schemes have been a privileged target of governments' attempts to reduce spending on welfare. Pensions generally constitute the largest single item of social expenditure, so that successful cost containment in this area of policy is particularly beneficial to governments' budgets. In addition, pensions are directly exposed to the twin pressures of economic and demographic change. Economic changes, like globalisation, are reducing governments' ability to generate revenues. On the other hand, population ageing is resulting in increased pension expenditure. This is a powerful incentive for governments to take action. It explains why pension reform has been high on the agenda in most advanced industrial countries over the last decade.

In general, however, continental European welfare states are proving to be less vulnerable to cuts than their Anglo-Saxon counterparts. One way to explain this is with reference to their higher degree of middle-class integration. The United States, and to a lesser extent Britain, were retrenching residual welfare states. In the United States, the losers of welfare reforms had little potential for political mobilisation, and were de facto unable to influence policy-making. In Britain, although the inclusiveness of welfare arrangements before the Thatcher decade was significantly stronger, a political system which concentrates power in the Cabinet helped to neutralise the effects of external opposition to cuts in welfare programmes.

1

Welfare retrenchment in continental Europe seems to be different. The higher levels of coverage and generosity of social programmes there make social policies meaningful to larger sections of the population, including politically influential middle-income voters. Either through informal mobilisation or threats of electoral punishment, pro-welfare interest groups have managed to maintain strong pressure on governments, and to moderate their retrenchment initiatives. In addition, few political systems in western Europe offer the same level of power concentration of the Westminster model. Instead, most of them provide veto points, which can be used by external groups to prevent the adoption of unwanted legislation. This is perhaps most clearly the case in Switzerland.

This book, in fact, originated from a comparison of welfare retrenchment in Britain and in Switzerland. In the early 1990s, Switzerland went through its worst economic downturn since 1945, and the neo-liberal ideas that had inspired the Thatcher reforms of the 1980s gradually gained ground among Swiss elites. Employers, the powerful banks and the political right wing were increasingly arguing in favour of a more radical approach in economic and social policy, based on lower social expenditure, a more flexible labour market, lower taxes and so forth. The conditions were ripe for a shift in public policy like the one experienced by Britain in the 1980s. Nevertheless, Swiss policy-makers had to operate in a substantively different political system with different political institutions.

In Switzerland, policy decisions are generally the result of compromises that are indirectly supported by some 80 per cent of the electorate. As political scientists have pointed out, this is not due to a particular listening attitude of Swiss policy-makers. Rather, it is the Swiss constitutional structure which makes provision for power-sharing and offers veto points, such as referendums, to unsatisfied minorities. The result is that Swiss governments have tended to incorporate potential dissent, in order to reduce the risk of being unable to get legislation accepted. For this reason, the legislative process in Switzerland is among the most lengthy in Europe, and innovative policies are rather unlikely. Typically, viable compromises can be achieved only via incremental change.

As policy-makers started embarking on a rethinking of the welfare state, it became clear that Swiss political institutions were going to constitute a formidable obstacle to the neo-liberal ambitions of economic and political elites. The sort of reforms they were advocating were unlikely to generate the level of consensus that is usually needed to legislate in that country. Reforms were likely to be unpopular with large sections of the electorate, and were thus at a high risk of defeat in referendums. A 'Thatcherite revolution' was probably impossible in the Swiss institutional context, but could policy change be achieved at all?

To try to answer this question was the initial stimulus for this study, which, in general, is more concerned with the impact of constitutional structures and political institutions on the process of welfare state adaptation. I chose to concentrate on the particular area of pensions because that is where such institutional effects are more likely to be visible. In most industrial countries, public pension schemes are widely supported by the population and have an impact on the lives of large sections of the electorate. As a result, pension reforms are likely to generate strong opposition. Those who oppose reform will tend to exploit institutional veto points where available. Arguably, this will make the institutional obstacle to retrenchment more visible. For it is not institutions *per se* that impede retrenchment. They can provide an opportunity to influence policy, but there needs to be a social group prepared to take up this opportunity; otherwise the potential impact of institutions on policy remains unnoticed.

Since the UK and Switzerland are two rather extreme versions of majoritarian and consensus democracy respectively, I decided to include in the analysis a third country, France. This is a country that is generally ranked close to Britain with regard to its government's ability to impose policy change. However, in the area of pension policy, the involvement of the trade unions in the management of social security and the strong level of public support enjoyed by the welfare state have contributed to reduce the extent of governmental control over policy-making. In addition, a division within the executive in the 1993–5 period further diminished the level of power concentration. The result was that, in that period, the French government was forced to accept compromises to a more substantial extent than is normally the case.

This book also aims to explain why given paths to pension reform are adopted in some countries but not in others. It argues that the political limits to welfare retrenchment are country-specific and that, as far as pensions are concerned, they depend on the interaction between political institutions and the design of pension schemes. The former provide opportunities to affect policy, the latter structure patterns of interests in relation to pension policy. Political institutions can generate veto points and opportunities to influence policy-making for external interests. Pension scheme design, in turn, affects the perception of actor's self-interests, and may or may not create opportunities for politically feasible reforms. The way in which these two institutional effects interact is likely to have a powerful influence on the direction of reform.

The first conclusion of this study is that governments committed to reform pensions, and operating in political systems which offer substantial veto points, are likely to pursue their retrenchment initiatives in combination with concessions targeted on key potential opponents, and that such strategies can work. In Switzerland, the inclusion of measures which had been demanded by the left and by the labour movement in a pension reform package managed to strengthen its electoral appeal. The reform was eventually accepted in a referendum. In France, a government weakened by a division within the executive and worried about an upcoming presidential election managed in 1993 to obtain the acquiescence of the most radical sections of the labour movement by including some carefully designed *quid pro quos*, which responded to long-standing demands of the trade unions.

The significance of this finding relates to the initial questions from which this study grew, i.e. whether fragmented political systems, such as Switzerland's, had the capacity to adopt politically difficult reforms in the areas of pension and social policy. In the case studies reviewed here, fragmented political systems did manage to secure the adoption of unpopular cuts in pensions, when these were combined with *quid pro quos* for key external actors. This suggests that welfare state adaptation is politically feasible in systems characterised by numerous veto points, but will be less unilateral and will tend to include retrenchment as well as improvements in provision.

This is not to claim that a focus on political institutions alone can produce predictions with regard to policy outcomes. By looking at these rules we can get a hint of how the positions of the various actors will be aggregated, but we can say little on the final outcome unless we know what each actor wants. Actors' preferences in pension policy, however, are structured to some extent by the institutional design of the relevant programme, so that a combined focus on political and pension institutions can improve the predictive capacity of this model.

This brings me to the second finding of this study, which refers to the existence of a common pattern of *quid pro quos* in pension reforms adopted in countries which have pension schemes of Bismarckian inspiration. In France, but also in Germany and in Italy, the recent pension reforms and the proposals for future policy change have tended to combine cuts in the generosity of the schemes with a restoration of the original character of pension policy. In particular, the non-contributory elements which were integrated in these schemes to achieve general social policy aims are being removed and taken on (including financially) by governments. In all three countries the separation of non-contributory and insurance-based benefits is a key demand of the trade unions, which typically regard social security as an insurance plan covering the entire working population, as opposed to an area of state policy. The inclusion of such measures in reform packages that are mainly concerned with reducing expenditure can secure trade union support, or at least acquiescence.

These institutional effects are likely to become more important in future, as the main political cleavage in social policy-making seems to be shifting from the left–right axis to an opposition between governments, to a large extent regardless of their political orientation, and a pro-welfare coalition of interest groups, which is often led by the labour movement. This has long been the case in France where the Socialist governments of the 1980s clashed with the unions on a number of occasions. As new left-of-centre governments have been voted into power in Europe, this shift in the dominant cleavage in the politics of social policy has become more evident. In Germany, Italy and, to a lesser extent, Britain, the left-of-centre governments of the late 1990s are committed to continue reforming their welfare states, and the main confrontation is between themselves and the labour movement. Economic conditions allow very narrow room for manoeuvre and as a result the left, even when in power, has little choice but to adopt retrenchment policies in the area of welfare.

If, as I argue, the main cleavage in social policy reform is shifting from the left–right axis to an opposition between governments and a pro-welfare coalition, then the institutional explanation of policy outcomes will acquire additional relevance and possibly replace the 'politics matter' thesis as one of the key approaches to social policy analysis. The degree of influence that pro-welfare interest groups have on policy depends to a large extent on the opportunities provided by the political institutions. Absence of veto points means that governments will be able to go much further in the restructuring of their welfare state. In contrast, political systems that offer veto points will find it more difficult to adapt their welfare states and pension systems to a changing economic and demographic environment. As a result, they will need to develop more sophisticated strategies to secure the adaptation of their welfare arrangements.

More generally, this book argues that, despite the emphasis in current research on public policy on institutional resistance to change, governments in different political systems have been able to devise specific strategies which managed to bring about substantial policy change. Carefully designed reform packages stand a good chance of being adopted even in fragmented political systems, but then lead to qualitatively different adaptation processes. Veto points can be neutralised by integrating potential opponents in policy-making, or by targeting some key concessions on them. After all, the landscape of social policy in Europe is perhaps not as frozen as it might seem. The new problems that have emerged in the 1990s have demanded a quick response, which most governments were unable to deliver. However, as learning processes begin to produce results, we might see an acceleration in the restructuring of the European welfare states.

The book begins by looking at the socio-economic pressures on pension schemes, in particular those related to demographic change. It provides a picture of the factual background against which current pension policy-making takes place (ch. 1). Next the focus moves to theory. The questions and the hypotheses which have been briefly presented in this introduction are spelt out in a more detailed manner, and they are related to some of the most influential views on social policy-making (ch. 2). There I put forward a model for the analysis of pension reform which focuses on political institutions as an independent variable of pension policy. Chapters 3 to 5 are accounts of the political processes that led to the adoption of pension reforms in Britain, Switzerland and France. As far as possible, I have tried to follow a similar structure in the presentation of the case studies. First, I look at the institutional and political context in which reforms have been adopted; second, I provide a description of the country's pension system; third, I concentrate on the pension policy-making process; and, finally, I focus on the link between what has been observed and the theoretical framework presented in chapter 2. Finally, chapter 6 highlights the key elements that emerge from the comparison of the case studies, and links them to the theoretical discussion of chapter 2.

# 1 Dimensions of the pension problem: institutions, economics and politics

The long-term sustainability of current pension arrangements is one of the major issues with which advanced industrial societies will have to deal over the next few decades. The projected increase in the size of the older population, combined with a reduction in the number of workers, constitutes a significant challenge to the viability of existing pension systems, which, according to many commentators, need to be substantially reformed. While these general views are widely accepted, there is little agreement as to what the actual size of the pension problem is now and will be in future. Those who have analysed the phenomenon have reached conclusions that range from apocalyptic scenarios in which, if nothing is done, the elderly will appropriate increasing large shares of national income with massive detrimental consequences for the welfare of younger generations (World Bank 1994a; Thurow 1996), to less pessimistic ones, in which the occurrence of an increase in pension expenditure is accepted as a likely development, but it is felt that this will not constitute a major economic problem (Johnson and Falkingham 1992; European Commission 1995).

The evidence reviewed in this chapter suggests that gloomy predictions of a 'demographic time bomb' have little credibility. However, it seems clear that, when the baby-boomers born after World War II reach retirement age, pension expenditure will increase quite dramatically over a relatively short period of time. Most likely, this will result in a financing problem.

What is more, concern for pension scheme finances has been heightened by recent economic and political developments. First, the ongoing process of economic internationalisation is putting pressure on governments to reduce, or not to increase, rates of taxation. To do otherwise would put the competitiveness of their national economies at risk, with potentially serious consequences for their countries' prosperity (Gough 1996; Rhodes 1996). Second, countries willing to participate in EMU need to respect a number of economic criteria. In particular, a government budget deficit higher than 3 per cent of GDP is not considered as acceptable. As a result, countries committed to joining and remaining in the European single currency (such as France, Germany or Italy) have been forced to take steps to reduce public expenditure. Pensions, generally the largest single item of social expenditure, are an obvious target for saving measures. These elements, combined with the threat of a substantial change in the demographic structure of the population, constitute a powerful pressure on governments to take action. In this study, the term 'pension problem' refers precisely to this series of pressures on pension policy.

This chapter discusses some of the aspects that contribute to defining the pension problem. Above all, it aims to establish what are the conditions in which the pension problem emerges and in which debates on the future of pensions take place, or, in other words, the factual background against which political actors operate. In this respect, it constitutes the basis on which to build an analysis of the politics of pension reform.

First, it provides an overview of provision for retirement in industrial countries. It looks at the differences between pension systems and at their origins. Starting points can be important for the course of reform, because, as is increasingly being recognised, they tend to channel developments and debates in some given directions. Second, it focuses on the socio-economic pressures that are likely to affect pension policy over the next few years. The discussion covers demographic and expenditure projections as well as the variation in the living standards of the retired population. This review of empirical evidence concludes that there are real pressures on governments to take action in the area of pension policy, in order to continue providing income security in old age. Third, the chapter looks at the main options for reform available to policy-makers. These are analysed mainly in relation to their economic effects, although it is clear that they have different implications in so far as politics is concerned. That is why the chapter concludes by making the case for an analysis of the politics of pension reform. Pension systems are highly sensitive distributional mechanisms. They transfer huge sums of money across generations, time, occupational groups, income groups, genders and so forth. Their distributional equilibrium reflects the power relationship between the different political actors who designed them. The result is that, once a settlement is reached, departures from it are likely to be extremely delicate exercises. In particular, when the objective of reform is to achieve savings, policy change is likely to create winners and losers. That is why pension policy in general and especially the recent pension reforms have been characterised by an impressive level of political controversy.

## 1.1     The institutional level: an overview of pension systems

As in other areas of social policy, there are substantial cross-country variations in pension systems,[1] even if the analysis is restricted to a fairly
homogeneous geo-political area, like western Europe. Similarity exists in
the sense that virtually all countries have legislated old age pension programmes. Beyond that, it becomes more difficult to find consistency
between different pension systems (Palme 1990: 147).

Several attempts to make sense of these variations have been made,
some of which are reviewed below. In particular, researchers have tried to
identify ideal-types of pension provision, which can be found in a more or
less pure form in a number of countries. To a large extent, this exercise
overlaps with the more general effort aimed at classifying welfare states, as
pensions typically constitute the largest social programme and are often
seen as the backbone of a welfare state.

The classification of welfare states in recent years has tended to revolve
around three types, or regimes (Esping-Andersen 1990), or four depending on whether or not one considers southern European welfare states to
constitute a distinctive category. This approach focuses mainly on the outcomes of social programmes, in terms of decommodification[2] and social
stratification. A socialist or social democratic regime is found in Nordic
countries. In this model, welfare arrangements (including pensions) cover
the whole population and perform a fair amount of vertical redistribution,
and access to benefits is less dependent on labour market participation
than is the case in other countries. A second model, referred to as
corporatist or conservative, is found in continental European countries.
The key social programmes cover the working population only and grant
earnings-related benefits which guarantee the maintenance of status
differentials at times of inactivity. Those who do not participate in the
labour market have to rely on often stigmatising social assistance schemes.
Finally, a liberal regime is found in English-speaking countries. Its most
distinctive characteristic is the preference for programmes targeted on the
poorest sections of the population. It reinforces social divisions because

---

[1] Throughout this study the notion of 'pension system' is used to designate the totality of
transfers to the older population which are either compulsory, provided by the state or
encouraged by legislation (e.g. through tax concessions). This excludes other sources of
income for the elderly such as earnings, private savings, social assistance and intra-family
transfers. A pension scheme, by contrast, is understood here as a single arrangement
which has the aim of providing income to older people. In virtually all industrial countries
pension systems consist of various pension schemes.

[2] Decommodification is defined as 'the degree to which individuals or families can uphold
a socially acceptable standard of living independently of market participation' (Esping-
Andersen 1990: 37).

the affluent have no stake in these programmes. In addition, since benefits are often very low, it does not constitute an alternative to individual provision. The existence of a fourth regime of southern European welfare states has been postulated (Leibfried 1992; Ferrera 1996b). Its key features are a highly fragmented income maintenance system with a strong emphasis on old age pensions, the persistence of clientelism and a stronger reliance on the family as an alternative to labour market participation.

While works aiming at classifying welfare states like Esping-Andersen's have tended to focus on outcomes, studies dealing only with old age pensions have typically concentrated on the institutional design of the various systems and on their evolution in a historical perspective. Reference is often made to two distinct models of pension provision which were introduced at the end of the nineteenth century in Germany, Denmark and New Zealand. In 1889, Germany instituted a pension scheme for industrial workers. The scheme was meant to guarantee retirees a level of income related to their earnings while in work. Denmark (1891) and New Zealand (1898), in contrast, introduced means-tested pension schemes targeted on the poor (Myles and Quadagno 1997; Overbye 1996a).

These two models of pension policy had two very different underlying objectives. In the German case, the scheme introduced by Bismarck was part of a political project aimed at containing the rise of the labour movement. The adoption of a pension scheme, as well as of other social programmes introduced more or less simultaneously, was meant to buy the allegiance of the rapidly emerging working class. As a matter of fact, Bismarckian social legislation was accompanied by laws which banned the political organisation of workers (Alber 1986: 5; Baldwin 1990: 59–65). Understandably, the schemes were confined to industrial workers, as other groups did not constitute a threat to social stability, and Bismarck had no immediate interest in improving their conditions. The Danish scheme, in contrast, did not have such an overt political aim. Its introduction constituted mainly a modernisation of the existing system of poor laws. Its objective was to alleviate poverty across the whole population (Baldwin 1990: 65–76). Given their different goals, the two original approaches to pension policy used different means as well. The German scheme was financed by contributions shared equally by employers and employees (with a state subsidy); it granted earnings-related benefits; and entitlement to a pension was based on having paid contributions. Its overall result was status maintenance in retirement. In Denmark, by contrast, the 1891 pension scheme was tax-financed and means-tested, and granted flat-rate benefits. As such, it continued in an ameliorated form the tradition of poor relief enshrined in the previous system of poor laws.

In subsequent years, other countries followed the example set by

Table 1.1 *Original model of pension policy in selected countries (first compulsory or comprehensive nation-wide scheme)*

| Social insurance (Bismarck) | Poverty prevention (Beveridge) |
| --- | --- |
| Germany 1889* | Denmark 1891 |
| Italy 1919* | New Zealand 1898 |
| France 1932* | UK 1908 |
| United States 1936 | Sweden 1913 |
| Switzerland 1948 | Norway 1936 |

*Note:* * for industrial employees only
*Source:* Adapted from Overbye 1996a.

Germany and Denmark. In general, the German lead was followed in continental Europe. In France this came as a result of the re-annexation of Alsace and Lorraine after World War I. As these two regions had been part of Germany before the war, they already had a compulsory system of social insurance. This was extended to the rest of France in 1930 (Saint Jours 1982: 95). In Italy a compulsory pension scheme, covering industrial employees only, was introduced in 1919 (Artoni and Zanardi 1997). Switzerland was a latecomer, as a compulsory pension scheme at the federal level was introduced only in 1948 (see ch. 4). In contrast, the Danish (and New Zealand) model was followed in other Nordic countries (Salminen 1993), though with some variations, and in other English-speaking countries (such as the UK in 1908), with the notable exception of the United States, which in 1936 introduced an earnings-related scheme closer to the Bismarckian tradition (Overbye 1996a). Table 1.1 shows the initial choices in the area of pension provision in a number of countries.

These two initial models of pension provision can also be seen as ideal-types in the analysis of past and current developments in pension policy. In fact the distinction between the two is often used to classify pension schemes and systems. In the literature, different terms are found in relation to these two models; however, perhaps somewhat anachronistically,[3]

[3] In fact, as the above discussion shows, the schemes that are commonly referred to as 'Beveridgean' were introduced well before the publication of the Beveridge report of 1942. In addition, in its predominant use in comparative social policy, the word 'Beveridgean' refers to tax-financed schemes, which is in contrast with Beveridge's preference for contribution financing (Silburn 1995: 92–3). This peculiar understanding of the term 'Beveridgean' in comparative social policy probably developed because of the focus on the overall objective of Beveridgean social policy – poverty prevention – rather than on the instruments he suggested using (see also Bonoli 1997a).

the two traditions can be conveniently labelled with reference to Bismarck and Beveridge, two key figures in the development of modern welfare states who had very different motives for their actions. The Beveridge plan, in fact, set out to achieve 'freedom from want' and as such it was consistent with the objectives of the Danish and New Zealand social reformers. As seen above, Bismarck was worried more about social stability in the context of rapid industrialisation and the rise of the labour movement.

Like all classifications, the one presented here is a crude simplification of the real world. In fact, other authors have suggested more complex ways of categorising pension schemes. Some (Ferrera 1993b; Overbye 1996b) further distinguish between (Bismarckian) insurance programmes which cover the whole population of a country (Switzerland, United States) and those in which different groups are covered by different arrangements (Germany, France, Italy). Niemelä and Salminen (1995) have put forward a four-type classification, which uses the basis of entitlement to discriminate between pension schemes (instead of the objective). The result is a categorisation in which pension schemes are grouped according to whether entitlement depends on citizenship, social condition (need), employment or private contract. The approach is not too dissimilar from the one reviewed above, the main difference being the distinction between means-tested and universal schemes and the introduction of private schemes.

While most countries initiated pension policy by adopting one or the other model discussed above, the overall trend in subsequent years, but in particular after World War II, has been towards a convergence in pension provision (Chassard and Quintin 1992; Overbye 1996a). In general, the first step taken in either of the two 'worlds' was to expand provision so as to cover larger shares of the population. In Bismarckian countries, this was done by progressively including other occupationally defined groups into the existing social insurance system. In 1911 Germany introduced a new scheme for white-collar employees, and one for farmers in 1957. In France, the *régime général*, which was meant to cater for the whole population, was set up in 1946 (see ch. 5). In Italy additional compulsory schemes for farmers, non-industrial employees and the self-employed were created throughout the 1950s and 1960s. In addition, with the notable exception of Germany, countries which initially followed the Bismarckian lead, such as France, Italy, Switzerland and the United States, introduced income-tested pensions, either within the insurance system or as additional schemes to provide for those who did not have a sufficient contribution record to afford them an adequate pension.

A similar trend towards enlargement in pension coverage can be observed in countries that started with means-tested pensions, which were expanded into universal schemes. In most countries this occurred after World War II. In the Nordic countries expansion took the form of a citizenship pension (Salminen 1993), while in the UK the same goal was achieved through a contributory scheme, which, because it grants flat-rate benefits that are below the social assistance level, remains closer to the Beveridgean ideal-type than to the Bismarckian one. Because universal flat-rate benefits were rather low, especially for those on relatively high incomes, the post-war period saw a rise in occupational provision in these countries. In some countries, like Sweden and the UK, supplementary earnings-related coverage was made compulsory for employees.

In most countries, the result of convergence has been a two-tiered pension system, in which a basic pension aims at guaranteeing a subsistence level to the whole population, while the second tier allows retirees to maintain a living standard close to the one they had while working (Chassard and Quintin 1992; Overbye 1996b). The notion of convergence seems accurate to describe developments in the functions fulfilled by pension systems. The guarantee of a minimum income combined with a partial replacement of earnings is a common feature to almost all pension systems. The exceptions are Germany, which does not guarantee a minimum pension, and Denmark which does not include a compulsory earnings-related element in its pension system.

Convergence, thus, has occurred mainly with regard to the functions of pension policy (poverty prevention and income maintenance). However, when analysis shifts from the functions to the details of the various components of pension systems, the variation that can be observed across industrialised countries is still impressive. Important differences exist with regard to benefit formulas, source of financing (taxation or contributions), financing method (funded or pay-as-you-go) and in the roles played by private and occupational provision. In general, the initial choice in terms of the Bismarck or the Beveridge model still affects the current shape of a pension system.

The institutional features of pension systems are important, as they can affect both the extent of the pension problem and the likely path to reform. Depending on the rules that govern pension provision, the impact of population ageing on pension expenditure can be magnified or reduced. These rules, moreover, are likely to affect the economic adequacy and the political appeal of the various possible measures that can be used to contain pension expenditure. In this respect, pension scheme design constitutes an important independent variable of pension policy.

## 1.2    The economic debate: ageing, pension financing and pensioners' welfare

Debates on the present and future of pension policy usually make reference to three different socio-economic developments which are likely to affect the financial viability of pension schemes. First, demographic ageing, or the increase of the proportion of older people in the total population, constitutes an ever present background to any discussion on pension policy and pension reform. According to currently available projections, in industrial countries, particularly in Europe, the population age structure is expected to change dramatically over the next fifty years as a result of a decline in birth rates, an increase in life expectancy and a reduction in the scale of migration, with possible consequences on the financial viability of pension schemes. Second, pension schemes' receipts and outlays depend on a number of developments in the sphere of production. In particular, increases in productivity and increases in labour market participation rates can have a substantial impact on the financing side of pension schemes, and possibly offset the negative effects of demographic change. These developments, which cannot be predicted with any accuracy, are nonetheless crucial in any discussion on the viability of pension schemes. Third, particularly in English-speaking countries, there is growing concern with regard to notions of intergenerational equity. It is assumed that the older population today constitutes a relatively affluent group in society. As population ageing will increase this group's financial requirements, it is considered fair that the elderly contribute to solve this problem, possibly by accepting reductions in pension expenditure and in their living standards (Longman 1987; Thurow 1996; for a critical discussion, see Quadagno 1989 and Walker 1994).

These demographic and economic variables constitute the overall background against which debates on the future of pensions and policy changes take place. They are the starting point of virtually any discussion on pension policy. Possibly because they are characterised by a significant degree of uncertainty, they can also be instruments in the hands of political actors aiming at redefining existing distributional equilibria in the area of old age pensions. In this respect it is important, prior to any discussion on the politics of pension reform, to establish what the reality of these variables is. On the basis of studies carried out by international agencies, this section will try to provide a picture of the socio-economic component in the pension debate.

Table 1.2 *Population over sixty-five as a percentage of total population in selected countries*

|             | 1995 | 2000 | 2010 | 2020 | 2030 | 2035 |
|-------------|------|------|------|------|------|------|
| France      | 14.5 | 15.5 | 16.3 | 20.2 | 23.3 | 24.3 |
| Germany     | 15.2 | 16.2 | 20.2 | 22.5 | 28.1 | 30.6 |
| Sweden      | 17.5 | 16.5 | 18.4 | 20.4 | 23.1 | 23.8 |
| Switzerland | 15.1 | 15.8 | 19.1 | 23.3 | 27.5 | 28.8 |
| UK          | 15.8 | 15.9 | 17.0 | 19.7 | 23.0 | 24.6 |
| USA         | 12.6 | 12.5 | 13.6 | 17.5 | 21.8 | 22.8 |

*Source:* World Bank 1994b.

### Demographic change

There is relatively widespread agreement among demographers about the fact that the proportion of older people in western societies is going to increase over the next decades. This is the result of recent trends in fertility rates, which have been declining since the 1960s, and in life expectancy, which has constantly increased since World War II. As table 1.2 shows, population projections produced by international agencies tend to confirm this view. However, they also highlight the existence of substantial differences between countries in the expected transition pattern.

The World Bank demographic projections reproduced in table 1.2 show the various patterns of expected demographic change in some industrial countries. While all countries will experience an increase in the proportion of older people, the demographic transition is expected to be more severe in Germany and Switzerland, where it is expected that by 2035 the older population will make up about 30 per cent of the total population. In contrast, in the United States, and to a lesser extent in the UK, Sweden and France, the transition seems to be less dramatic. In all countries, however, the demographic structure of the population around the year 2030 is likely to be very different from what it is at present. This is likely to have substantial policy implications, particularly in the area of pensions.

On the other hand, it is certain that these projections have to be looked at with caution, particularly when they refer to long-term developments. What they say depends on assumptions made on the likely developments of three key variables which can be fairly volatile and difficult to predict – fertility rates, life expectancy, migration – and the current age structure. Demographic projections are particularly sensitive to assumptions made with regard to future fertility rates,[4] as this determines the size of the new generations that feed into the age pyramid and over time affect the size of the different age groups. Fertility rates, however, are also particularly difficult to predict (Johnson and Falkingham 1992: 21; OECD 1988a: 16). The overall trend in fertility rates in western countries has been one of decline for the past century. However, after World War II there was an upswing in fertility, followed by a decline since the 1960s. There are a number of factors behind these developments. Economic expectations are usually considered to be the main determinant of people's decisions with regard to having children (Ermisch 1983). Nevertheless, it seems clear that other factors have played an important role in recent developments in fertility, and are likely to do so in future. The availability of contraception, the increased participation of women in the labour market and the character and scale of family policies are all factors that have probably influenced recent trends in fertility.

The World Bank's and OECD's population projections are based on the assumption that fertility rates will remain constant until 2005 and that they will then gradually increase and converge (on 2.1) in 2030. Similar assumptions are made by other agencies as well. However, recent developments, particularly in the Nordic countries, suggest that fertility rates may be more volatile than expected. For instance, in the case of Sweden, fertility increased from 1.6 in 1983 to 2.1 in 1990, but dropped back to 1.6 in 1996 (Calot and Sardon 1996). The upswing has been explained with reference to Sweden's work-friendly family polices, such as free child care and generous maternity leave, as a result of which Swedish women do not experience a trade-off between work and motherhood like many of their continental European counterparts (Esping-Andersen 1996b: 78). On the other hand, the recession of the 1990s and the fact that the generosity of the Swedish welfare state is increasingly being questioned are possibly the reasons behind the recent decline in fertility (Calot and Sardon 1996).

Changes in life expectancy, unless they are substantial, have a smaller impact on the age structure of a population, as they affect only the upper end of the age pyramid (Johnson and Falkingham 1992: 21). In addition, trends in life expectancy seem relatively easy to predict. In general, life expectancy has increased gradually in the past and can be expected to continue along the same lines (OECD 1988a: 16). The World Bank's population projections assume an increase in life expectancy at birth of about five years between 1995 and 2035. With regard to the problem of

---

[4] The fertility rate is defined as the number of children per women in the reproductive age range (fifteen to forty-five).

pension financing, however, what matters is not life expectancy at birth, but at the age of retirement. A study looking at twelve European Union countries has shown that the two can be quite different. Since the end of World War II, increases in life expectancy at the age of sixty accounted for less than 50 per cent of the total increase in life expectancy for men, and for about 25 per cent for women (Sturm 1992: 24). This suggests that the impact of increases in life expectancy on the relative size of the older population will not be as substantial as that of developments in fertility.

Finally, migration can also have a substantial impact on the age structure. Nevertheless, in so far as the economic impact of population ageing is concerned, migration is not likely to play an important role. In Europe, in fact, high levels of immigration occurred at times of labour shortage, which is not the case at present. Labour shortage is likely to occur only if there is a dramatic upswing in economic activity, which would by itself considerably reduce the difficulties involved in coping with population ageing.

In sum, there seems to be a relatively high degree of uncertainty with regard to long-term population age structure projections. Since the fertility rate is the most relevant factor and yet the most difficult to predict, projections are reliable only if they look at the generations who have already been born. For instance, the ratio between the above-retirement-age population and the working-age population is not going to be affected by changes in fertility for the next fifteen to twenty years, i.e. until when today's new-borns are going to enter the labour market. Current projections of the population above fifteen to twenty years of age, thus, should be considered as relatively reliable until around 2015. Beyond this time-horizon it is extremely difficult to produce useful projections. With regard to the next two decades, however, we can say that most countries will almost certainly see an increase in the relative size of the retired population. This development is likely to have an impact on the financial viability of pension systems.

### Projecting pension expenditure

Age structure projections provide only one element for the assessment of the future viability of retirement systems. In fact, a number of other factors will affect receipts and outlays of pension schemes, the most important of which are increases in productivity and changes in labour force participation rates. The projections given in table 1.3 take these factors into account, assuming that current pension legislation is applied consistently throughout the relevant period. Variations reflect the differences in the expected pattern of demographic ageing as seen in

Table 1.3 *Projected public pension expenditure as a percentage of GDP in selected countries, 1995–2060*

|             | 1995 | 2000 | 2010 | 2020 | 2030 | 2040 | 2050 | 2060 |
|-------------|------|------|------|------|------|------|------|------|
| France      | 10.6 | 9.8  | 9.7  | 11.6 | 13.5 | 14.3 | 14.5 | 14.2 |
| Germany     | 11.1 | 11.5 | 11.8 | 12.3 | 16.5 | 18.4 | 17.5 | 16.5 |
| Sweden      | 11.8 | 11.1 | 12.4 | 13.9 | 15.0 | 14.9 | 14.5 | 14.8 |
| Switzerland | 6.8  | 7.1  | 8.4  | 9.0  | 11.7 | 12.0 | N/A  | N/A  |
| UK          | 4.5  | 4.5  | 5.2  | 5.1  | 5.5  | 5.0  | 4.1  | 3.6  |
| USA         | 4.1  | 4.2  | 4.5  | 5.2  | 6.6  | 7.1  | 7.0  | 7.4  |

*Source:* Roseveare *et al.* 1996: 17; data for Switzerland: author's own calculations based on World Bank 1994b and the same assumptions as in Roseveare *et al.* 1996 (see text).

table 1.2. This means that expenditure projections depend to a large extent on the assumptions made for demographic projections. However, the degree of variation here is even more substantial than in the simple demographic projections. While Germany is expected to reach expenditure levels of around 18 per cent of GDP in 2040, France and Sweden are forecast to spend around 14–15 per cent of GDP in the same year. In this comparison, the most striking case is the UK, where public pension expenditure is expected to remain at around the current level of 5 per cent of GDP until 2040, and then start declining.

Like age structure forecasts, projections of pension expenditure and financing should be looked at with caution. First, as seen above, there is little certainty on the validity beyond the year 2015 of the demographic projections on which they are based. Second, in order to produce expenditure projections one needs to make additional assumptions on variables which are extremely difficult to predict in the long term, such as labour force participation rates (LFPRs), increases in productivity and the extent to which such increases will be reflected in pension scheme outlays.

The OECD projections reproduced in table 1.3 are based on the assumption that LFPRs will remain constant after the year 2000. This might turn out to be too pessimistic, as recent developments in labour force participation suggest that we might see an expansion of LFPRs over the next few decades. There are two reasons for this. First, there are considerable variations in LFPRs in Europe. To a large extent this is due to differences in women's involvement in the labour market, and current trends seem to suggest that women's involvement in paid work will increase in future, especially in countries where it is comparatively low (Schmähl 1990: 167). Second, the demographic transition is expected, in some countries at least, to imply a significant reduction in the size of the working-age population. If this trend is not accompanied by a corresponding reduction in labour demand, it is likely that LFPRs will increase and absorb part of the currently unemployed population. As the baby-boomers retire after 2005, they will free up more jobs for younger generations, so that the unemployment rate might decline and the proportion of the population employed might increase correspondingly.

A second important assumption refers to increases in productivity and to the extent to which these increases are reflected in benefits and on contribution/taxation revenues. The OECD projections reported above assume an increase in productivity of 1.5 per cent per annum. How much of this increase will be reflected in pension benefits and contribution/taxation revenues depends on national pension and tax legislation. In countries such as the UK, where increases in wages have almost no impact on benefits (with the exception of SERPS; the basic pension is flat-rate and indexed according to prices), increases in productivity have a substantial positive impact on the country's ability to finance pensions. In contrast, in countries like France or Italy, where benefits are earnings-related, part of the increase in productivity will result in an increase in benefits. In addition, if pension schemes are financed only through employment-related contributions (France), it is also important to know whether the increase in productivity is reflected in wages, as it does not otherwise contribute to the financing of pensions. With regard to France, one study has shown that between 1970 and 1993 the growth rate of wages was close to that of GDP. However, between 1970 and 1976 wages rose faster than GDP, between 1976 and 1981 they increased roughly at the same rate, but since 1981 salaries have risen significantly slower than GDP, on average by 1 percentage point per year (de Foucault 1994: 8). If this trend persists, increases in productivity might not be particularly helpful in paying for future pensions.

Overall, expenditure projections are useful to the extent that they provide a picture of the likely trend that pension expenditure is going to follow in a given country, although they are too uncertain to give a reliable measurement of the actual size of pension expenditure at any given time. In this respect, what one can conclude on the basis of the OECD projections is that there will be an increase in pension expenditure over the next few decades, and that such an increase will be more dramatic in some countries than in others. Beyond that, we enter an area of uncertainty in which data cannot be used as a basis for policy decisions. What is important, however, is that these trends are generally regarded by governments as a compelling reason for reforming their pension systems. In addition, even if there are going to be substantial increases in productivity over the next few decades, the political and distributional sides of the pension problem might nevertheless remain topical. As noted in an earlier OECD report, 'the shift in the demographic structure is manageable even assuming a quite moderate rise in real income, but then requires a major redistribution of resources between generations' (OECD 1988b: 41). This means that the future viability of pension systems will depend also on the willingness of the working population to share part of its income with retirees. To some extent their support for public pension schemes is likely to depend on the way in which they look at the retired population and on their notions of appropriateness in relation to pension provision.

*Pensioners' living standards and the debate on generational equity*

If the effectiveness of old age policy is measured by the extent to which the living standards of older people have improved over the years, state intervention in the area of pensions has been a success story in most countries. It is widely accepted that during the post-war period pensioners as a whole have moved from being a relatively deprived group in society to one enjoying conditions of relative affluence. This is a result of the overall expansion in pension provision that has taken place over the last fifty years in western European countries. Public schemes have become more generous and coverage has been extended. In OECD countries between 1960 and 1985 expenditure on old age pensions as a proportion of GDP increased by 146 per cent, mainly as a result of changes in eligibility and in the level of benefits (OECD 1988b: 26). In addition, in almost all western European countries, there has been an important expansion of occupational pensions, and more recently of private plans, as a result of which the overall intergenerational transfer has increased over the years.

The relatively favourable economic situation enjoyed by many older people, combined with the concern associated with the expected increase in the proportion of elderly people in industrial societies, has sparked a debate on the issue of fairness and equity in intergenerational transfers. OECD studies show that, because of differences in cohort size and in pension contribution rates, some generations end up being net contributors to the state system while others are net beneficiaries. The debate is not confined to pensions, but it covers other areas in which expenditure is related to age (such as health care and social care) as well as the debt policy of a government. A recent OECD report summed up the results of a comparative study as follows: 'The calculation reveals generational imbalances in favour of living generations. If policies do not change generations that are born after the base year 1993 are likely to have a significantly greater tax burden than present generations' (OECD 1995: 38).

These considerations have entered political debates, mainly in English-speaking countries and particularly in the United States. It has been argued that older people are enjoying an affluent retirement at the expense of current working generations, and particularly of the young who are having to put up with squeezes in education budgets needed to finance public pensions and other social programmes (Thurow 1996). The policy implication of this analysis is that radical steps to contain and possibly reduce pension expenditure must be taken now, in order to redress the unfairness brought about by the substantial growth in pension provision over the past decades. From an economic point of view, the affluent status of older people allows room for manoeuvre to politicians to achieve substantial savings.

Existing studies on the living standards of older people support the overall claim that pensioners are better off now than they were in the past, and that they can be considered as a relatively affluent group in society. These overall trends, however, conceal country variations, and, within countries, differences between income groups. The evidence provided by the EU Observatory on older people in Europe in the late 1980s highlights the persistence of poverty among the elderly despite an overall improvement in their living conditions: 'Despite generally rising living standards and the achievement of high net replacement ratios in some member states, the national reports reveal a continuing poverty problem among a minority of older people, with the size of the minority varying considerably between countries' (Walker 1993: 16).

Using national definitions of poverty (typically people living at or below the social assistance level), Walker identifies three groups of countries. The first group includes countries which have poverty rates below 10 per cent: Denmark, Luxembourg, Ireland and Germany. Second, France, the Netherlands, the UK and Belgium have medium poverty rates which range between 10 and 30 per cent. Finally a third group includes the southern European welfare states for which it is difficult to find reliable information, though it seems that poverty rates are most likely to be relatively high (Walker 1993: 16–18).

These findings are broadly confirmed by other cross-national studies on the living standards of older people. In a comparison of the effectiveness of income transfers in ten welfare states, Mitchell (1991) found relatively high poverty rates among older people in Switzerland (18.6 per cent) and in the UK (15.6 per cent). Much more successful in eradicating poverty among the older population were France (poverty rate of 1.4 per cent) and Sweden (0.0 per cent).[5] Whiteford and Kennedy (1995) also found persistently fairly high rates of poverty among older people in a number of countries. This is particularly the case in the United States (34.0 per cent among single older people) and, to a lesser extent, in Germany (11. 5 per cent). These studies clearly highlight the existence of substantial differences in older people's living standards in virtually all countries, and of variably large sections of the older population having disposable incomes lower than commonly accepted poverty lines.

Differences in living standards of elderly people are to a large extent related to gender. A study by Rake (1996) covering France, Germany and the UK has found that, in all three countries, male-headed one-person households and two-person households fare far better than female-headed one-person households, though in France this occurs to a lesser extent than in Germany or in the UK. In addition, in all three countries, elderly women rely more on state pensions and in particular on means-tested provision than their male counterparts. In contrast, male pensioners and couples receive a bigger proportion of their income from occupational pensions or investment. Gender-based income inequality among older people, in part, reflects income inequality which exists in the labour market and women's longer life expectancy. However, it also reflects the fact that the assumptions on which most pension schemes are based usually imply continuous careers, which are more rarely found among women than among men. Moreover, in countries where occupational and private pensions are widespread, women are less often covered by these additional arrangements. In Britain, for instance, only a quarter of those who have taken out a personal pension are women (ibid.: 10). In Switzerland occupational pensions cover virtually the totality of male but only around 80 per cent of female employees. Occupational pensions are compulsory only above a certain earnings level which, because of lower wages and stronger reliance on part-time work, is more rarely exceeded by women.

This brief summary of evidence concerning the living standards of older people suggests that it is misleading to treat the elderly as a homogeneous group in discussions regarding income distribution, as the differences within that group are more important than the difference between the active population and older people. This has important consequences for the debate on intergenerational equity. As Johnson and Falkingham put it, 'Any discussion of intergenerational conflict for

---

[5] Poverty rates refer to the proportion of single people aged over sixty-five with incomes below 50 per cent of average national disposable income (Mitchell 1991: 68).

welfare resources establishes a false dichotomy as economic inequality within age groups is greater than between age groups' (1992: 59).

The vision of an affluent generation of pensioners enjoying good life at the expense of hard-pressed younger workers is not supported by the available evidence. As a result, the claim that the prosperity currently enjoyed by older people would allow for a radical reduction in inter-generational transfers without serious social consequences does not seem convincing. In contrast, the relatively good standards of living enjoyed by many pensioners are extremely fragile and for most of them dependent on the quality of state provision. Arguably, there are no painless solutions to the pension problem. Any shift in the current distributional equilibrium is likely to generate substantial controversy. At the same time, however, the room for manoeuvre available to governments is limited.

## 1.3     Options for reform

The 1990s have witnessed the emergence of pension reform as a major issue in virtually all industrial countries. This is not only a result of the expected demographic transition. In general, low rates of economic growth and high unemployment have affected pension schemes' receipts. In addition, in a number of countries, governments have responded to rising numbers of jobless people by allowing older workers to pre-retire (this is especially the case in France and Germany). The combined effect of these two trends has been a swift worsening in pension schemes' budgets, which has put pressure on governments to act. In this respect, pension reforms can also be seen as a reaction to an immediate economic situation rather than the anticipation of expected changes in the popula-tion's demographic structure.

Over the past few years, a majority of western European countries have taken steps to reform their public pension schemes. Generally, these changes consisted of reductions in the generosity and/or the scope of public pensions, with a view to reducing current and future expenditure. The measures adopted vary quite substantially across countries. For instance, they range from the introduction of incentives for individuals to provide privately for their retirement, to increases in pensionable age, or changes to the indexation mechanisms of existing pensions. On occasion, more complex measures have been taken, which affect the pension formula in various ways, generally with the effect of reducing the average level of benefits. This section provides a review of the most commonly mentioned measures which can reduce or contain pension expenditure. Some of them have been used in various combinations by different coun-tries, while others remain abstract proposals. To some extent the list below can be seen as the repertoire of measures from which policy-makers can select the solutions which best meet their economic and political needs.

### Shifting financing from pay-as-you-go to funding

There is a relatively widespread consensus among international agencies that the way forward in pension policy lies with an expansion of funded financing.[6] This should be achieved through the development of a multi-tiered pension system, in which the state provides a basic level of income security only, with the other functions of a pension system catered for by the private sector (OECD 1994; World Bank 1994a). In most western European countries, the introduction of such a system means a radical reduction in the generosity of pay-as-you-go public pension schemes, which provide earnings-related benefits most often far above the subsistence level, and an expansion of funded private pension schemes.

Critics of this approach have argued that a shift from pay-as-you-go to funding in pension policy would not improve a country's ability to cope with the demographic transition. The size of the intergenerational transfer would be the same; the only difference would be in the mechanisms that produce this transfer. In a pay-as-you-go scheme, it is the tax system. In a funded scheme, it is the sale of assets plus the returns to the invested capital (Johnson and Falkingham 1992; Gilliand 1988). This argument holds only if the funds accumulated by funded schemes are invested within the country where the pensioners live. If this is not the case, then foreign workers are going to contribute to financing the living expenses of retired population. This fact might acquire some relevance if pension funds invest in Third World countries, which have a more favourable age structure. In this case, the shift in the generational balance might be countered by having younger workers in Third World countries support ageing western populations.

In addition, while in a closed economy the macro-economic impact of ageing is not affected by the funding method of pensions, from a micro-economic point of view, the difference can be quite substantial. The revenue side of a pay-as-you-go system, especially if financed by employment-related contributions, is more sensitive to variations in aggregate wages than to changes in GDP. As seen above, increases in GDP are not always reflected in wages, which means that increases in national income

---

[6] In a pay-as-you-go pension scheme, current benefits are financed by current contributions. In contrast, in a funded one, current contributions are set aside and invested in order to finance the future retirement of current contributors. In general, public schemes are of the pay-as-you-go type, while private ones are funded.

might be of little use to the financing of pensions. A deterioration in the dependency rate means that a higher proportion of workers' earnings will have to be used to finance current expenditure on pensions. In contrast, in a funded scheme, older people become capital owners, and live on the profits produced by the capital they own, plus the revenue produced by selling it to the working generations who will retire later on, and so forth. In this way two components of GDP, wages and profits, are contributing to the financing of pensions.

On the other hand, funded schemes have the disadvantage of being more sensitive to inflation. In the UK, in the late 1970s and early 1980s the erosion of savings for retirement was a major concern for policy-makers. In addition, pension funds are also sensitive to fluctuations in capital markets. It has been pointed out that an excessive reliance on funding combined with population ageing might actually contribute to these fluctuations. When the large baby-boom cohorts reach retirement age, they will be selling their assets, and thus exert a downward pressure on asset value (Johnson and Falkingham 1992: 148). The result might be that defined-benefit schemes might be unable to meet their obligations whereas defined-contribution ones will end up paying lower than expected pensions[7] (ibid.; Ermisch 1990: 47).

A more immediate problem involved in shifting from pay-as-you-go to funded financing of pension is the issue of 'double payment' for current workers (Pierson 1997b). The current working generation would be required to continue financing the retirement of the older population through the pay-as-you-go system, but at the same time it would have to start saving for its own old age. If the pay-as-you-go schemes were discontinued, this would leave large numbers of older people without coverage. The double payment issue is a formidable obstacle to the shift in the financing method. A limited expansion of funded provision is possible, but workers who are already making substantial contributions to the pay-as-you-go system cannot be expected to fully fund their own retirement. In the late 1990s, some countries which relied almost exclusively on pay-as-you-go financing, such as France and Italy, have expanded funded provision through the introduction of tax incentives. This movement, however, has been rather limited and private provision remains voluntary.

---

[7] In defined-benefit schemes, the amount of the pension is expressed as a percentage of a salary (final or the average of a given number of years). This level is guaranteed regardless of the performance of the invested capital. In contrast, in defined-contribution schemes, there is no guaranteed level for pension benefits, which depend entirely on the amount paid in contributions and the interest earned on that amount.

*Increasing the age of retirement*

A very effective way to improve prospects for pension financing is to raise the age of retirement. This measure increases revenues, because it increases the size of the working population by retaining older workers, and decreases expenditure by reducing the number of beneficiaries. Unsurprisingly, increases in retirement age have been adopted or are under discussion in a majority of industrial countries. In countries which had different retirement ages for men and women, it is generally the latter who have seen delay in their pensionable age (United Kingdom, Switzerland).

The obvious downside of increases in the age of retirement is the impact on the labour market. First, this will delay the replacement of older workers at a time when young people are finding it difficult to enter and remain in the labour market. Second, in many sectors of the economy, older workers are increasingly seen as unable to deliver the productivity and flexibility levels demanded by current levels of competitiveness. As a result, measures which might prevent employers from using retirement or early retirement as a measure of human resource management might have a detrimental impact on a country's economic competitiveness.

*Targeting of benefits*

Given the big variations in living standards that exist among older people, it may be argued that state provision should be limited to an income- or means-tested pension which would be paid only to those who have been unable to build up a sufficient amount of savings to finance their own retirement. In fact, various forms of income-testing have been adopted in countries with flat-rate tax-financed basic pension schemes (Australia, Canada, Denmark and New Zealand; see Myles and Quadagno 1997: 256). This option, however, is not available when reforming Bismarckian pension schemes, which provide contributory earnings-related schemes. In these countries (Germany, France, Italy) the entitlement to a pension gained through the payment of contribution is regarded as a near-property right. Besides, the targeting of pension benefits creates the risk of moral hazard. Workers might perceive the availability of a means- or income-tested pension as a disincentive to save for their own retirement (Dilnot 1997).

*Changes in the benefit formula*

To change the formula for the calculation of benefits is probably the most straightforward way to achieve savings in pension expenditure in earnings-related schemes (Myles and Quadagno 1997). There are three variables which determine the amount of a pension: the reference salary, the qualifying period and the accrual factor. Governments can influence pension expenditure by changing any of these variables. The reference salary generally varies between career earnings and earnings in a number of 'best years'. In general, governments have tended to extend the relevant period for the calculation of the reference salary to the whole career of a worker (Italy, Sweden). The qualifying period refers to the number of contribution-years that are required in order to be entitled to a full pension. In most countries, the qualifying period is forty years, although some (Austria, Switzerland) require forty-five years of paid contributions for a full pension. Finally, the accrual factor is the proportion of the relevant earnings that is replaced by a pension per contribution-year. Typically, accrual factors are set between 1 and 2. Accrual factors can also be reduced in order to achieve savings.

*Changes in the indexation mechanism*

Shifting to a less generous indexation mechanism can produce very substantial savings in the long run, with relatively little visibility in the short term. Indexation concerns both the value of flat-rate and earnings-related benefits, as well as the calculation of the reference salary in earnings-related systems, and in this respect is an option available in all systems. Typically, countries have moved from wages to prices as a basis for the indexation of pensions (Britain, France). Germany has shifted from gross to net wages, so that increases in contributions will automatically result in lower pension benefits (Schmähl 1993). A different indexation mechanism is used in Switzerland, which upgrades benefits according to the arithmetic average of change in wages and salaries.

## 1.4    From the economics to the politics of pensions

This chapter has focused on the technical aspects of pension policy and reform. It gives a picture of the pressures that affect governments and of the options that they can use to respond to these pressures. The technical dimension of the pension problem, however, is not the only source of difficulties in pension policy-making. Pension reforms, in fact, are highly sensitive political exercises. Because their goal is to achieve savings, they alter established distributional equilibria. If savings are to be achieved, there are bound to be losers in a pension reform. Such people, unless they are compensated in some other way, are likely to oppose reform, and depending on their effective power might succeed in preventing the adoption of new pension legislation, or in imposing a watering-down of the proposed measures. Policy-makers, thus, need to pay exceptional attention to the political side of pension policy.

The way governments go about reforming pension systems in the political arena varies quite substantially between countries and sometimes within the same country at different times. There are examples of pension reforms which have been negotiated with the trade unions, such as the one in 1995 in Italy, and others that were strenuously fought by the labour movement, such as the British 1986 Social Security Act. Similarly, the outcomes of pension policy-making have displayed a significant degree of variation over the last few years. The United Kingdom has implemented some of the most radical measures in the early to mid-1980s, and the problem of financing public pensions in the long term has been virtually solved (though, as will be seen in chapter 3, other problems have emerged there). In contrast, in most continental European countries, the measures adopted have somewhat eased budgetary pressure on pensions, but further intervention will probably be needed.

The amount of political controversy generated by the pension issue can be substantial. On occasions, governments have been forced to withdraw plans for pension reforms as a result of massive protest movements. This was the fate of the 1994 attempt at pension reform by the Berlusconi government in Italy, and of the pension element of the 1995 Juppé plan in France. In both cases, governments tried to impose a reform package without prior negotiation with trade unions. These differences in governments' strategies and in the public's response to changes in pension legislation are one of the key concerns of this study. They are not explained by the socio-economic variables reviewed in this chapter; their existence suggests that we should look at the politics surrounding the adoption of pension reform.

# 2  Understanding the politics of pension reform: a theoretical framework

The political dimension of the pension problem is to a very large extent a question of how the diverging preferences expressed by different groups in society will be aggregated. The ability of each individual group to influence policy will depend on a range of factors, such as its power resources, the political appeal of its cause and so forth. A crucial variable, however, is likely to be the extent to which political institutions allow non-governmental actors the opportunity to influence policy-making.

Relying mainly on the work of new-institutionalists, this chapter aims to set out a framework for understanding the paths to reform chosen by different countries. Its key independent variable is the degree of power concentration granted to governments by political institutions, although it is also pointed out that the design of pension schemes can provide powerful incentives for governments to act in given directions. Social and political variables are not totally neglected either, although the selection of cases allows us to control for most of these non-institutional variables. Prior to reform, Britain, Switzerland and France were experiencing budget deficits, and, at the time of reform, all three political systems were dominated by right-of-centre majorities committed to retrenching in the area of pensions. In all three countries, governments expected substantial increases in pension expenditure due to population ageing. Since most non-institutional variables are kept constant in the sample, the analysis of pension reform in these three countries is likely to highlight the impact of political institutions on government capabilities and on the ability of political systems to bring about and sustain policy change.

The theoretical framework is built 'piece by piece'. First I look at the state of the research on the determinants of social policy-making, based on the analysis of the expansion of welfare states. In line with Pierson (1994, 1996), I argue that much of what has been written on that subject needs to be reformulated if it is to be applied to current change. Then the focus moves to new-institutionalist analysis of policy change, both in the area of pensions and with regard to more abstract theoretical implications. In particular, I concentrate on the institutional structures that

29

determine the degree of governmental control and external influence over policy-making, or veto points. In the concluding section, I argue that different configurations of veto points are likely to be associated with different strategies in pension reform.

## 2.1    The logic of social policy-making

The theoretical literature on welfare state development, by and large, has been concerned with explaining the growth and the expansion of social programmes in industrial countries. Generally, studies falling under this category have addressed two basic questions: why did welfare states develop, and why did they develop differently in different countries? These two questions have kept students of social policy busy for around three decades and now, with the benefit of hindsight, their work can be summed up under three headings: the 'logic of industrialisation' approach, the 'politics matters' school and the new-institutionalist approach.[1] Since these theories focused primarily on the determinants of social policy, they are the natural place to start a discussion on current changes in pension policy. At the same time, however, they need to be reconsidered in the light of today's circumstances.

### The 'logic of industrialisation' approach

The initial efforts to theorise the determinants of social policy go back to the 1960s. One of the first theories developed was the 'logic of industrial-isation' approach, put forward by authors like Cutright (1965) and Wilensky (1975). They viewed the welfare state as a byproduct of eco-nomic development. In a functionalist perspective, social policy was seen as a response to the needs generated by industrialisation. This thesis was supported by statistical analyses covering large numbers of countries (sometimes over sixty) which proved the existence of a significant correla-tion between economic development, measured by per capita GDP, and the level of social expenditure of a country.

The 'logic of industrialisation' approach is an accurate first approxima-tion of the causes of welfare development. However, as more comparative information on welfare provision was made available, it became clear that country variations went well beyond what could be explained by differences in the level of economic development. Particularly, the con-trast between Sweden and the United States, two countries which had reached comparable degrees of economic development, but with sharp

---

[1] This categorisation of theories of the welfare state is borrowed from Pierson 1996.

differences in the level of social protection, emphasised the weakness of the 'logic of industrialisation' approach. In addition, the measurement of the 'welfare effort' of a country, based solely on expenditure, was also criticised, since it did not take into account important notions such as conditions for entitlements, degree of redistribution or coverage (Esping-Andersen 1990).

### The 'power-resources' model

Focusing on the Swedish case, and to a lesser extent on other Nordic countries, a second strand of welfare theory emerged in the early 1980s. Authors like Stephens (1979), Korpi (1983), Esping-Andersen (1985, 1990) and Castles (1982) developed what is known as the 'politics matters' or 'power-resources' model. Its general hypothesis is that the strength of the labour movement and of left-wing parties is a key determinant of the level of welfare state development in a country. According to them, the successful mobilisation of the working class is the crucial factor in the explanation of different levels and models of social protection. Left-wing parties can, once in government, prompt the adoption of generous and universalist social policies which best serve working-class interests.

Empirical studies of welfare state development have generally confirmed the existence of a significant positive relationship between the strength of the left and the labour movement on the one hand, and various measurements of welfare effort (not necessarily spending) on the other. Esping-Andersen (1990), for instance, found a significant correlation between left-power mobilisation and the degree of decommodification achieved by various welfare states. Castles, focusing on the impact of political parties only, concluded that strong parties of the right have hindered welfare state expansion, while the existence of social democratic parties has served as a stimulus (1982: 85). With regard to pensions, Myles (1984) found a correlation between the power of the left and his index of pension quality, which takes into account a wide range of variables.

### Institutionalist analyses

While the power-resources model helped explain Swedish exceptionalism, students of American social policy were increasingly turning to state institutions as a key explanatory factor in the development of welfare arrangements. These analyses, generally referred to as institutionalist (or new-institutionalist; see below, section 2.3, 38–43), have put forward three key hypotheses in relation to the determinants of welfare state development. First, countries which developed a strong state apparatus relatively early are associated with high levels of social protection; second, existing social policies have a substantial impact on future developments; and, third, countries in which political institutions allow minorities substantial access to power are less likely to develop big welfare states. These three claims are found in various combinations in the institutionalist literature on the welfare state.

Heclo (1974), for instance, highlights the importance of state capabilities, inherited policies and the role played by administrators in initiating social reforms. Skocpol and Amenta (1986: 147) emphasise the impact of existing policies on current politics, through a mechanism they call 'policy feedback'. In her subsequent work, Skocpol applies new-institutionalist political theory to the United States, a case which is not successfully accounted for by the 'logic of industrialisation' approach nor by the power-resources model. The comparatively small size of the American welfare state is explained with reference to the traditional weakness of state institutions. Particularly at the time of industrialisation, state bureaucracy was underdeveloped and did not have the capacity to set up and run extensive social programmes as was the case in Europe. Instead of being instigated by the state, in the United States social policies were sponsored by political parties. This resulted in the introduction of social programmes more or less targeted on specific groups, such as Civil War veterans, who were likely to respond with electoral support (Skocpol 1995).

More recently and in a comparative perspective, Immergut (1992) and Huber et al. (1993) have put forward the hypothesis that constitutional structures have a substantial impact on the level of state welfare of a country. More specifically, they argue that, in countries in which interest groups are allowed substantial access to the policy-making process, and in which minorities have the opportunity to prevent the adoption of legislation thanks to the existence of veto points, solidaristic welfare reforms are more difficult to implement. Immergut (1992) contrasts the different course of health policy in Sweden, France and Switzerland. In the latter, the lack of a public health insurance scheme or a national health service is explained with the fact that, thanks to the availability of referendums, interest groups that opposed state intervention in the area of health care (such as doctors or mutual societies) were able to prevent the adoption of such legislation. The Swedish success in establishing a national health service, conversely, is explained with reference to the dominance of the executive in policy-making. A similar conclusion is reached by Huber et al. (1993), who found a correlation between various indicators of the size of welfare states and power concentration with the executive branch of government. Their approach is particularly interesting as it accounts for the comparatively low levels of social protection found in Switzerland and in the United States.

### Is retrenchment different?

The three strands of comparative welfare state theory reviewed here are concerned with the expansion of social policy in industrial countries. However, by looking at the factors that affected the expansion movement, we can expect to gain some useful insights on the more general question of what the determinants of social policy-making are, and in this respect their findings could be relevant to the understanding of the current phase of welfare state restructuring. There are, however, a number of problems concerning how theories which were developed for the analysis of welfare expansion can be applied to current restructuring, which is primarily characterised by retrenchment in the level of social protection.

First, the weaknesses identified in relation to how these theories explain the expansion phase remain relevant. For instance, a socio-economic explanation of welfare retrenchment would argue that cutbacks are likely to be more substantial in countries which are experiencing serious financial problems in sustaining welfare expenditure. This view seems accurate as a first approximation, as in many countries welfare restructuring has been prompted by economic recession and by recurring budget deficits. However, if one looks at the details of current change in social policy, one will find that there is relatively little correspondence between the seriousness of economic and financial problems experienced by governments, and their actions in the area of welfare. For instance, with regard to pensions, the UK was among the first industrial countries to take radical steps to reduce state expenditure on this programme, and yet in international comparison it stood out for its lower projected increase in expenditure associated with population ageing (see, for example, OECD 1988b). The key weakness of the 'logic of industrialisation' approach remains its inability to account for much of the observed cross-national variation in social policy-making, which stems, arguably, from its neglect for political, institutional and cultural factors. In a similar way, a 'politics matters' analysis, which was not particularly adequate in explaining welfare developments in the United States, if applied to current social policy change, fails to account for the overall persistence of welfare arrangements in countries like Britain and the United States, which have witnessed a collapse of left-wing and trade union influence during the 1980s (Pierson 1994: 29).

Besides these known weaknesses of comparative welfare state theory, however, there are some more fundamental problems in applying its findings to current change. First, the overall economic context of social policy-making has changed. During the expansion of welfare states, governments had a relatively high degree of control over their economies, for example through Keynesian demand management. In contrast, the current international trends of economic and political integration mean a reduction in national governments' ability to influence national economies (Scharpf 1997a). The result is that, while theories of expansion could limit their search for determinants to the nation-state, accounts of current change must find ways to incorporate the constraints imposed by the international economy and by supranational institutions.

In addition, unlike policy changes which expanded the reach of welfare states, retrenchment is generally an unpopular exercise (Pierson 1994, 1996, 1997b). According to Pierson this is to a large extent due to the fact that social programmes have modified the socio-economic and political context in which they operate. As a result of the welfare state, a certain level of state-guaranteed economic security has become the norm in most western societies. If governments want to reduce that level, they are likely to encounter powerful resistance from relatively large sections of public opinion. Moreover, social programmes have created their own constituencies, which include substantial sections of the electorate (pensioners, families, middle classes, social workers and so forth). These groups will tend to oppose and mobilise against cutbacks which are likely to worsen their economic condition. Different levels of public support for expansion and retrenchment are likely to generate different politics and patterns of coalition formation. Theory, thus, must be amended in order to take these facts into account.

In Pierson's view, the differences between expansion and retrenchment in social policy are substantive. The implication is that the two trends require distinctive conceptual frameworks:

Retrenchment is not simply the mirror image of welfare state expansion. Why should we assume that theories designed to explain outcomes in a particular context and involving the pursuit of particular goals will still apply once the political environment and the goals of key actors have undergone radical change? The question of whether theories of welfare state expansion offer insights into the retrenchment process is still open, but . . . major modifications are probably required. (Pierson 1996: 156)

Pierson's argument is supported by empirical evidence. First, the overall persistence of welfare arrangements in countries like the United States and the UK despite the collapse of the left in the 1980s suggests that new political actors have emerged in support of the welfare state. These need to be integrated into any theoretical framework which aims to account for current change. Second, welfare retrenchment in continental

European countries is proving extremely unpopular and is generating much more controversy than was the case during the expansion of welfare states. Even in countries like France, which have a traditionally weak labour movement, supporters of the welfare state were able to force the government to drop plans for pension reform in 1995. According to many commentators, the electoral defeat suffered by the right-of-centre coalition in 1997 was due to a very large extent to its open commitment to retrenching the generous French welfare state (see ch. 5). This contrasts with the overall popularity of welfare expansion, and is likely to produce different patterns of political confrontation.

Yet, some aspects of retrenchment are not totally unknown to traditional welfare state theory. To a very large extent, retrenchment constitutes an alteration of existing distributional equilibria. As a result of welfare retrenchment, some groups in society are likely to improve their position while others are likely to be worse off. The perceived resulting patterns of advantage and disadvantage will shape the position of various groups in the political arena, and will obviously have an impact on policy outcomes. Mechanisms of translation of interests into politics are central to analyses such as the power-resources model, and to many new-institutionalist studies which emphasise the influence that institutional structures have on access to policy-making for various groups (Immergut 1992; Huber *et al.* 1993). They are likely to bear much relevance to the understanding of current change.

With Pierson, thus, I argue that the challenge currently facing analysts of social policy-making is to find out in what ways and to what extent the changes in the socio-economic and political environment have affected the causal relationships identified by the students of welfare state expansion. The mechanisms they have highlighted have not disappeared, but they operate in a different environment and might produce slightly different effects.

## 2.2    Retrenchment in the area of pensions

Welfare retrenchment can be defined as policy changes that result in reductions in the generosity, coverage or quality of social programmes. Retrenchment is a key feature of current social policy-making, although it rarely occurs in a pure form, as in practice recent reforms have tended to combine retrenchment measures with other policy changes, often geared towards meeting changing social needs. Retrenchment is primarily an enterprise which aims to alter existing distributional equilibria. Its key consequence is a reduction in the amount of redistribution (vertical, horizontal or in some other direction) performed by the state in the area of social policy. In this respect, the distributional outcome of welfare retrenchment is likely to entail an improvement for some and a worsening for others.

This is particularly true in the area of public pensions reform. Pension schemes are arrangements which transfer resources between sections of the population (generations, income groups, etc.). In this respect, and unlike in other areas of social policy, in pension policy there is very limited scope for efficiency savings, particularly since administrative expenditure for public pension schemes is extremely low compared to other forms of provision for retirement. The logical consequence of this is that reductions in pension expenditure must be financed by reductions in the level or the coverage of current schemes, leaving some groups of beneficiaries (or would-be beneficiaries) worse off as a result. Retrenchment in the area of pensions, thus, is very much a zero-sum game.

### Contextual effects

In this respect, retrenchment is not entirely different from expansion. The construction of welfare states in industrial countries was also characterised by struggles over the allocation of resources, which often resembled zero-sum games. The introduction of universal pay-as-you-go pension schemes in western Europe after World War II meant that the funds distributed through pension benefits had to be collected from the then working population. The history of the development of the European welfare states shows how political and social actors were generally aware of the distributional consequences of their decisions, and how they fought to protect their interests (Baldwin 1990).

These struggles over the definition of distributional equilibria, however, took place in an economic context that was radically different from today's. To a very large extent, the expansion of welfare states was financed by high rates of economic growth, which allowed governments to expand their revenues without having to increase rates of taxation. As a result, the redefinition of distributional equilibria which characterised welfare state expansion did not have any clear losers, as those who were paying for improvements in provision were nonetheless seeing their post-tax incomes rising. Retrenchment, in contrast, occurs in a context of declining and generally low rates of economic growth. As a result, the zero-sum game character of redistribution becomes much more evident to those who take part in it, and in particular to those who lose out in policy change.

Contextual differences between welfare state expansion and retrenchment are reflected in the politics generated by the two exercises. While the expansion of welfare states was characterised by a general appreciation by electorates, this does not seem to be the case in the current phase of retrenchment. The extension of coverage and the improvement of provision in a context of fast economic growth did not generate radical opposition. In fact, these measures were often supported by large coalitions of different interests, including bourgeois parties (Baldwin 1990; Ferrera 1993b). The popularity of social programmes created a powerful incentive for political actors to be associated with social reformism, and made coalition building easier. In contrast, current attempts to reduce the scope and generosity of social programmes have often been met with disapproval by many political actors and large sections of the public.

### The impact on politics

The general unpopularity of cuts in social programmes makes it difficult for governments to generate support for such measures, and encourages defection from a retrenchment-oriented coalition. Moreover, the overall unpopularity of retrenchment constitutes an asset in the hands of political actors who support current arrangements. Recent events in various western European countries have shown that even weak labour movements are able to generate massive informal protest against governments committed to retrenching social programmes. France is a case in point. With a rate of unionisation below 15 per cent and substantial internal divisions, the French labour movement is considered among the weakest in the industrial world. Yet, when it comes to mobilising public opinion on matters related to social protection, the French unions have repeatedly proved to be able to inflict massive damage on a non-cooperative government (see ch. 5). Governments, thus, are caught between two contrasting pressures. On the one hand, current trends of economic globalisation, ageing and changes in social structures are forcing them to reduce, or at least to contain, the level of social expenditure. On the other hand, the overall unpopularity of welfare retrenchment and the objective difficulty involved in imposing changes of distributional equilibria are likely to constitute a formidable obstacle to the adoption of retrenchment measures.

One of the most significant results of this situation is the loss of relevance of the left–right axis as a dimension of confrontation in current social policy-making. The political orientation of governments does not seem to account for different courses of action with regard to current social policy-making. Left-of-centre governments in France, Italy and Britain in the late 1990s have all adopted measures which can be classified under the rubric of retrenchment. This is in spite of persisting differences between left and right on the level of discourse and attitudes of politicians (George *et al.* 1995; George 1998). It seems, thus, that the room for manoeuvre allowed by socio-economic and supranational constraints to governments is increasingly limited, and that traditional left-wing values, albeit still present in the discourse of much of the European left, are being abandoned in their policy-making (George 1998).

The lack of clear distinctive positions between left and right in relation to the welfare state means that the key dimension of political confrontation in social policy is unlikely to be the traditional left–right axis. Instead, in most European countries, the current battles over the welfare state are fought between governments, to a large extent regardless of their political persuasion, and a coalition of interests that defends the existing settlement. In continental Europe it is the labour movement that plays the pivotal role in this coalition. In contrast, in Britain and in the United States, pro-welfarist interests are represented by a wide range of issue-related pressure groups.

This shift in the politics of social policy-making is bound to affect the way in which we explain policy change in the welfare state. In particular, if the strength of the political left was a key determinant of welfare state expansion, this factor is likely to play a minor role in the current phase of retrenchment. In contrast, what is likely to play a major role is the degree of access that various interest groups have to policy-making, which in turn is likely to depend on two different variables: their relative internal strength and the rules which in each country govern the policy-making process and establish the pattern for the aggregation of conflicting preferences. A conceptual framework which has the ambition to account for current change in pension policy must take these two factors into consideration.

## 2.3    Institutions and policy-making

The 1990s have been characterised by an increasing awareness among political scientists of the extent to which institutions structure political interaction and contribute to the definition of policy outcomes.[2] Building on research published in the 1980s which emphasised the role of the state as an independent variable in the explanation of political change (see, for example, Skocpol 1985), this strand of public policy analysis has concentrated on identifying key institutional features that affect the way in which

---

[2] There is a substantial corpus of literature which falls in this category. Among the most frequently cited works are Hall 1986; March and Olsen 1989; Thelen and Steinmo 1992; North 1990; Immergut 1992; Weaver and Rockman 1993a. Hall and Taylor (1996) and Kato (1996) offer comprehensive literature reviews on institutions and policy-making.

actors interact in the formulation of policy, and as a result have an impact
on policy outcomes. These studies constitute a corpus of literature
named 'new-institutionalism',[3] after the title of a seminal article by
March and Olsen (1984).

The concept of 'institutions' is defined in different terms by different
authors.[4] However, in general, it is understood in fairly broad terms.
Typically it refers to the 'formal and informal procedures, routines,
norms and conventions embedded in the organizational structure of the
polity or political economy' (Hall and Taylor 1996: 938). In practice, the
concept of institutions includes a set of rules and structures which range
from the constitutional order of a country to the unwritten conventions
that contribute to shaping the political game.

The central claim made by new-institutionalists is that institutions can
be considered as an independent variable or as important intermediate
variables in the analysis of public policy formation. In their view, the
power and the interests of political actors constitute only the first tier of a
causal explanation of policy-making. Their impact on public policy is
significantly mediated by the institutional setting in which they operate.
As Hall puts it, 'the organization of policy-making affects the degree of
power that any one set of actors has over policy outcomes' (1986: 19).
Moreover, institutions are likely to influence the definition of actors'
interests: 'organizational position also influences an actor's definition of
his own interests, by establishing his institutional responsibilities and
relationship to other actors' (ibid.).

The study of the impact of institutions on policy-making is an enterprise which highlights the limits of democratic politics. Institutional
variables are seen as setting the boundaries within which policy-makers
can operate. They contribute to determining the number and the range
of options for policy change that are politically feasible in a given
country. In this respect, institutions help to account for the lack of convergence in policy-making among countries of similar developments of
industrial development, which are facing similar problems (Kosonen
1994; Bonoli et al. 1996). The country-specific character of institutional limits to policy-making explains the persistence of national
differences in spite of the increasing interdependence between sove-
reign states.

---

[3] This trend is contrasted with the 'old' institutionalism which dominated political science
debates until the late 1950s. Within this strand, the main emphasis was put on institutions which were studied from a strictly formal point of view. To some extent, 'old' institutionalism overlapped with the study of constitutional law (March and Olsen 1984;
Stone 1992: 157).

[4] Thelen and Steinmo (1992) offer a review of various definitions of institutions found in
the literature.

Institutions limit the scope of feasible change in two distinct ways, which correspond to two substrands of the new-institutional literature. First, some authors have highlighted the existence of *path dependence* in policy formation, a concept which refers to the impact that decisions taken at the introduction of a new policy have on future developments (North 1990; Pierson 1994, 1997a). A second strand of institutional analysis has focused on the issue of *government capabilities*, or governments' ability to bring about and sustain change in policy, depending on the political institutions of a country (Weaver and Rockman 1993a; Tsebelis 1995; Scharpf 1997b). The relevance of these concepts for the study of pension reform is assessed below.

### Path dependence and pension reform

The concept of path dependence was developed by economists to account for the persistence of inefficient technologies despite the availability of better alternatives.[5] The most frequently quoted example is probably the development of the QWERTY keyboard layout. This keyboard is not the most efficient for high-speed typing but, given the fact that it is used universally, a shift to a better alternative would entail prohibitive costs. In this respect, a decision taken about a century ago is still affecting, and limiting, technological developments in typewriting. A more general argument about path dependence is made by North (1990). In order to account for the lack of convergence in economic performance among industrial countries, he uses the notion of path dependence with reference to the persistence of institutions that do not allow optimal economic performance.

Instances of path dependence have been identified also in the area of pension policy. Pierson talks about 'lock-in' effects, or mechanisms 'that greatly increase the cost of adopting once-possible alternatives and inhibit exit from a current policy-path' (1994: 42). In his view, a key example of a lock-in effect is the choice of a pay-as-you-go financing method for public pensions. A shift to a funded system, in fact, would require the generations currently in work to pay double pension contributions, as they would have to finance their own retirement and, at the same time, the pensions that are currently being paid. In the UK 1986 pension reform initial plans for scrapping a pay-as-you-go pension scheme (SERPS) and replacing it with a system of funded private pensions were dropped also because of the increased cost due to double payment (see ch. 3).

[5] For an account of the genesis of the concept of path dependence among economists and its translation in political science, see Pierson 1997a.

Myles and Quadagno (1997) have found a relationship between the design of pension schemes and forms of retrenchment which constitutes an example of path-dependent policy change. In an ingenious article they have pointed out that recent pension reforms in industrial countries have tended to follow two different patterns and that these patterns are related to the type of pension scheme which is being reformed. Schemes of Bismarckian inspiration, i.e. those which offer earnings-related benefits on a contributory basis, have tended to be changed by strengthening the relationship between contributions and benefits (Italy, Germany, France). In contrast, schemes belonging to the Beveridgean tradition, which grant flat-rate benefits often on a non-contributory basis, have been cut back by restricting eligibility. For instance, Australia, Canada, Denmark and New Zealand have all introduced some form of income- or means-testing of their basic pension.

The trend observed by Myles and Quadagno highlights the limits that pension scheme design poses to reform. Politically, it would be extremely difficult to means-test a contributory scheme of Bismarckian inspiration. This option, in contrast, is easily implemented in tax-financed systems. As a result, policy-makers who have to deal with financial imbalances in Bismarckian systems have to find alternative ways to reduce expenditure. Apparently, the solution chosen is a reinforcement of the link between contributions and benefits. Since this option respects the ethos of Bismarckian social insurance, it is likely to be more acceptable to the relevant actors and to the public in general.

A similar conclusion is reached by Ferrera (1996a) in his analysis of patterns of welfare retrenchment in various European countries. After having identified four regimes of welfare provision, Scandinavian, continental, Anglo-Saxon and south European, he argues that the use of increased targeting as a retrenchment option will be most easily implemented in Anglo-Saxon countries (UK and Ireland). Since these two systems are mainly based on flat-rate provision at a relatively low level, increased targeting can be achieved through the non-adaptation of benefits to increases in people's living standards. In this institutional context, governments do not need to take a proactive approach to increase income-testing; if they simply omit to upgrade benefits, people will increasingly turn to means-tested provision.

The institutional design of pension schemes is a powerful determinant of reform, in the sense that it limits the number and the range of possible options, and it points policy-makers looking for political feasibility in some pre-determined directions. The authors discussed here have found different associations between given institutional features and the course that pension reform is likely to take in various countries. Despite their emphasis on institutions, all these studies in fact highlight the importance of politics in the adoption of a pension reform. Institutional features become relevant only in so far as they make some solutions more politically attractive than others.

Path-dependence arguments, such as those reviewed here, highlight the limits of policy-making, and provide helpful tools for the analysis of structural persistence in public policy. Path-dependent change does not mean absence of change. It refers to a limited range of options available to policy-makers, which is determined by the shape of structures already in place. The implication of the path-dependence argument, if taken in its strictest version, is that policy change is possible, but is to a large extent pre-determined. It is a position which downplays the importance of politics and of power relationships within democratic polities, and the scope for subverting existing equilibria. This view somewhat contrasts with another substrand of new-institutionalist thinking, which focuses on the differing capabilities of governments to bring about policy change, and emphasises the impact of institutions on the political game.

### Government capabilities and pension reform

In recent years, a growing corpus of new-institutionalist literature has been concerned with the issue of government capabilities.[6] In general, its findings have shown that the degree of control that governments can expect to exert on policy-making varies substantially across democratic polities. In particular, the existence of veto points, i.e. points at which a suitable coalition of actors can stop the policy-making process, has emerged as a major limitation on governments' ability to control policy outcomes. In contrast, the absence of veto points is associated with strong power concentration with the government and a much stronger ability to bring about change in policy-making.

The existence of veto points and the resulting pattern of power distribution in political systems is likely to be an important factor affecting governments' approaches to the pension problem. Since pension reforms are primarily exercises which alter distributional equilibria, the availability of veto points will provide opportunities for opponents to block the adoption of new pension legislation. In order to prevent them from doing so, governments operating in institutional environments which offer numerous veto points are likely to develop strategies aimed at neutralising their impact on policy. In the absence of such strategies, policy change might be unachievable.

---

[6] See, for example: Immergut 1992; Weaver and Rockman 1993a; King 1995; Scharpf 1997b; Tsebelis 1995. With Weaver and Rockman, I understand the concept of 'government capability' as 'a pattern of government influence on its environment that produces substantially similar outcomes across time and policy areas' (1993a: 6).

Patterns of institutionally determined power distribution are also likely to affect the way in which path-dependent development occurs. If path dependence is due to the political difficulties involved in shifting away from established structural equilibria, then we can expect governments with strong capabilities to be more successful in avoiding path-dependent developments when this suits them. A focus on government capabilities is likely to emphasise the potential for change which exists in political systems with strong control over policy-making.

## 2.4    Veto points in democratic polities

Veto points have been identified at various levels of the policy-making process. Some are situated in the constitutional order, which can allow non-governmental actors access to the definition of policy, for example through a constitutional court, a referendum system or a strict separation of powers between the executive and parliament. Veto points, however, can exist also on a more informal level. If a political system is used to negotiate with the trade unions before the adoption of changes in economic and social policy, then, in that system, the approval (or acquiescence) of the labour movement can become a de facto veto point through which the legislative process has to pass if it is to succeed.

The main constitutional mechanisms that produce veto points in democratic polities are reviewed below. These are of great relevance to the pension reform issue. As pension reforms involve the alteration of existing distributional equilibria, those who are going to lose out are likely to exploit veto points where available, in order to affect the course of policy-making or simply to try to block the adoption of legislation perceived as disadvantageous.

### Separation of powers

An important dimension which distinguishes political systems is the degree of control that the government can exert over parliament. In this respect, political scientists distinguish between parliamentary systems, where the government is elected by and responsible to parliament, and separation-of-powers systems, in which the two authorities are elected separately and can operate independently from each other (Lijphart 1984; Weaver and Rockman 1993a). The exemplar countries of these two models are Britain and the United States respectively. Switzerland is a hybrid of these two models, but in policy-making it shares many of the features that are typical of the separation-of-powers system.

Typically, governmental control over parliament is stronger in parliamentary systems. There, the executive is elected by a parliamentary majority, which prevents the occurrence of 'divided government', i.e. a situation in which the executive and the legislative branches are controlled by different parties (or coalitions). Second, in separation-of-powers systems, the government cannot be brought down by a no-confidence vote. This means that members of parliament can vote against their government without having to worry about its survival. Third, in parliamentary systems the government can resign and even dissolve parliament and call an early election. Often, the simple threat of doing this can constitute a powerful argument to help convince members of parliament to back the government on a controversial bill.

A disciplined parliament, thus, is more likely to exist in a parliamentary system. In this respect, governmental decisions are better insulated from pressure coming from interest groups which lobby parliament. The United States, a separation-of-powers system, is a typical case in which lobbying of parliamentarians can result in Congress turning down legislative proposals which originated from the presidency. Clinton's failed attempt to introduce compulsory health insurance in 1994 is a case in point.

A similar situation is found in the Swiss political system, which constitutes a hybrid between the parliamentary and the separation-of-powers models. The government is elected by parliament, but for the duration of the electoral term it cannot dissolve and cannot be brought down by parliament. The result is a policy-making process in which parliament can overrule and amend decisions taken at the executive level, without any consequence for the government's survival. Rather like the US president, Swiss ministers have to convince members of parliament to back their bills without the threats that are available to colleagues operating in parliamentary systems, such as resignation or dissolution. Separation of powers, thus, produces a potential veto point that can be used by the losers in policy changes. Their ability to influence parliamentarians is likely to be enhanced by the reduced government control over the legislature.

### Bicameralism

The existence of a second chamber of parliament constitutes an additional point at which legislation needs to be accepted. However, whether bicameralism can amount to an additional veto point depends on the electoral rules and the resulting composition of each of the two chambers. When the two chambers are elected on the same basis (Italy, Belgium, Netherlands), the majorities produced in each of them are also likely to be identical. As a result, there is little likelihood that bicameralism make a difference. In contrast, when the two chambers are elected on the basis of different rules

(Germany, Switzerland, United States), a second chamber, with a different party composition, can provide a veto point for unsatisfied groups.

This is most notably the case of Germany, where the lower chamber (Bundestag) is directly elected but where members of the upper chamber (Bundesrat) are designated by the governments of the *Länder*. For much of the 1990s the Bundestag was controlled by the right-of-centre coalition headed by Chancellor Kohl, while the Bundesrat was dominated by the Social Democrats. The result was that, in a large number of areas, the government was unable to adopt legislation unless it was capable of gaining the approval of the opposition. This constituted an important limitation on the room for manoeuvre available to the government and a powerful incentive to seek consensual and negotiated solutions (Schmidt 1996).

### Proportional representation (PR)

The electoral system does not directly provide veto points by itself, but can create favourable conditions for their emergence. In general, first-past-the-post electoral systems tend to enhance the representation of the largest party, to be associated with a lower number of parties (often only two) and to produce strong, single-party majorities (examples: UK, United States). In contrast, proportional representation with multiple-member constituencies tends to be associated with a large number of parties represented in parliament, and with coalition governments.[7] Examples are the small European countries (the Netherlands, Switzerland, Denmark, Sweden).

Coalition governments, in turn, are more likely than single-party governments to offer veto opportunities to actors who oppose legislation, especially when legislation being considered is widely regarded as unpopular. Coalition governments are composed of parties which will compete against each other at the next election. As a result, coalition members have a relatively strong incentive to defect, as this will promote them as the defenders of widely supported policies, and possibly be electorally rewarding (Weaver and Rockman 1993a: 24).

### Referendums

Few countries provide for voters to intervene directly in the policy-making process through the use of referendums. This is most notably the case of Switzerland, where any act passed by parliament can be challenged at the polls if opponents are able to produce 50,000 signatures to

---

[7] The link between electoral laws and party system has been qualified by Duverger as one of the few that in political science 'approximates a true sociological law' (Duverger 1963).

that effect. This constitutes a powerful veto point that can be exploited by the losers in any alteration of redistributive arrangements. As one would expect, political actors resort to the use of referendums rather often, when unsatisfied with legislation passed by parliament.

According to Lijphart, referendums do not necessarily constitute an opportunity for unsatisfied groups to influence policy-making (1984: 31). Referendums, he points out, can also be used by governments to generate majorities in the public and to silence unsatisfied minorities, and thus be an instrument for imposing the government's views. What matters, however, seems to be who has the ability to call a referendum. Since referendums in Switzerland do not take place at government discretion, but are either compulsory or called by external groups, they can provide a veto opportunity to unsatisfied groups of voters (Kobach 1993).

### Balanced dual executive

While many parliamentary systems have a dual executive, consisting of a head of state and a head of government, in most cases the former plays only a ceremonial role. In the case of France, however, the president, directly elected, has more substantial influence in the definition of policy (Duverger 1987). In addition, since presidential and parliamentary elections do not occur at the same time and have different frequencies, it is possible to have situations in which parliament and the presidency are controlled by different camps, which results in executive power-sharing between a president and a prime minister who have different political orientations. Although in matters of internal policy the approval of the president is not formally required, it is obviously politically difficult for a prime minister to embark on an unpopular pension reform without the backing of the presidency, particularly in France. In this respect, the division of executive power can provide a veto opportunity if president and prime minister belong to different political camps.

### Veto points, power concentration and accountability

The existence of one or more veto points of those mentioned in this list is likely to restrict the scope of what is politically feasible in a given polity. Actors who are dissatisfied with the legislative proposals put forward by the majority can exploit the opportunities provided by existing veto points in order to prevent the adoption of unwanted legislation. Often, the simple threat of making use of veto opportunities is enough to force governments to renounce their plans. The number of veto points can be seen as a rough indicator of executive's ability to control policy-making and to impose policy change despite external opposition. The higher the number of veto points, the less a government will be able to influence policy outcomes.

It has been argued, however, that the concentration of power resulting from the absence of veto points is not necessarily an element of strength for governments who wish to impose unpopular measures. The absence of veto points does concentrate power, but by the same token it also concentrates accountability, and thus makes electoral punishment for unpopular measures more likely. The two effects tend to counterbalance each other and the overall result is uncertain and highly contingent (Pierson 1994; Weaver and Rockman 1993a; Pierson and Weaver 1993). Theoretically, this argument is convincing. However, it can be taken further in an attempt to identify the conditions that create one or the other of the two effects – concentration of power or of accountability – dominate over policy-makers' concerns. The relative importance of these two effects is likely to depend on at least three different factors.

First, the importance of the accountability effect depends on how intense party competition is in a given political system. For the fear of electoral punishment to play a role in restricting the reforming ambitions of a government, there has to be an opposition party which can credibly put itself forward as an alternative. If there is no likelihood of a change of government in the near future, policy-makers are less likely to be sensitive to the accountability effect. For instance, in the Britain of the 1980s, a division in the anti-conservative camp contributed substantially to neutralising the potential impact of electoral punishment and as a result to reducing the weight of the accountability effect. This certainly helps to account for the uncompromising style in policy-making which was typical of the Thatcher governments of the 1980s (Jessop et al. 1988; Riddel 1989; Kavanagh 1990).

Second, the accountability effect is also likely to play a relatively smaller role in proportional representation electoral systems than in FPTP ones, as the losses due to electoral punishment are less likely to result in big losses of parliamentary seats. FPTP systems amplify the impact of swings in the public mood.

Finally, the relative importance of the power and accountability concentration effects is likely to vary according to the political cycle. Typically, one would expect the power concentration effect to be stronger at the beginning of an electoral term, and accountability concentration to be stronger in the run-up to an election, as politicians become more sensitive to the public's perception of their actions.

Overall, the importance of the accountability effect seems to be stronger in the United States than in most European countries. The

United States combines the conditions that enhance the importance of the accountability effect: a bipartisan system in which both parties are equally capable of winning important elections, a FPTP electoral system and, perhaps most crucially, an almost permanent state of electoral campaigning due to the two-year lag between presidential and parliamentary elections. In Europe, these conditions are combined in different ways, and one can expect the impact of the accountability effect to vary with time. The electoral cycle is likely to play an important role in this, although in fact, in so far as pension reform is concerned, it is unlikely that governments will embark on a possibly unpopular policy a short time before an important election. In this respect, we can expect that, most of the time in most European countries, the impact of power concentration on policy-making will be felt more strongly than the accountability effect. The final assessment of the relative importance of divergent effects produced by power concentration, however, should be left to a case-by-case analysis of specific instances of policy change.

The existence of veto points in a political system can be conceptualised in terms of increased uncertainty. Governments operating in an institutional setting characterised by a high density of veto points are less able to control the final outcome of the legislative process. Uncertainty affects both the ability to control the content of legislation and to make sure that legislation is adopted at all. External actors can threaten to make use of their veto power unless bills are amended, and as a result impose some of their own priorities, or, if dissatisfied, can make use of the relevant veto points with a view to impeding the adoption of unwanted legislation.

Veto points can be a formidable obstacle for pension reform. Cuts in provision for retirement are likely to make some groups of the population worse off. These, in turn, will tend to exploit existing channels of access to the policy-making process in order to prevent the adoption of legislation, to minimise their losses or to demand some form of compensation. In this context, governments are likely to develop strategies aimed at controlling the uncertainty brought about by the existence of veto points. In order to respond to demographic and socio-economic pressures they need to devise retrenchment packages which are politically feasible in their institutional setting. This means that legislation must be able to attract enough support from the actors who can make use of existing veto points. Government policy needs to be carefully calibrated so as to be able to achieve the two objectives of tackling the pension problem and generating sufficient support from relevant actors.

This enterprise is obviously highly complex, and the failures of pension reform initiatives in France and Italy in the 1990s have shown that governments do not always manage to strike the right balance between these two objectives. Nevertheless, the observation of successful instances of pension reform reveals a series of strategies that governments have adopted in order to maximise their chances of seeing a pension reform adopted. The type of strategy chosen seems to be associated with the number and the type of veto points that exist in a political system.

## 2.5    Political institutions and policy-making strategies

Traditionally, political systems characterised by a high density of veto points have responded by integrating external groups in policy-making. By having potential opponents on board, governments in these countries have managed to defuse their potential to block the law-making process. Perhaps this is most notably the case in Switzerland, where a consociational style in policy-making has developed to a large extent as a response to the existence of referendums (Neidhart 1970; Kriesi 1995; Lehner 1984; Lehmbruch 1979, 1993). Other countries, however, when the political situation increases the number of veto points, have also adopted strategies of integration. For instance, the German government has dealt with the incongruent majorities in the two chambers of parliament by devising legislation able to attract support from the opposition party (Schmidt 1996).

Similar strategies of integration of potential opponents have been attempted in pension reforms in institutional contexts characterised by high levels of power fragmentation. The controversial nature of pension reform and the extent of demographic and socio-economic pressures do not always allow much room for manoeuvre for governments seeking a consensual solution. As a result, often, policy-making strategies in pension reform have been limited to offering some *quid pro quos* targeted on key opponents, particularly on those who can threaten to make an effective use of existing veto points, in order to buy their support, or at least their acquiescence. In some instances, key opponents who were granted some form of *quid pro quo* as part of retrenchment packages (most often the trade unions) did not formally approve the reform package, but refrained from trying to prevent its adoption. This was the case in the French 1993 pension reforms when some of the unions' demands were included in a pension reform that was otherwise geared towards reducing pension entitlements. In 1993 France was in a situation of executive power-sharing between a Socialist president and a Gaullist prime minister.

In contrast, pension reforms adopted in contexts characterised by few veto points and a high level of power concentration with the executive tend to display a higher degree of coherence and to comply more firmly with the government's declared priorities and ideological orientation. Little effort is made to secure approval from potential opponents and reform has to be imposed to a substantial extent. The result was that, in these instances, the imposition of controversial measures generated widespread opposition. In one case, the French 1995 public sector pension reform, the government was eventually forced to withdraw its plans in the face of a massive protest movement. In the UK, the 1986 pension reform succeeded, but was opposed by an impressive coalition of interests which included not only the opposition and other left-wing groups, but also actors who were traditionally supportive of Conservative government policy, such as the Confederation of British Industry.

Undoubtedly, the existence of veto points constitutes a powerful incentive for policy-makers to seek a consensual solution. However, the high potential for controversy embodied in the pension reform issue means that governments find it exceptionally difficult to devise fully consensual pension reforms. As a result, the tendency is towards the inclusion of *quid pro quos* targeted on key opponents in view of neutralising their veto power. This strategy can in fact be rather successful in securing the adoption of retrenchment packages, although it obviously constitutes a limitation on government room for manoeuvre in designing a pension reform.

Governments' decisions concerning how to deal with the pension issue will depend on their perception of the likelihood of a veto opportunity being exploited by particular actors. This, in turn, is likely be determined by the existence of veto points but also by the judgement the government makes of the mobilising capacity of the relevant interest groups. A trade union movement able to stage massive demonstrations, to block strategic sectors of economic activity and, perhaps most crucially, to receive support from the public against unpopular government policies can provide an incentive for a government to negotiate, just as does a series of veto points in the political system.

The consequence of the adoption of different policy-making strategies in different political systems is likely to concern the overall pattern of welfare state adaptation. The evidence provided in the next three chapters suggests that the combination of retrenchment with *quid pro quos* targeted on key actors tends to be responsive to a wide range of pressures on the welfare state. Pure retrenchment constitutes a response to the financial problems of social programmes. However, the emergence of new needs and aspirations in modern societies – like, for example, gender equality – is also putting pressure on arrangements designed decades ago. The need to combine retrenchment with *quid pro quos* in political systems with a high density of veto points provides an opportunity to contain expenditure and at the same time to modernise the welfare state. Political institutions and veto points are likely to affect not only policy-making strategies, but also policy outcomes, by encouraging qualitatively different processes of welfare state adaptation. This hypothesis is discussed in chapter 6 on the basis of the evidence presented in the next three chapters.

# 3  Britain: pension reform through majority rule

By international standards, the 1986 British pension reform constitutes one of the most radical departures from the traditional west European post-war approach to pension policy. As a consequence of this reform, British employees can now opt out of the state second-tier pension or of their occupational pension and make individual provision for their retirement through a private and personal pension. The significance of this change is twofold. On the one hand it constitutes a major shift from the state to the market in pension provision, with the implication that the redistributive function and the role of guarantor played by the former are substantially reduced. On the other hand, the introduction of the opting-out clause means that fewer people are now paying into the state scheme which impairs its ability to meet existing and future pension commitments and thereby provides an incentive to the remaining employees to opt out of the state system. The impact of the 1986 Social Security Act has been substantial. Partly as a result of it, the UK is the only major industrial country which does not have a financial problem in meeting future pension commitments (see tab. 1.3). On the other hand, other problems have emerged, like the lack of adequate coverage for employees on low incomes or in intermittent employment, which personal pensions are unable to provide.

It is useful to recall that the debate and the adoption of the British reform occurred in a particular ideological and political climate. The mid-1980s were characterised by the strong dominance of the Conservative Party in politics, and by the general ascendancy of neo-liberal ideas with regard to the respective roles of the state and the market in modern societies. To some extent, the pension reform was part of a wider move to reform the British economy and society, which, under the heading of 'popular capitalism', included measures such as privatisation of state-owned firms and of public housing, deregulation of financial services and incentives for home and share ownership.

The ascendancy of neo-liberal ideas in the mid-1980s has prompted a number of commentators to argue that, contrary to government's claims, the 1986 pension reform was adopted for ideological reasons, rather than to anticipate a pension crisis due to population ageing (Nesbitt 1995; Walker 1991). For instance, according to a leading expert in British pension policy:

> It is not the burden of aging as such that concerns the Thatcher government, or even the cost of pensions; it is the public burden ... Concern about the aging of the population in Britain has been amplified artificially as an economic and demographic imperative in order to legitimate ideologically driven policies aimed at reducing the state's role in welfare. (Walker 1991: 31)

Walker's thesis is supported by international comparisons. If one looks at the financial situation of the British pension system throughout the 1980s, one will find that it is among the least worrying among industrial countries (OECD 1988b), and yet the UK was among the first countries to adopt radical retrenchment in the area of pensions. In addition, as will be seen below, the government's own analysis of demographic projections is not always clear as to why future pension commitments will not be sustainable. There is something missing, however, in this ideological explanation of the 1986 British pension reform. Walker's thesis assumes a linear link between economic ideas and public policy, but fails to address the issue of why the Conservatives espoused a given set of ideas in relation to pension policy; and, perhaps more crucially, how were they able to carry them through into actual legislation.[1]

This chapter attempts to answer these two crucial questions on the basis of the theoretical framework presented in chapter 2. Particularly, the UK's political institutions and its standard patterns of policy-making are treated as two important independent variables, as well as the institutional design of the pension system. It is argued that a peculiar combination of these institutional factors made possible and encouraged the adoption of a particularly radical pension reform, which is seen as part of a wider reform movement which goes under the rubric of popular capitalism.

## 3.1    The politics of majoritarian democracy in the UK

British policy-making is characterised by the relatively unchecked dominance of the party in government. This is to a substantial extent due to the particular constitutional structure of government in the UK, which emphasises the influence of the majority party over policy. This process

---

[1] To integrate the 'role of ideas' in explanatory models of policy-making is one of the big theoretical challenges currently facing political scientists. Remarkable attempts are those by Hall 1989 and Jobert 1994.

takes place in two distinct stages. The first is at the polls, where, thanks to a first-past-the-post electoral system, the party which obtains a plurality of votes in the electorate is likely to reach an absolute majority in Parliament (see tab. 3.1). Second, once the majority party has formed a government, there is no written constitution to limit the scope of its actions. Because of the strong tradition of party discipline in British politics, underpinned by institutions such as the 'whip', Parliament does not constitute an effective check on the government's actions. The result is a political system which allows the government comparatively wide room for manoeuvre in policy-making. Continental European countries, where electoral systems generally require political parties to form coalition governments, are examples of polities in which the control of the majority on policy is less substantial.

According to political scientists, in the UK the main check on what the government does is in fact party competition (see, for example, Budge 1996). Dissatisfaction with government policies may lead to a transfer of votes from the ruling party to the opposition, resulting in an alternation in government between parties of different ideological persuasions. Governments seeking re-election, thus, are expected to adopt policies that take into account a wide range of external interests, precisely in order to reduce the risk of electoral defeat. In practical terms, however, party competition did not always work as an effective limitation on the government's actions. This was particularly the case during the Conservative governments of 1979–92. Instead of smoothing the content of policy in order to appeal to wide sections of the electorate, the Thatcher governments of the 1980s actively pursued radical and controversial policies. Probably because of a split in the opposition during the 1980s, the role of party competition as a check on government policy lost its effectiveness. Party competition provides an effective balance to government's power only as long as there is a competing party which can credibly threaten to win the upcoming election. During the 1980s this threat was not strong enough. The structural weakness of the Labour Party and the division in the anti-Conservative camp between two parties gave the Thatcher governments a substantial degree of freedom to pursue their own objectives.

As a matter of fact, during the Thatcher years a substantial number of policies adopted after World War II saw a clear reversal. In economic policy, demand management of Keynesian inspiration was replaced by monetarism and a preference for economic *laissez-faire* (Hall 1992). In social policy the desirability of having a welfare state was questioned. In pension policy, it was the public/private mix in provision for retirement that would be mostly affected. This reversal in policy was made possible

Table 3.1 *British general election results, 1979–97*

| | Conservative Party | | Labour Party | | Liberal Democrats | |
|---|---|---|---|---|---|---|
| Year | percentage of vote | number of MPs | percentage of vote | number of MPs | percentage of vote | number of MPs |
| 1979 | 43.3 | 339 | 36.9 | 268 | 13.8 | 11 |
| 1983 | 42.4 | 396 | 27.6 | 209 | 25.4 | 23 |
| 1987 | 42.3 | 375 | 30.8 | 229 | 12.8 | 17 |
| 1992 | 41.9 | 336 | 34.4 | 271 | 17.8 | 20 |
| 1997 | 31.5 | 165 | 44.4 | 418 | 17.6 | 46 |

*Source: Keesing's Archives of World's Events 1979, 1983, 1987, 1992, 1997.*

and perhaps encouraged by the structure of British formal institutions. The absence of veto points in the political system, and a first-past-the-post electoral system coupled with a divided opposition, allowed the Thatcher governments to pursue extremely controversial policies without incurring substantial electoral losses. As I argue throughout this chapter, Thatcher was able to fully exploit the advantages of power concentration, and at the same time neutralise the accountability effect.

### First-past-the-post (FPTP) electoral system

The most obvious consequence of the FPTP electoral system in the UK is the fact that it allows a party with a plurality of votes in the electorate to have a majority in Parliament. This is precisely what repeatedly happened during the Thatcher years. As table 3.1 shows, the Conservative Party never obtained more than 43.5 per cent of the vote, yet it had absolute majorities in Parliament throughout the 1979–97 period. Political parties which have a strong regional basis are favoured relative to those which are of medium strength nation-wide. This appeared clearly in the 1983 election results, in which the Alliance, with more than 25 per cent of the vote, won only 23 seats, whereas Labour, with less than 2 percentage points more, won 209 seats. The two major parties tend to concentrate their support in some areas, and to be extremely weak in others, while the Alliance (now the Liberal Democrats) are more likely to end up second (this was the case in 303 constituencies in 1983). Traditionally, the North of England, Wales and Scotland support Labour, while the South-East has been the key Conservative stronghold.

A second implication of the FPTP electoral system is the fact that governments do not need broad, cross-class support in order to win elections. A plurality of votes is enough. This feature of FPTP seems to have been crucial in influencing the direction of British policy during the 1980s. As the former prime minister herself put it: 'It [is] important to have a philosophy and policy which because they are good appeal to sufficient people to secure a majority' (Thatcher, quoted in Riddel 1989: 1). In fact, if one looks at the major reforms adopted by the various Thatcher governments, one will find that many have the quality of being palatable to a relatively large section of the electorate. This is the case of reforms that facilitated the establishment of the Conservative vision of 'popular capitalism' such as encouraging home and share ownership, privatisation of state-owned firms and the introduction of private personal pensions.

More precisely, however, these policies tended to have an asymmetric impact on the population; this asymmetry most often depended on income and on ideological persuasion of individuals. In other words, those who had sufficient financial means and were prepared to go along with the project of a 'popular capitalism' put forward by the Thatcher governments did rather well throughout the 1980s. The number of individuals involved was quite substantial. The privatisation of council houses resulted by 1988 in an increase by 3 million in the number of home owners, of whom many had bought their house with a substantial discount (up to 50 per cent). The number of individual shareholders soared from 3 million in 1979 to 9 million in 1989 (Riddel 1989: 111–24).

The political significance of the various reforms falling under the rubric of 'popular capitalism' was a reinforcement of the 'social base'[2] of Thatcherism. In other words the neo-liberal reforms of the 1980s did have a positive economic impact on a relatively large section of the population, which in turn became more inclined to stay in or to join the Conservative camp. This interpretation of Thatcherism is not new. Jessop et al. (1988) have suggested the existence of a link between the content of government reforms in the 1980s and the permanence in power of the Conservative Party, on the basis of a coherent strategy which consistently directed the course of policy.

### A Thatcherite project?

Jessop et al.'s analysis of Thatcherism starts from a critique of the ideological interpretation, which basically sees the change of direction in policy as being due to a shift in the values and beliefs which animated elites and

---

[2] The concept of 'social base' is defined in terms of the 'set of social forces which support – within an institutional framework and policy paradigm – the basic structure, mode of operation and objectives of the state system in its role as the official representative of civil society' (Jessop et al. 1988: 156).

public opinion. According to them, the main weakness of an ideological interpretation lies with the fact that 'it could neglect the structural underpinnings of Thatcherism in the economic and in the state systems and its specific economic and political bases of support' (Jessop *et al.* 1988: 73). In contrast, Jessop *et al.* view Thatcherism as a political strategy adopted by the Conservative Party in response to the 'continuing relative decline of the British economy and, more particularly, to its political repercussions' (ibid.: 163). The key element of this strategy is its 'two nation' character. In other words, it is based on a division between two sections of the population: on the one hand the 'productive', understood as those individuals who are able to extract resources from a competitive market, and on the other hand the 'parasitic', who rely for their livelihood on the state or on non-competitive arrangements. Policy changes consisted in the adoption of measures which rewarded the 'productive' at the expense of the 'parasitic', by performing a transfer of resources from the latter to the former. This transfer took the form of various policies, such as privatisation of state enterprises, de-regulation of financial services, sales of council housing and, of course, the partial privatisation of pensions. In return, those who were favoured by the policies adopted by the various Conservative governments came to constitute the social base of Thatcherism, i.e. a coalition of interests which would support the government when elections were fought.

The main problem with Jessop *et al.*'s interpretation is its insistence on the coherent and deliberate nature of the Thatcherite project. In fact, policy-making under Thatcher was characterised by a high degree of experimentation and by the tendency to go a step further in the adoption of policies such as privatisation or marketisation of public services (Hayward and Klein 1994: 112; Riddel 1989: 5). In addition, the claim that 'popular capitalism' reforms alone explain the permanence in power of the Conservative Party does not seem plausible. Even though the new policies might have generated fresh support for the government by those who gained from them, elections are affected by numerous factors of a very different nature and are only partly influenced by individual perceptions of changes in personal economic well-being. Nevertheless, it seems plausible to consider that, when the neo-liberal policies were elaborated, their likely electoral repercussions were taken into account. In this context, the idea of targeting the benefits of policy on some given groups more likely to respond with electoral support might have played a role. Interestingly, share ownership was not spread evenly across the political spectrum. In 1987, 38 per cent of Conservative Party supporters bought shares as opposed to a much lower 14 per cent among Labour supporters (Riddel 1989: 124). In addition, among the few Labour supporters who did buy shares, between 1983 and 1987, the swing in voting from Labour to the Conservatives was more substantial than in the rest of the electorate (Saunders 1995). While 'popular capitalism' alone does not explain the Conservative Party's permanence in power, their wish to stay might help to explain 'popular capitalism'.

Despite some limitations, the contribution of Jessop *et al.*'s approach in the context of this study lies in its ability to relate Thatcherism to the concept of majoritarian democracy. The connection between the two notions is the common reference to a situation in which a majority in a democracy is able to determine the course of policy with little influence from the rest of the population. Thatcherism, thus, can be viewed as an extreme version of majoritarian democracy, because of the openly confrontational attitude in policy-making, and because of the refusal to use the existing (though limited) instruments which have traditionally helped to generate consensus: namely, in the 1980s no Royal Commission was appointed in Britain (Hayward and Klein 1994).

The durability of Thatcherism is also connected to the majoritarian character of the British constitutional structure. As Jessop *et al.* themselves point out, 'the mechanisms of first-past-the-post electoral system [and] the elective dictatorship of prime ministerial power under the British constitution . . . provided the crucial political preconditions for Thatcherism' (1988: 176). In this respect, it can be argued that Thatcherism, understood as a two-nation strategy, found a fertile ground in Britain thanks to the majoritarian character of British institutions.

In sum, it seems that Thatcherism was made possible, or at least facilitated and perhaps encouraged, by the majoritarian character of British democracy. The most obvious factor is certainly the electoral system. Following Jessop *et al.*'s interpretation, the Thatcher governments adopted policies which were expected to reinforce their social base, by making it better off economically and by enlarging it. The 1986 pension reform must be seen in this context, i.e. as an element of a bigger strategy aimed at constructing and regenerating a social base of support for the leadership.

## 3.2     The British pension system

Like those of most other European countries, the British pension system is characterised by a two-tier structure. The first tier consists of a universal, flat-rate contributory state pension, commonly referred to as the basic pension. It is meant to provide pensioners with a minimum level of income only. In addition, British employees must belong to an earnings-related scheme. This can be provided either by the state or by the employer, in the shape of an occupational pension fund (the 1986 Social Security Act added a third option: a private personal pension).

During the twentieth century, the British pension system underwent a number of substantial changes. The overall trend until the mid-1970s was one of expansion of provision for the elderly. The basic features of the current arrangements were laid down after World War II, when the Labour government adopted the proposals made in the Beveridge report. The main concern for Beveridge was to guarantee a minimum subsistence level to every citizen. He also insisted on abandoning the pre-war practice of means-testing, which was regarded as highly stigmatising and had been extremely unpopular in the inter-war period. The report argued in favour of contributory benefits in order to establish a clear link between financing and entitlements. Both contributions and benefits had to be flat-rate and kept to a minimum level, so that voluntary provision would not be undermined (Silburn 1995: 92–3). The actual implementation of the Beveridge report by the Labour government in 1946 included some additional provision not envisaged by Beveridge, such as a the granting of full pensions immediately instead of adopting a twenty-year transitional period (Brown 1990: 26). In the 1950s, the flat-rate contributions approach came under increased scrutiny. Contributions could not be increased beyond a certain limit or would not otherwise be affordable for low-earners, and yet the financial requirements of the National Insurance fund were growing (Baldwin 1990: 232). In 1958, a Conservative government introduced a limited earnings-related element in the calculation of contributions and benefits.

The basic pension is currently granted to men over sixty-five and to women over sixty years of age,[3] who retire from regular employment and who have paid National Insurance contributions. If the contribution record is incomplete, the amount of the pension is reduced correspondingly. In order to qualify for a full pension, contributions must have been paid or credited for around nine-tenths of the claimant's working life. There is an addition for a dependent spouse of around 67 per cent of the single person's pension. Until 1980, the value of the basic pension was regularly increased in real terms so as to keep up with the evolution of earnings. From 1980 onwards the basic pension has remained constant in real terms, which means a decline in its replacement rate. In 1983 the amount of the single pension corresponded to 32 per cent of average male earnings, while in 1993 the same figure was 22 per cent (Atkinson 1994: 8).

---

[3] Retirement ages are going to be equalised at sixty-five over a relatively long period of time. The first cohort of women who will start drawing a state pension at sixty-five will be the one born in 1955.

The other important reform which determined the structure of the pre-1986 pension system was the 1975 Social Security Act. On that occasion, National Insurance contributions were made totally earnings-related, and a State Earnings Related Pension Scheme (SERPS) was introduced. The 1975 reform was the conclusion of two decades of debates on the issue of 'superannuation'. The main problem lay with the recognition that the level of the basic pension was in fact insufficient to guarantee an adequate standard of living to most pensioners. While those working for big employers were usually covered by an occupational pension, this was not the case for many other pensioners who had to rely solely on the state pension. The idea of a comprehensive second-tier pension gathered support among public opinion, so that both major parties started producing proposals for a new arrangement. Because many employees already had access to satisfactory occupational provision, none of the political parties seriously contemplated the idea of replacing existing pension funds (Heclo 1974: 265). Interestingly, in the early 1950s and 1960s the Conservative leaders considered the possibility of making private provision compulsory for everyone, but private insurers did not meet such proposals with enthusiasm, because they feared that it would mean stricter government interference in their activities (ibid.: 280).

The final shape of SERPS was the result of a compromise between the different positions of the relevant actors. It did guarantee compulsory superannuation for all employees, but allowed those who wished to remain members of their occupational funds to do so. Also in future, employees would be entitled to contract out of the state scheme if their employer provided an occupational scheme which met certain conditions. The SERPS scheme granted an additional pension corresponding to 25 per cent of earnings during the best twenty years (the pension formula was modified by the 1986 SSA).

Both the basic pension and SERPS are financed mainly through National Insurance contributions. These are paid by employers (13.7 per cent) and employees (7.75 per cent) as a percentage of gross salary up to a ceiling.[4] If an employee is contracted out of SERPS to join an occupational scheme, the contribution rate is reduced by 2.5 percentage points for the employee and by 4.5 points for the employer (all figures refer to the period prior to the 1986 pension reform). The payment of National Insurance contributions entitles employees to claim a number of contributory benefits (including unemployment benefit). It should be noted,

---

[4] The figures refer to Class 1 contributions, which are paid by employees only. Self-employed people pay flat-rate contributions.

however, that National Insurance payments are not earmarked for specific programmes, but they all contribute to the National Insurance Fund. In fact, the fund is de facto considered as part of the general government budget, so that the difference between income from contributions and expenditure on benefits (usually negative) is made up with government money.

With the introduction of SERPS, the state intervened to regulate the occupational pension sector, which up to then had enjoyed a relatively high degree of freedom. In order to be able to contract out of the state scheme (i.e. to receive the rebate on National Insurance contributions), pension funds have to provide a guaranteed minimum pension (GMP), which corresponds to the amount an employee would receive from SERPS, had he or she not contracted out. The state provides insurance against the risk involved in such long-term commitment. Earlier, the 1973 SSA had set up a supervisory body, the Occupational Pension Board (OPB), charged with overseeing pension funds and advising the government on occupational pension policy (Hannah 1986: 64). The board is composed of representatives of employers and employees and of members of the actuarial profession.

### Pressures for change

In the debate which led to the adoption of the 1986 SSA, two main issues played a key role: the problem of expected rising pension expenditure, due to population ageing and to the maturation of SERPS; and the inadequate level of pensions paid to employees who left an occupational pension before retirement (usually job-changers) commonly referred to as early-leavers.

As Brown notes, preoccupation with the cost of pensions has been a constant feature of pension debates in the UK (1990: 206). The introduction of SERPS in 1978 added a new component to pension expenditure, which was likely to increase significantly over the following years because of the maturation of the scheme. This, together with the intellectual climate of the early 1980s, contributed to making the future cost of pension provision a topical issue. In the first half of the 1980s a number of reports, articles and influential interventions referred to the expected rise in pension expenditure (Nesbitt 1995: 40). Particularly active were institutes and think-tanks which were sympathetic to new-right ideas, although the most influential documents were those published by the government.

In 1982 the Government Actuary produced a report entitled *National Insurance Fund Long Term Financial Estimates*, which included projections

Table 3.2 *Projected employer/employee combined contribution rates for state pensions in Britain (percentage of gross earnings)*

| Year | Indexation on prices | Indexation on earnings |
|------|----------------------|------------------------|
| 1985 | 12.5 | 12.5 |
| 1995 | 11.9 | 13.3 |
| 2005 | 11.9 | 14.3 |
| 2015 | 13.3 | 17.0 |
| 2025 | 14.7 | 19.9 |

This projection was based on the following assumptions: fertility rate of 2.1 in the period concerned; unemployment rate of 6 per cent; 25 per cent improvement in mortality; and average real earnings growth of 1.5 per cent per year.

*Source:* UK, DHSS 1984b: 6, tab. 5.

of future expenditure and receipts of the state pension scheme. In the report it was argued that the standard contribution rate was expected to rise from 15.4 per cent in 1985 to 16.7 per cent in 2005 and to 21.9 per cent in 2025, and to increase by a further 2 per cent. The projection was based on the assumption that earnings and flat-rate benefits would increase at 8 per cent (average) a year while earnings-related benefits would increase at 6 per cent afterward. In the comment to these figures, it was pointed out that 'if flat-rate benefits . . . were uprated over a long period at a lower rate than earnings . . . the increase in the standard rate of contribution might be less steep and it might even not increase at all depending on how big was the difference between earnings and benefit increases' (UK, Government Actuary 1982: 5). With the benefit of hindsight, and considering the fact that flat-rate benefits have been uprated according to prices since 1980,[5] the projections of 1982 do not seem to reveal a particularly alarming picture.

The demographic issue was picked up again two years later, when the DHSS (Department of Health and Social Security) published a background paper dealing with the issue of projected expenditure on pensions (UK, DHSS 1984b). The document was presented as an updated version of the projections made by the Government Actuary in 1982, but was based on notional contributions for pensions (i.e. the part of National Insurance contributions needed to finance the pension element of social

[5] It should be noted that at the time of the publication of the Government Actuary report (1982), it was generally assumed that the indexation of flat-rate benefits in line with prices was a temporary measure (Nesbitt 1995: 36).

security) as opposed to the actual contribution rate (which also includes contributions to unemployment insurance and other contributory schemes). This difference makes a comparison between the figures presented in the two reports impractical. The 1984 background paper presented a range of possible scenarios based on different assumptions with regard to fertility rates, mortality, unemployment, real earnings growth and benefit indexation. Table 3.2 gives the result of the central projection with benefits upgraded according to prices and earnings respectively.

Because of the different bases used in the two projections, it is difficult to compare these figures with those published by the Government Actuary two years earlier. However, the government's interpretation of the new figures was more concerned with the future cost of pensions. This was made clear in the introduction to the 1984 background report, signed by the then secretary of state for social services, Norman Fowler, who commented on the findings of the report in the following terms:

One of the main messages about the future in the Government Actuary's projections is that expenditure on pensions is set to rise significantly as pensioners increase in number and live longer, and as more of them get higher pensions . . . some may say that looking ahead to the next century is too uncertain . . . In pension policy twenty or thirty years is a relatively short time. We will not be thanked by . . . future generations if we do not address now the problems which they may face. (Fowler, in UK, DHSS 1984b)

The government's interpretation of the projections was thus one of relative urgency. The expected increase in pension expenditure was seen, or at least presented, as a compelling reason to cut back on current commitments of the state pension scheme. Both the projections and the way in which these were interpreted by the government were challenged by a number of different interest groups and commentators. This was not only the case of the opposition and of other groups traditionally antagonistic to the Conservative governments, but also of independent commentators and academics (Abel-Smith and Townsend 1984; Reddin 1984).

*The early-leavers problem*

Pension schemes were designed at a time when stable full-time employment was the norm in western societies. Since the mid-1970s, however, stable patterns of employment have become increasingly rare. In 1983, it was estimated that some 95 per cent of employees change job at least once (*The Economist* 11 June 1983). The issue of compatibility of the UK pension system with these tendencies in the labour market structure gained prominence in the pension debate prior to the 1986 SSA. The main problem was the preservation of pension rights for those employees who left an occupational pension scheme before reaching retirement age (early-leavers) typically because they changed jobs. At the time (before the 1985 SSA, discussed below), early-leavers were particularly disadvantaged relative to those who remained in the same scheme for their whole career. The law (1973 SSA) provided three options for those who intended to leave an occupational scheme. First, job-changers could have their pension entitlement transferred to their new employer, but only if an agreement between the old and the new employer could be reached. Alternatively, the employee could receive an entitlement to a 'deferred pension', which would be paid at the time of retirement and be based on the contribution record achieved before leaving the scheme, but not revalued since. The third option was the simple retrieval of one's own contributions, with no interest. According to estimates, the first option, potentially the most satisfactory, was being used by only 5 per cent of early-leavers, while the third affected some 75 per cent of them (*The Economist* 11 June 1983).

The problem of early-leavers was brought on to the agenda by a report of the Occupational Pensions Board (1981) which included some figures estimating the extent of early-leavers' losses. The estimate was based on the assumption that earnings were going to increase by 7.5 per cent a year. Under such conditions an employee who changed job at forty-five was left with a pension of 60 per cent of what a stayer would have received. If someone changed job three times, he or she might have ended up with a pension of 50 per cent of that of a stayer, despite having paid the same amount in contributions. The OPB report insisted on the need for improving the situation of early-leavers, and in particular it recommended changes in the preservation of deferred pensions, suggesting that pension rights in defined-benefits schemes be increased in line with earnings (ibid.: 69).

To a large extent the issue of early-leavers was dealt with by the 1985 Social Security Act. This new piece of legislation provided the right for employees to a 'transfer value' in respect of their accrued contributions (although the new employer would not be obliged to accept the transfer). It introduced an obligation for pension funds to disclose information to members on the situation of their accrued contributions, and provided for deferred pensions to be increased in line with inflation. This series of measures were the first step towards the establishment of a competitive market in provision for retirement. As argued by some commentators, the 1985 SSA aimed at creating suitable conditions for the introduction of personal pensions (Nesbitt 1995: 123; Brown 1990: 222).

## 3.3      The pension debate in the early 1980s

The intellectual and political climate of the early 1980s in Britain was dominated by neo-liberal ideas of supremacy of the market over the state as an instrument of resource allocation. The overall discourse of the Thatcher governments was a key factor in this, as was the participation in the debate on social and economic policy of a number of London-based research institutes, commonly referred to as think-tanks, which shared and pushed forward neo-liberal ideas. It has been argued that, during the 1980s, these institutions played a key role in policy-making. Novel ideas on how to shift responsibilities away from the state and to the private sector frequently originated from these think-tanks (Desai 1994; Hayward and Klein 1994). In the area of pensions, an important role was played by the Centre for Policy Studies (CPS), which in 1983 published a paper entitled *Personal and Portable Pensions for All* (Vinson and Chapell 1983). This was the first important published document which advocated a radical shift in pension policy by setting out a reform proposal. The paper argued for the introduction of personal pensions, mainly on ideological grounds. Some of the ideas expressed in that paper were in fact contained in subsequent government proposals for new legislation.

Politically, the period before the adoption of the 1986 SSA was characterised by the overwhelming victory achieved by the Conservative Party in the 1983 election. The party emerged with a majority of 144 seats, which gave the government a position of extreme strength in Parliament. This had an impact on policy, which became more uncompromising than before (Nesbitt 1995: 57).

The shape of power relationships in the British political system of the mid-1980s can be qualified as an extreme version of majoritarian democracy. As pointed out above, the various Thatcher governments have typically profited from the opportunities offered by the UK's political institutions. The period between 1983 and 1987 is, because of the strength of the parliamentary majority, the one in which the search for consensus was least needed and the majoritarian character of the British democracy reached its highest level. This, arguably, did have an impact on pension policy.

### The 'Inquiry into Provision for Retirement'

The official debate on a major reform of the British pension system started in November 1983, when the then secretary of state for health and social services Norman Fowler announced the setting up of an 'Inquiry into Provision for Retirement', in order to 'study the future development, adequacy and costs of state, occupational and private provision for retirement in the United Kingdom, including the portability of pension rights' (UK, DHSS 1983: 4).

The team which carried out the Inquiry was chaired by Norman Fowler himself, which gave the Inquiry a strong political connotation. In the United Kingdom policy change is often initiated by the work of *ad hoc* commissions. Particularly, Royal Commissions were used to generate consensual approaches to a given policy problem. Alternatively, the Inquiry could have taken the shape of an independent committee such as the Beveridge Committee. However, Norman Fowler decided to opt for a more overtly political form. As he pointed out, the task of the Inquiry was to generate neither consensus nor new ideas, but 'proposals which I could get past my colleagues' (Fowler, quoted in Nesbitt 1995: 69). According to Nesbitt, the choice of an alternative format for the Inquiry would not have allowed Norman Fowler the same degree of control over the policy-making process (ibid.: 68).

The main team of the Inquiry was composed of twelve members, half of whom were Conservative ministers. Represented in the team were other government departments, such as the DTI (Department of Trade and Industry), the Department of Employment and the Treasury. The remaining members were representatives of the insurance industry and experts, such as the Government Actuary (Nesbitt 1995: 71). It is striking to note how little representative of the interests involved was the team, which did not include individuals supposed to represent employees and pensioners.

These, as well as other groups, were consulted by the team in the following months. In November 1984 submissions of written evidence were invited and, in the two-month period of consultation, more than 1,500 different items were submitted. The duration of the consultation procedure, however, was widely regarded as inadequate. Strong criticism came from pressure groups which felt they had no opportunity to influence the course of policy, such as the CPAG (Ward 1985), but also from independent commentators (*Financial Times* 3 June 1985; Nesbitt 1995: 73).

The Inquiry did not produce a final report, although the Green Paper published in June 1985 (UK, DHSS 1985b) can be regarded as its outcome. Two other documents were published in the context of the Inquiry. The first was a background paper containing data on current and future cost of state pensions as well as statistics on pensioners' living standards (UK, DHSS 1984b). The second, more significant, was a consultative document (UK, DHSS 1984a) which set out the overall objectives of the government in the area of pension policy. The main points were the right for employees to have their own personal pension; a contribution-defined opt-out criterion (such as the GMP for defined-benefits contracted-out schemes); the provision of special arrangements to avoid demographic destabilisation of occupational schemes; and the commitment not to ask employers to contribute to personal pensions in excess of the National Insurance rebate.

## 3.4    The 1986 Social Security Act

The government's intentions in the area of pension policy were spelt out in the Green Paper *Reform of Social Security*, which was published in June 1985 (UK, DHSS 1985b). The main points of the paper were the gradual phasing out of SERPS, although all entitlements earned to date would be preserved, and the introduction of personal pensions. The Green Paper did not meet with much approval from the various actors concerned. The most controversial issue was the idea of phasing out SERPS, which was opposed by groups antagonistic to the government (such as the Labour Party, the TUC and the anti-poverty lobby) but also by more unlikely opponents, such as the CBI, the NAPF and, perhaps most significantly, the Treasury (see below, 71–2).

In the face of mounting criticism, Norman Fowler eventually decided to drop plans for the abolition of SERPS. In the White Paper *Programme for Action* (UK, DHSS 1985a), the subsequent step in the formulation of policy, the cuts proposed were limited to a reduction in the generosity of SERPS benefits. The pension formula was to be changed so as to reduce the amount of standard benefits, and provision for widows was also to be reduced. The White Paper maintained the introduction of personal pensions, and made provision for a 2 per cent additional rebate to employees who joined a personal pension scheme.

The debate that led to the adoption of the 1986 SSA was highly complex and controversial. The various actors involved put forward a number of very different proposals and some of them changed their demands during the policy-making process. In order to reconstruct the course of policy, and to ascertain the level of participation of the relevant actors in decision-making, this section outlines government policy in the period prior to the adoption of the 1986 SSA, and looks at the reactions of the most influential actors.

*Government policy, 1984–6*

The position of the government is itself the result of interaction and of aggregation of the preferences of the different entities which compose it and of the interests represented within it. In this respect, mechanisms of compromise and consensus building are at work within the government as well as in the overall process of policy-making. In the case of the 1986 pension reform, three key governmental actors took part in the definition of policy. Prime Minister Margaret Thatcher, because of her position of leadership, was obviously able to affect the course of policy. Second, the DHSS, headed by Secretary of State Norman Fowler, was the department with direct responsibility with regard to both the formulation and the implementation of policy. Third, the Treasury frequently intervened in the policy-making process when matters of spending arose.

The Treasury, in fact, is often regarded as one of the most powerful government departments in the UK. In general, its main concern lies with balancing the budget, and in the past the Treasury has often been able to veto expensive economic policies (Hall 1986: 62). It appears that the Treasury did play a substantial role in the definition of pension policy. The review of social security was constrained within a zero-cost requirement, set by the Treasury (Nesbitt 1995: 69). This meant that new programmes would have had to be financed by restrictions in existing ones, within the social security system. In fact, in the course of the Inquiry into Provision for Retirement, the representative of the Treasury in the team intervened on various occasions to block attempts made by Inquiry members to discuss issues relating to taxation (ibid.: 71).

The extent of disagreement within the 1983–7 Conservative government should not be exaggerated. In a one-party government with a strong leadership, internal divisions are relatively easily dealt with. In addition, with regard to the 1986 pension reform, there was a substantial degree of agreement on the principles and on the overall direction of pension policy. Assumptions relating to the proper balance of state and private provision, the value of freedom of choice and of market-based competition were widely shared by Cabinet members. Such views were reflected in the 1983 election manifesto, which argued that a Conservative government would 'reintroduce measures to give substantial tax incentives to personal pensions, and to enable members of occupational schemes to make additional voluntary contributions to a pension plan that is completely separate from their employers' scheme' (Conservative Party 1983). Internal dissent emerged only when the implementation of ideology-driven solutions resulted in increased state expenditure.

The overall direction of pension policy was the result of decisions taken in relation to specific issues. In the debate which preceded the adoption of the 1986 SSA and in the elaboration of policy, four different aspects were seen as particularly important to the effectiveness of reform. These were: the current and the future cost of pensions; the situation of early-leavers;

the introduction of personal pensions; and the future of SERPS. The decisions taken in these four areas determined the content of the reform and its overall character. Their details are examined below.

*Cost* With regard to the issue of cost, there seemed to be overall agreement within the government on taking steps to reduce projected costs of the state scheme. The Treasury stressed that 'after the turn of the century numbers [of persons above pension age] will rise rapidly as those born during the baby boom of the 1950s and 1960s reach retirement age' (UK, Treasury Department 1984: 14). Similarly, virtually all the DHSS publications concerned with pension policy put forward the view that to maintain pay-as-you-go arrangements in their current shape would be irresponsible to future generations. For instance, the Green Paper argued that: 'We should not place on our successors the responsibility for meeting all our financial expectations in retirement. Instead we should ensure that everybody is able to save and invest for his own additional pension' (UK, DHSS 1985b: I, 4).

The critique of the pay-as-you-go system, which was one of the key bases for the 1986 SSA, also had a moral dimension, which seemed to be consistent with the notion of individual responsibility embedded in liberal-conservative ideology. The Treasury's pragmatic interest in keeping state expenditure on pensions under control was matched by the moral concerns of the ideologues, who saw the state compulsory pay-as-you-go system as an infringement of economic freedom.[6] As a result, the issue of cost did not raise much controversy *within* the government: the general agreement was on keeping state spending as low as possible. However, such correspondence between the requirements of neo-liberal ideology and the Treasury's pragmatism in budget balancing was not found everywhere in the 1986 SSA. In other areas of pension policy these two imperatives were in conflict.

*Early-leavers* The second important issue which characterised the pre-1986 pension debate is the comparatively disadvantageous situation experienced by early-leavers, i.e. employees who left an occupational pension scheme before reaching the age of retirement. The terms of reference of the Inquiry included the study of the 'portability of pension rights' (UK, DHSS 1983), and, from the early stages of the legislative process, the problem of early-leavers was seen by the government as connected to the introduction of personal pensions and the creation of a competitive market for pension provision. Under such conditions, ideally, employees

---

[6] For a discussion of notions of personal freedom and responsibility in the area of pensions in a new-right perspective, see Morgan 1984.

would be able to move their accrued pension rights from one provider to another at their convenience and without incurring any loss. In fact, the 1985 SSA (see above, 64), which was intended precisely to deal with the issue of early-leavers, introduced the right to a 'transfer value' for members of occupational schemes. This corresponds to the amount of accrued contributions and must be disclosed to the employee at any time. As pointed out above, legislation passed in 1985 had the twofold objective of dealing with the problem of early-leavers and preparing the conditions for the introduction of personal pensions, by creating a level playing field for competing pension providers (Brown 1990: 222; Nesbitt 1995: 122).

*Personal pensions* There was substantial agreement within the government on the desirability of introducing personal pensions. This fitted in well with both the neo-liberal ideology and political concerns with resource allocation. In addition personal pensions provided an answer to the most pressing socio-economic issues discussed above. In the government's view, personal pensions did not represent a burden for future generations, since they were funded. In addition, by creating a free and competitive market for pension provision, they provided a solution to the problem of early-leavers.

The government, however, and in particular Norman Fowler, were keen to emphasise the individual choice dimension of personal pensions. As Fowler put it in an interview: 'What I wanted to do was to make it clear that what we were talking about was *your* pension, *you* had ownership and pension holders had rights' (Fowler, in BBC 1996). Similarly, the White Paper stressed that 'the right to a personal pension gives all employees a new dimension of choice' (UK, DHSS 1985a: 16). In addition, the government insisted on pointing out that there was a substantial popular demand for personal pensions. The DHSS commissioned a Gallup poll on social security, from which it emerged that two-thirds of employees who were not members of an occupational scheme thought that it was important or very important to have access to a second-tier pension (UK, DHSS 1985b: III, 75). This was reiterated in the White Paper: 'the evidence suggests that many more people would like to have their own occupational or personal pension' (UK, DHSS 1985a: 3).

There was, thus, an important ideological component in government insistence on personal pensions, which suggests that these were indeed seen as an element of popular capitalism. While initially these seemed to be seen mainly as an instrument to deal with the issues of projected cost and of early-leavers, it became increasingly clear that the government viewed personal pensions as worth introducing in their own right. In Norman Fowler's own words:

I would have proposed personal pensions irrespective of what had happened to SERPS because personal pensions seemed to me to be simply an extra option as far as the public was concerned. It of course was deeply unpopular with the occupational pension industry. It was an option we would have wished to give to people come what may. (Fowler, in Nesbitt 1995: 76)

Personal pensions thus became an element in the wider context of 'popular capitalism', which was part and parcel of the Conservative Party ideology and political strategy. Personal pensions were not necessarily aimed at the middle classes although, as it turned out, they do benefit more those who are not on low incomes[7] (Waine 1995: 326). However, together with home ownership and share ownership, pension ownership was going to contribute to the creation of a constituency who would resist changes in legislation likely to worsen the economic advantages of their position. Given the policy orientation of the major parties at the time, this amounted to a reinforcement of the Conservative's social base.

*SERPS* The future of SERPS was by far the most controversial issue in the pension debate during the 1980s, both within the government and in general debates. Norman Fowler envisaged a pension system based on a two-tier structure, in which a strong basic pension would be coupled with compulsory and totally funded private pensions. State provision would thus be limited to a minimum, so that there was no reason to maintain SERPS (Fowler, in BBC 1996). Despite controversy within the Cabinet, Norman Fowler managed to transpose his vision almost intact into the Green Paper. The argument of the excessive future cost of SERPS was reiterated (UK, DHSS 1985b: I, 22). In addition, the state additional pension was criticised since it 'discourages the development of occupational pensions because of the complexity of the state scheme's provision on contracting out and the open-ended commitment that employers have to take on' (ibid.: 22). As a result, the government concluded that the best policy option was the gradual phasing-out of SERPS. The possibility of reducing its importance was considered but dismissed, since 'the impact of restricting SERPS is essentially negative. It restricts the scope of state provision but puts nothing in its place' (ibid.: 24).

The abolition of SERPS attracted criticism from a significant and probably unexpectedly high number of actors. In addition to the Labour Party and traditionally left-wing groups (such as the TUC and the anti-poverty lobby), substantial criticism came from interest groups traditionally sympathetic to the Conservative government such as the CBI and NAPF

---

[7] That is because, for someone on a low income, the rebate on National Insurance contributions would be so small that a substantial part of it would be needed to meet the cost of charges.

(Nesbitt 1995: 88; *Economist* 21 September 1985). Moreover, there was no unanimity on the issue even within the government. In fact, even before the publication of the Green Paper, the Treasury had signalled its opposition to plans for abolishing SERPS. The episode was described by Norman Fowler as an 'all-out battle' with Chancellor of the Exchequer Nigel Lawson (Fowler, in BBC 1996). The reason behind the Treasury opposition to the abolition of SERPS was the 'double payment' problem, which occurs whenever pension financing is shifted from pay-as-you-go to funding (see ch. 1). In fact, while contribution rebates would have had to be granted immediately, the state would have still been liable to fund current pensions and those of people near retirement age. This would put additional pressure on the state budget, and was seen as unacceptable by the Treasury.

Given the extent of criticism raised by proposals to abolish SERPS, and given internal dissent,[8] the government decided to opt for a less radical solution: a reduction in the value of future SERPS pensions. This change of direction was announced in the White Paper. It was justified with the argument that 'the aim of pension policy should be to seek as much agreement as possible' (UK, DHSS 1985a: 3). In addition, it was argued that, while not constituting an optimal solution, the reduction of SERPS was acceptable because it made it possible to achieve the government's two key objectives: 'to see the emerging cost of SERPS reduced' and 'to ensure that the conditions are created whereby individual pension provision can expand' (ibid.: 4). The proposals contained in the White Paper were translated into final legislation almost unchanged, in spite of continuing criticism from external groups.

### Reactions to government policy

*The Confederation of British Industry (CBI)* The position of British employers in relation to change in pension provision was characterised by a fundamental ambivalence. On the one hand, as an interest group concerned with competitiveness and levels of taxation, the CBI was sympathetic to the government's aim of shifting responsibility for pension provision from the state to the private sector. On the other hand, however, British employers have responsibility for occupational pension schemes, and in this capacity they have tended to oppose measures which were likely to affect the stability of pension funds, which are a form of collective provision but are highly valued by employers. As some commentators have pointed out, occupational schemes constitute an efficient

---

[8] According to Norman Fowler, his plans were opposed 'most significantly of all by the Treasury' (Fowler, in BBC 1996).

instrument in human resources management,[9] as they encourage employee loyalty to the company, and provide a means for tax-efficient self financing (Lusenti 1989: 396; Schmähl 1991: 35).

Consistent with these priorities, the CBI supported a three-tiered pension system. In the submission of evidence to the Inquiry, British employers argued that the basic pension should be kept as a safety net, that the structure of the second tier should remain unchanged, with pensions provided either by the state (through SERPS) or by occupational pensions, and that personal pensions should be made available and encouraged through fiscal incentives as a voluntary third tier of provision (CBI 1984: 2). In this way, the introduction of personal pensions would not have undermined the stability of occupational schemes.

On the issue of the projected costs of SERPS it was argued that 'provided the economy continues to grow . . . it would appear that the current commitments for State and occupational pensions can be met in the future within acceptable cost . . . The CBI therefore does not believe that there is a need to dismantle the current state earnings related system' (CBI 1984: 3). The submission also suggested that some reduction in SERPS benefits could be more appropriate, such as in the case of widows' pensions and in the 'twenty best years' rule, which could be changed to 'lifetime earnings'.

The CBI showed strong opposition to the proposal of introducing personal pensions as an alternative to membership of an occupational scheme. The main problem was the fact that personal pensions were likely to attract younger employees, and thus undermine the demographic balance within occupational schemes.[10] This, it was argued, would make it impractical for employers to provide occupational pensions. As a result many would contract back into the state scheme, with the result of achieving the opposite effect of what was intended (CBI 1984: 7). Strong opposition was also displayed against the idea of employers' contributions to externally provided personal pensions on behalf of the employee, as this would imply having to meet the cost of pension provision without enjoying the advantages provided to an employer by having a pension fund as an instrument of human resource management.

---

[9] This aspect is stressed in the CBI submission to the Inquiry: 'From the employer's point of view the objectives of pension schemes include attracting and motivating employees as well as retaining them' (1984).

[10] Many defined-benefit schemes were set up in the post-war period and had not yet reached maturity by the mid-1980s. This meant that these schemes were functioning (many still are) on a partial pay-as-you-go basis, with younger employees de facto subsidising current retirees, who did not contribute for long enough to fully fund their own retirement. Many occupational schemes, thus, perform a redistributive function from younger to older employees. If large numbers of young employees were to leave occupational pensions, this might have constituted a serious problem for their financial viability.

When the Green Paper was published, the CBI made clear its opposition to the government's plans. Particularly, the suggested phasing-out of SERPS was attacked for the double payment problem. This would have meant a higher rate of pension contributions (National Insurance and occupational), as employers and employees would have had to fund current SERPS pensions and the future (occupational or personal) pensions of current employees. As a result, the CBI reiterated the suggestions made in the original submission of evidence of a reduced version of SERPS instead of its abolition (CBI 1985).

The White Paper met with more approval, as the plans for scrapping SERPS had been abandoned. The paper was described as 'broadly in line with CBI recommendations' (CBI 1986). However, the demographic stability of occupational schemes was still a cause for concern for British employers. In particular, the 2 per cent tax incentive for personal pension buyers was attacked as it was likely to encourage younger employees, attracted by a higher take-home pay, to opt out of their occupational scheme. The CBI requested that the 2 per cent tax incentive be made available only to employees who contracted out of the state scheme, or, alternatively, to all contracted-out employees. The first option was the one adopted by the government.

*The National Association of Pension Funds (NAPF)* The NAPF, an association representing British occupational pension funds, perceived the government's plans for reform as a threat to the stability of their activities. Like the CBI, the NAPF was concerned that the introduction of contracted-out personal pensions would have a detrimental impact on the demographic balance of occupational funds. In the various submissions of evidence and reactions to government proposals, the NAPF expressed sometimes strong criticism against the idea of contracted-out personal pensions and little satisfaction with the government's motives.

The reaction to the CPS paper, which was one of the first appearances of the concept of personal pensions in the debate, was particularly negative. As the then chairman of the NAPF put it at an annual conference of the association: 'Let us hope that the Centre for Policy Studies document is never taken seriously by any politician who sees half a chance to win a vote or two' (Oldfield 1983, quoted by Nesbitt 1995: 54). The same aversion to personal pensions was expressed in the submission of evidence to the Inquiry. In that document it was argued that current occupational pensions were in fact personal, since 'the benefits for and in respect of each individual are based on *his* service and *his* salary', and the only difference with a personal pension is that 'the individual does not have his own pot of gold' (NAPF 1984, emphasis in the original). The same paper went on to argue that defined contribution schemes, such as personal pensions, would involve much bigger risks for employees than was the case with current arrangements, as the amount of the pension they will draw will depend on unpredictable investment returns. Like the CBI, the NAPF was prepared to accept personal pensions only as a third-tier arrangement, and not in the proposed contracted out form (ibid.).

Predictably, the NAPF's reaction to the Green Paper was particularly negative. First the speed of the policy-making process was attacked: 'the introduction of legislation on pensions should be held back until there has been sufficient time for full consultation'. The proposals were described as a 'threat to the stability of the partnership between the occupational pensions movement and State provision' (NAPF 1985). The paper recommended that the government reconsider its plans for the abolition of SERPS, and expressed concern about the commitment made by the Labour Party to reverse such legislation once back in office. The overall tone of the NAPF reaction was to insist on the need for a more consensual approach to pension reform, which would attribute a bigger role to consultation and seek agreement from the opposition, in order to avoid a reversal of legislation with a future Labour government.

*The Labour Party* The 1983 election manifesto set out the main priorities of Labour Party policy on pensions. These included the restoration of the link between the basic pension and increases in earnings (removed by the Conservative government in 1980); and the movement towards a common retirement age of sixty for both men and women (Labour Party 1983). The distance between these positions and the direction of government policy was such that there was little scope for the Labour Party to influence legislation. The sort of minor changes that the government might have agreed to introduce were insignificant in relation to the differences between the two parties.

When Norman Fowler announced the content of the Green Paper, the Labour Party reacted with strong disapproval. Michael Meacher, the then shadow secretary of state for social services, described the proposals as the 'erosion of the fundamental principle of a welfare state for all citizens' and as 'the reintroduction, for the first time this century, of Victorian values in an invidious distinction between deserving an undeserving poor'. The government was also attacked for the stated intention of abolishing SERPS, since the 1983 election manifesto did not mention any such plans. Finally, the validity of the demographic projections was challenged, in particular with reference to the forecasts made by the Phillips Committee in 1954, which turned out to be excessively pessimistic (Hansard 3 June 1985). The policy response to the Green Paper was

formulated at the 1985 annual conference, which adopted a document
'condemn[ing] the Government plans to abolish the state earnings
related pension scheme' and which included a commitment for a future
Labour government to re-introduce a state earnings related pension
scheme if it were abolished (Labour Party 1985: 308).

The decision of the government to abandon its plans for the abolition
of SERPS did not manage to bridge the gap between the two parties. In
1986, Labour Party policy on pensions was to block the implementation
of the 1986 SSA if in government before April 1988, and to repeal the act
if elected after that date (Randall's Parliamentary Services 1986). In fact
in the 1987 election manifesto, there was no mention of what a Labour
government would do with regard to personal pensions, which suggests
that the potential electoral appeal of such schemes was being recognised
by Labour Party officials as well. The manifesto included, however, a
commitment to reverse two other major changes introduced by the
Conservative government: an increase in the basic pension above the rate
of inflation and eventually the return to the inflation/earning indexation
formula; and, in relation to the changes brought about by the 1986 SSA,
the restoration of the former pension formula for SERPS (Labour Party
1987).

In subsequent years the Labour Party came to accept the existence
of contracted-out personal pensions, a reversal of this policy being
extremely impractical. However, some modifications were envisaged in
the early 1990s. The 2 per cent tax rebate was to be abolished, and personal pensions, in order to be approved, were to be required to guarantee
a minimum pension, i.e. subject to the same sort of requirements applied
to defined benefits occupational schemes (Meacher 1991).

*The Trades Union Congress (TUC)*    Like that of the Labour Party,
the TUC's priorities in the area of pensions were substantially different
from those of the government. In the early 1980s, TUC policy aimed to
'establish a comprehensive State social security scheme that provides a
range of benefits which ensure an adequate standard of living for people
in retirement' (TUC 1982: 63). The value of the basic pension was to be
increased to 50 per cent of average gross earnings for a couple, and to a
third for a single-person pension. These improvements could have been
financed through an increase in employers' contributions, which, it was
argued, were too low by European standards, and by an increase in the
tax-financed part of National Insurance (ibid.: 64).

These priorities were entirely out of line with those of the government,
so that, when the Inquiry was launched, the TUC had little opportunity
for fruitfully intervening in the policy process. Understandably, much of

the TUC's discourse and activities during the three-year period prior to the adoption of the 1986 SSA emphasised the total refusal to co-operate with the government on the introduction of personal pensions. As stated in the TUC's submission of evidence to the Inquiry: 'The TUC has no intention of assisting those who wish to reduce the protection to pensioners and workers in agreed final salary [defined-benefits] schemes. We do not accept that millions should be returned to the vagaries of the market-place and poverty for the unlucky' (TUC 1984b).

Opposition to personal pensions was reiterated at the TUC 1984 Annual Conference. A document was adopted in which the danger represented by personal pensions for the demographic stability of occupational schemes was emphasised. Instead, the TUC's approach was to increase the value of the basic pension and to support the 1975 SSA framework, or the combination of SERPS and occupational pensions as second-tier providers (TUC 1984a).

The TUC response to the Green Paper was thus in line with its approach in the previous months. The support for the 1975 SSA framework was reiterated, with emphasis on the wide extent of public support for occupational provision, as they give employees 'some control on their pension arrangements. In contrast, the personal pension holder would have no voice and would be simply an individual subscriber among thousands' (TUC 1985). The TUC also decided to support the Labour Party's commitment to re-introduce SERPS once in office (ibid.), and launched a campaign to try to persuade the government to drop its plans (*The Guardian* 22 July 1985).

*The anti-poverty lobby* The term 'anti-poverty lobby' usually refers to pressure groups and charities which are actively engaged in providing services to people in need, as well as in trying to influence policy debates in the relevant areas. These are part of a pro-welfare coalition which is relatively influential in the United Kingdom, and plays an important role in political debates on the future of the welfare state. In the case of pensions, the most influential pressure group is Age Concern. In the early 1980s, its overall orientation in pension policy was towards a Scandinavian-like pension system. In particular, the pressure group supported an increase of the basic pension and a change in its eligibility rules, so as to make it not dependent on a contribution record (Age Concern 1982).

It its submission to the Inquiry, Age Concern did not display a particularly strong aversion to personal pensions. However, it was pointed out that there were more pressing issues to be dealt with than the introduction of personal pensions: 'the more serious problem is that many people are not covered by company schemes and face retirement on inadequate state benefits' (Age Concern 1984: para. 1.3). Consequently, the support for an increase in the basic state pension was reiterated. In relation to the early-leavers problem, the charity suggested adopting full indexation and full transferability of preserved pensions (ibid.).

Age Concern's reaction to the Green Paper was highly critical. In particular, plans for the abolition of SERPS were attacked, as personal pensions would not guarantee the same level of income security as the state scheme. As David Hobman, then director of the charity, put it: 'We fear for the pensioners of the future, who will be left in the jungle of making their own pension arrangements. Personal pensions will never give the safeguards of SERPS' (Age Concern 1985). After the publication of the White Paper, Age Concern welcomed the retention of SERPS by the government, but was not satisfied with the treatment of women in the modified scheme, as the abolition of the twenty-best-years rule was likely to affect them to a greater extent than men (Age Concern 1986).

## 3.5    Key elements of the 1986 pension reform

The new law, which was passed in July 1986, introduced a number of changes in the British pension system as well as in other areas of social security.[11] The changes affected the whole area of second-tier pensions, by modifying the state scheme (SERPS), by changing some of the rules governing occupational provision and, most significantly, by introducing the possibility for employees to take out personal pensions.

First, the new law reduced the amount of future SERPS pensions, by changing the pension formula and by decreasing the value of widow(-ers) pensions. The benefit, up to then calculated as 25 per cent of relevant earnings, is being gradually decreased until 2009 to 20 per cent. In addition, the basis for the calculation of the pension was extended from the average earnings in the twenty best years to whole career earnings, with effect from 1998 (when SERPS would be twenty years old). Finally, widows' and widowers' pensions were reduced from 100 per cent of the spouse's entitlement to 50 per cent. As Brown pointed out, one of the effects of these measures was to make SERPS less competitive in relation to occupational and private pensions, which the government intended to promote (1990: 234).

---

[11] The pension reform was undoubtedly the most significant part of the 1986 SSA. Other important changes included the introduction of an *income support* scheme, which replaced a number of means-tested benefits; the creation of a *social fund* which provides loans for particular circumstances (such as maternity or funerals); and the requirement for housing benefits recipients to pay a proportion (20 per cent) of the rent.

With regard to occupational pensions, the 1986 SSA introduced provision which facilitated the development of defined contribution schemes, by specifying a contribution-defined opt-out criterion. This was meant to encourage small employers who might have been deterred from setting up an occupational scheme by the fact that they had to guarantee a minimum pension (GMP). In addition, the calculation of the GMP would be based on the new rules of SERPS, and the minimum period of membership in order to qualify for preservation of pension rights (introduced by the 1985 SSA; see above, 64) was reduced from five to two years. A 2 percentage point contribution rebate was granted to newly contracted-out occupational schemes. Finally, it was decided that membership of an occupational scheme could not be made compulsory by employers, although they could assume that, unless notified differently by an employee, the latter wished to be a member of the relevant scheme.

Finally, the most problematic aspect of the new law concerned the introduction of personal pension schemes. Personal pensions are provided on a competitive basis by insurance companies, as well as by other financial institutions. Employees can then shop around to find the pension which best suits them. This constitutes a third option for the provision of an earnings-related pension. Employees are obliged to make supplementary pension provision, and can chose between the state scheme (SERPS), an occupational scheme (if the employer provides one) or a personal pension.

In order to encourage employees to take out the new personal pensions, the 1986 SSA provided some fiscal incentives. First, as was the case for contracted-out occupational schemes, employees were entitled to a rebate in National Insurance contributions of 5.8 percentage points (2 per cent on employees' contributions and 3.8 per cent on employers' contributions). In practice, both employers and employees continued paying the full contribution rate, and the DHSS (now the DSS) then pays the amount of the rebate into employees' personal pensions.[12] This measure was intended to prevent possible hostile employers from refusing to pay contributions to an external body. In addition, a temporary 2 per cent rebate was granted to new buyers of personal pensions (until April 1993). This incentive was available only to employees who belonged to SERPS, in order not to encourage exit from occupational schemes.

In 1986 there was considerable uncertainty about the number of employees who were going to take out a personal pension. The official estimates made by the Government Actuary forecast 500,000 new

---

[12] In 1993, this was reduced to 4.8 per cent, in line with reductions of the rebate for occupational pensions.

Table 3.3 *Pension coverage for British employees (thousands of employees paying class 1 contributions at the standard rate)*

|      | SERPS  | Occupational pension | Personal pension |
|------|--------|----------------------|------------------|
| 1987 | 10,878 | 8,042                | –                |
| 1988 | 10,043 | 7,904                | 1,288            |
| 1989 | 7,973  | 8,030                | 3,397            |
| 1990 | 7,679  | 8,270                | 4,172            |
| 1991 | 7,436  | 8,202                | 4,810            |
| 1992 | 6,653  | 8,068                | 5,340            |
| 1993 | 6,335  | 7,804                | 5,667            |
| 1994 | 6,527  | 7,476                | 5,732            |

*Source:* UK, DSS 1996: 280 (table H1.03) and 287 (table H2.01).

contracted-out pensions, in either occupational or personal pension schemes. On this basis, the 2 per cent temporary rebate was expected to cost some £60 million in lost revenue to the Exchequer. The reality proved to be quite different. As table 3.3 shows, the number of personal pension holders soared from over 1 million in 1988 to more than 5 million in 1992. The cost to the Exchequer proved to be much bigger than expected. In the period 1987–93, the 2 per cent temporary rebate cost some £2.5 billion in lost revenues, while the grand total (including all rebates) reached £9.7 billion (Waine 1995: 328).

Two factors arguably contributed to this unexpected popularity: first, the importance of the incentive package offered by the government and, second, the intensity of the advertisement campaign carried out both by the government and by the pension industry. The hostile attitude of the government to state provision and in particular to SERPS certainly contributed to convince many members of this scheme to opt out of it. The rapid expansion of personal pensions was not unproblematic. In particular, the quality of the advice given by pension salespersons to prospective buyers was not always of an appropriate standard. The insurance industry was admittedly unprepared to handle the rapid development of this new sector, so that salespeople had to be trained in a very short time and frequently were not competent to correctly advise prospective buyers (BBC 1996; Waine 1995). Most of those who were badly advised were people on low income, for whom the rebate was not important enough to be attractive in comparison to SERPS, or people who were advised to leave their more generous occupational schemes (Waine 1995: 326).

The 1986 British reform was successful in so far as it managed to shift provision for retirement for a substantial section of the population from the state to the private sector, which was consistent with the government's priorities at the time. By reducing the generosity of SERPS, it also intervened to reduce the future cost of providing for the retirement of those who elected to remain with the state scheme. To a large extent, the privileged position of the UK in international comparisons of the future cost of public pensions is a result of the actions taken in 1986. The other side of the coin, however, is a pension system in which low-earners fare particularly badly. The low level of SERPS entitlements and the high costs of personal pensions mean that people on low income have little opportunity to make adequate provision for their retirement. Unlike in the rest of Europe, thus, the UK's pension problem is not about containing cost, but about extending coverage.

## 3.6    Developments in the 1990s

The issue of cost having been dealt with satisfactorily with the reforms of the 1980s, pension policy in the 1990s has been mainly about improving the security of funded pension schemes and the adequacy of provision for those on low income. These issues were brought up by two important events which received significant media coverage: the Maxwell scandal, which consisted of the loss of up to £1 billion by the Mirror Group's pension fund as a result of imprudent investment in the group's own companies (Davis 1997: 37), and the widespread misselling of personal pensions by insurance companies. These events highlighted serious shortcomings in British pension legislation, and were behind policy-making throughout the decade.

The Maxwell scandal brought to the attention of the general public the problems associated with the management of pension funds and their security. The legislation in force at the time allowed a great degree of freedom to pension fund trustees as to how to invest the fund assets. As a result, the Mirror Group's pension fund was able to lend to and invest in companies owned by Maxwell far in excess of what would have been appropriate according to rules of prudent investment. The companies subsequently became insolvent, and assets were lost. The Maxwell case highlighted the need for stricter regulations of trustees' investment practices in order to improve the security of pension funds.

The issue of security was dealt with primarily with the 1995 Pensions Act. The act introduced a 5 per cent limit on self-investment and the obligation for trustees to ensure that limits on self-investment and on loans to the employer are respected. Accountability to scheme members has been improved by requiring that at least one-third of the trustees are elected by them. Finally, the act established a new

Occupational Pensions Regulatory Authority and a compensation fund which intervenes in case of pension schemes becoming insolvent and guarantees the payment of pensions (Davis 1997; Gough and Shackleton 1996). The 1995 Pensions Act also included the equalisation of retirement age for men and women at the age of sixty-five. This was in response to rulings of the European Court of Justice in the early 1990s.

The early 1990s also saw the realisation that personal pensions had been widely missold, either to people who were covered by occupational pensions that offered better conditions, or by people on low income or with discontinuous career patterns, who would have been better off in SERPS. It is estimated that hundreds of thousands of individuals might have been wrongly advised. The problem of misselling was dealt with by the regulators (the Securities and Investment Board and the Personal Investment Authority), which have ordered personal pension providers to identify and compensate clients who were badly advised. Compensation will, in most cases, meet the cost of re-instating the client in the scheme (occupational or SERPS) which he or she had been wrongly advised to leave. The total cost of compensation could be as high as £3 billion (Gough and Shackleton 1996).

The misselling of private pensions has brought up a more fundamental problem relating to the adequacy of personal pensions as a savings vehicle for people on low income or with discontinuous career patterns. For them, the fixed costs of a personal pension are often too high to make it worthwhile to save in this way (Davis 1997: 60; Field 1996: 34–40). The Labour government elected in May 1997 has taken the view that new forms of protection need to be introduced to guarantee a satisfactory pension coverage for these groups. In a December 1998 Green Paper, the government put forward two key proposals designed to improve pension coverage for those who are at the bottom end of the income scale (UK, DSS 1998).

First, the Green Paper proposes to replace SERPS with a state second pension, which would grant flat-rate benefits to those who are not covered by a personal or an occupational pension. Being a flat-rate pension, it will be more advantageous for those on low income. Someone on yearly earnings of £9,000 can expect a benefit worth twice as much as what they would have received with SERPS. The state second pension will also allow contribution credits for individuals who are not engaged in paid work because they are performing caring tasks. The shift from SERPS to the state second pension will take place over a five-year phasing-in period.

Second, the government intends to introduce a new form of funded pension, known as the 'stakeholder pension', which is going to be subjected to strict regulations concerning the charge structure. Pension schemes will qualify as 'stakeholder pensions' if they meet criteria such as a maximum level of operating charges set by the government, if they do not charge entry or exit fees and if they do not impose penalties for missing payments. Employers will then be obliged either to offer membership in an occupational pension, or to 'ensure that employees who cannot join an occupational scheme have access to a stakeholder pension scheme at their place of work' (UK, DSS 1998: 57). Employers will not, however, be obliged to contribute to a stakeholder pension in excess of the contracted-out rebate. It is expected that stakeholder pension schemes will be set up by associations of members, such as trade unions, employers and insurance companies.

Both the state second pension and the stakeholder pension address the issue of inadequate coverage for those who are on low income and with discontinuous career patterns. If adopted, the measures discussed above would significantly improve the quality of pension coverage for these groups. British pension policy in the 1990s, unlike in the previous decade and in continental European countries, has not been about reducing or containing pension expenditure. On the contrary, the main theme of policy-making has been an improvement in provision, to some extent in response to overreaction to the cost problem in during the 1980s. At the end of the 1990s, the challenge for the Blair government is to achieve a more adequate pension coverage without losing the big advantage of not having to worry about the long-term cost of pensions.

### 3.7    Majoritarian politics and pension reform

The decision-making process which led to the adoption of the 1986 SSA is a paradigmatic case of majoritarian policy-making. The official bodies involved in the debate, such as the Inquiry into Provision for Retirement, were securely controlled by the government, and particularly by the secretary of state for social services. This allowed the government wide room for manoeuvre in the early stages of the definition of a new pension policy. The result was that the government was able to produce a Green Paper with relatively detailed suggestions for policy change before explaining its approach to external interests.

The confrontation with interest groups took place mainly between the publication of the Green and the White Papers, over a six-month period. In fact, such a short time did not allow much interference in government plans, though eventually the latter was forced to drop a key element of its plan, i.e. the abolition of SERPS. This was a major concession by the government, which, nonetheless, does not necessarily constitute an instance in which the UK government abandoned its typical majoritarian approach to policy-making. It is true that a majority of the relevant interest groups opposed the abolition of the earnings-related scheme, but it is also true that this issue was source of disagreement within the government as well. As seen above, the abolition of SERPS was strongly supported by the DHSS and equally strongly opposed by the Treasury. The result was a division within the Cabinet between two important departments, which introduced an element of power fragmentation and considerably reduced the potential for majoritarian policy-making. The position of the Treasury, and its capacity to block the implementation of unwanted legislation, can be conceptualised in terms of a veto point. In these circumstance, thus, the UK's political system did include a veto point which was effectively used.

A second important feature in pension policy-making throughout the 1980s is the lack of agreement among the relevant actors on whether or not the British pension system needed to be reformed. In the two other countries studied here, the pension issue is generally viewed in the same terms by the various relevant actors, which usually disagree only when it comes to putting forward solutions to commonly accepted problems. As seen above, in Britain the case for retrenchment of public pension provision was far from being unanimously accepted. Particularly the left and the labour movement were not persuaded by the government's argument that the system needed radical reform. Similarly, other interest groups, such as the CBI, did not feel that the pension commitments involved by SERPS were going to represent an excessive burden (CBI 1984: 3). In this context, what is striking is the fact that the British government managed to push through a relatively radical reform, despite the lack of shared views on the pension problem. In other European countries, the political sensitivity of pension reform usually requires a widespread sense of urgency before governments can take action. In this respect, the British government benefited from the absence of veto points in the UK's constitutional structure and from the majoritarian tradition in policy-making.

Third, the British pension reform of 1986 stands out for the asymmetry of its impact on various sections of the population. Unlike the pension reforms adopted in other European countries, the British 1986 Social Security Act cannot be qualified as simply unpopular. It made provision for personal pensions which were subsequently taken out by some 5 million people, and this, if anything, is a clear indicator of popularity, even though because of misselling not all of them will be better off than if they had stayed in a collective arrangement.

On the other hand, employees with low salaries and non-continuous career patterns, and particularly women, were the main losers in the 1986 pension reform. The state scheme SERPS included some de facto redistributive measures, such as the fact that it took into account earnings during the best twenty years, which benefited employees who did not have a full contribution record. The reduction from 25 per cent of reference salary to 20 per cent in the pension formula constituted an additional loss for employees who because of age, career patterns, salary or personal beliefs did not find it convenient to take up a personal pension.

Finally, employees covered by occupational arrangements, a large and influential section of the British electorate, were not affected by the savings measures adopted in the 1986 SSA. Thanks to the structure of the British pension system, and particularly to the division between occupational and state second-tier provision, the government was able to target savings on a section of the population only, which substantially reduced the risk of electoral punishment. The differentiated impact of reform on various sections of the population is a typical feature of the social and economic policies of the 1980s. It must be seen in connection with the majoritarian character of British democracy. Those who felt they were going to lose out in the reform of 1986 had little opportunity to influence the course of policy. On the other hand, the government did not need to worry too much about the electoral repercussions of its retrenchment measures. The support of those who felt that they were going to be better off with or unaffected by the new arrangements compensated for the loss of popularity due to cutbacks in state pensions.

The Thatcher government, thus, managed to exploit the opportunities provided by the institutional design of its pension system, which made possible the targeting of savings on a section of the population only. In doing this, it was assisted and perhaps encouraged by the structure of British political institutions which, by not providing veto points to external opponents, allow a significant degree of governmental control over policy-making. Moreover, the choice of such a strategy in pension reform was consistent with the electoral concerns of the government. As seen at the beginning of this chapter, the British electoral system rewards policies able to attract the support of a sufficiently large minority, if the rest of the electorate is divided as was the case throughout the 1980s.

# 4    Switzerland: the politics of consensual retrenchment

With regard to political institutions and to patterns of exclusion and inclusion in policy-making, Switzerland can be considered as the mirror image of the UK. Because they provide a series of veto points, Swiss institutions allow a significant degree of influence to external groups. Most notably, this is the case of the referendum system, whereby any act passed by parliament can be challenged at the polls if 50,000 signatures are collected supporting a referendum. In addition, well-established decision-making procedures tend to include a wide range of different and often conflicting interests, and to produce compromises that are more or less acceptable to as many actors as possible. This peculiar approach to policy-making constitutes an important limitation to the room for manoeuvre available to the government in virtually all areas of policy. Pension policy, of course, is no exception.

The 1995 Swiss pension reform was adopted after more than a decade of intense negotiations between political parties and the social partners. Despite a series of attempts at reaching a mutually acceptable compromise, a totally consensual solution was not found. Eventually, however, the reform included both expansion and retrenchment elements, a combination that proved instrumental in guaranteeing the final adoption of the pension bill. The retrenchment measures alone would have been at a much higher risk of defeat in a referendum. This strategy has been used in other welfare reforms in the early 1990s, and can be seen as a response to the institutional constraints that limit policy-making. The combination of improvements in provision, on which there was widespread agreement, with controversial retrenchment elements has contributed to the successful adoption of reform also in the areas of unemployment benefits and health insurance (Bonoli 1997b).

This chapter looks first at the key features of consensus democracy in Switzerland, on the basis of existing studies. It then describes the structure of the Swiss pension system and provides an account of the developments that led to the adoption of the 1995 pension reform. The final section explores the link between consensus politics and welfare retrenchment.

86

## 4.1    The politics of consensus democracy

To explain the roots and the underpinnings of consensual policy-making
has been a constant preoccupation in the work of Swiss political scientists.
Thanks to their efforts we now know relatively well how consensual politics works, how it originated and, perhaps most importantly, what its limits
are. In fact, the main challenge in understanding Swiss politics is probably
to avoid an excessive idealisation of the Swiss model. The term 'consensus' itself can be misleading in this respect, because it conveys an image of
general and widespread agreement and harmony in politics. Of course, it
is not like this. Swiss policy-makers disagree on policy as much as any of
their counterparts in other countries. Nevertheless, they have developed a
number of mechanisms which reduce the impact of disagreement and
favour the adoption of mutually acceptable solutions. The search for a
common platform among key actors is a basic rule in policy-making.

Swiss institutions, however, are unique in many respects. Besides referendums, there are other unusual elements by international comparison.
First, the government (Federal Council) is a 'collegial' institution. This
means that, unlike in other democracies, there is neither a single individual head of government nor a head of state,[1] these two functions being
fulfilled jointly by the seven members of the Federal Council. Decisions
within the Federal Council are taken through majority voting, and individual ministers are expected to conform to the majority view, regardless
of their initial opinion. The result is that the Federal Council is a place for
consensus building in so far as it includes members of the four largest
parties across the political spectrum. Compromise is a necessity in the
government coalition if it is to survive. Second, Switzerland has a symmetric bicameral parliamentary system, modelled on that of the United
States. Legislation has to be accepted by both chambers. The upper
chamber, the Council of States, represents the member-states of the confederation, or cantons. Each canton, irrespective of its size, has two
members in the Council of States. In contrast, in the lower chamber, the
National Council, cantons have a number of MPs which is proportional
to the size of their population. Third, the Swiss constitutional order is
characterised by a strict separation of powers between the government
and parliament. This means that the executive has comparatively little
control over decisions taken by parliament, which creates an additional
opportunity for external groups to influence legislation. These elements –
referendums, collegial governance symmetric bicameralism with a strong

---

[1] There is in Switzerland a 'President of the Confederation'; however, this position has an
exclusively representative function. The presidency is assumed by each Federal Council
member, by yearly rotation.

influence of the cantons and separation of powers – constitute a series of potential veto points that bills have to overcome in order to be adopted.

Political scientists are virtually unanimous in arguing that the availability of referendums to unsatisfied minorities is a key factor behind the development of consensual politics (Kriesi 1995: 90; Katzenstein 1984: 144; Neidhart 1970).[2] The fact that Swiss voters have the opportunity to call a referendum on any piece of legislation, provided they collect the appropriate number of signatures, has been a major element in the development of a consensual political system. Neidhart (1970) goes even further, and argues that referendums are *the* reason why Swiss policy-makers act more consensually than most of their European counterparts. He substantiates his claim by looking at the origin of consensus-building procedures, which go back to the late nineteenth century. In 1890, the government was defeated in a referendum on a proposal for the introduction of compulsory health insurance, which had nevertheless received wide support in parliament. As a result of this event, it introduced consensus-building mechanisms, such as a formal consultation procedure, precisely in order to minimise the risk of being defeated at the polls. In addition, the inclusion of 'unnecessary' parties in the ruling coalition began as a response to an obstructive use of referendums. Until 1891, in fact, the Liberal Democrats (PRD) were able to rule the country alone, but found it difficult to adopt legislation because of the obstructive strategy played by the Conservative-Catholic Party (now PDC). Between 1871 and 1891 the Conservative-Catholic Party called twenty referendums on acts passed by parliament and won fifteen. This created a situation of legislative impasse, which was solved by the ruling PRD by incorporating the Conservatives in the ruling coalition (Kriesi 1995: 207–9). Referendums are certainly a powerful force behind consensual politics. Typically, every effort is made to avoid the polls, as a defeat generally means a considerable waste of time and a loss of legitimacy for federal authorities, who are as a result unable to legislate in the relevant area for a number of years.

Referendums, however, are not the only factor responsible for the emergence of consensual democracy, as similar policy-making arrange-

---

[2] According to Lijphart (1984), referendums are not an element of consensus democracy, because they can favour majorities as well as minorities. This view, however, does not distinguish between different types of referendums, which can have different political implications (Kobach 1993: 60). When a referendum is called by the government, it can be used to legitimise the view of the majority (like De Gaulle's referendum on the independence of Algeria); in contrast, when referendums are either called by unsatisfied groups or compulsory (as is the case in Switzerland), they provide an additional opportunity for minorities to prevent the adoption of unwanted legislation, and can thereby increase their influence on power.

ments developed in other countries which do not have a referendum system. Katzenstein (1984, 1985), though he recognises the impact of institutions (1984: 144) has offered a structural-economic explanation. Small European countries, because of the size of their economy, are extremely dependent on world markets and cannot rely on protectionism. The result is that they have developed a system of compensation for economic change which implies concertation between conflicting interests and the development of corporatist arrangements. The Swiss version of democratic corporatism is dominated by export-oriented business, but the well-established inclusive decision-making procedures tend to magnify the influence of the labour movement (ibid.: 118). Lijphart, finally, relates the emergence of consensual patterns of policy-making to the degree of societal segmentation found in a country. The presence of deep religious and linguistic cleavages is managed by integrating the various groups in decision-making (Lijphart 1984).

### Decision-making procedures

The legislative process in Switzerland comprises a series of stages at which the various relevant actors have the opportunity to intervene and make sure that their preferences are taken into account. When new legislation is initiated by the government, as was the case with the pension reform analysed here, the preparatory work is done by the civil service. The relevant department of the federal administration (in the case of pensions, the Office of Social Insurance, OFAS) has the authority to decide the form of preliminary work. Legislation can be drafted by officials; however, if the decision is relatively important or likely to be controversial, it is usually drafted by an *ad hoc* expert commission.[3]

Expert commissions are the first and perhaps most crucial element in the consensus-building mechanism and in the elaboration of legislation.[4] Typically, expert commissions include civil servants, representatives of organised interests (usually employers and trade unions and other interests if relevant), academics and representatives of a number of cantons, and can include politicians. They have the task of producing the first draft of a bill, and serve a double function: to bring in the expert knowledge needed by the government and the civil service, but also to assess the

---

[3] In the case of pension policy there is a permanent expert commission, which is always responsible for drafting new legislation known as the AVS (Assurance Vieillesse et Survivants) Federal Commission.

[4] According to a survey carried out by Kriesi among policy-makers, the initial stages of the law-making process are regarded as the most important in so far as the result is concerned. Typically, a viable compromise is reached there, and it is relatively difficult to depart from that compromise at later stages (1995: 175).

political feasibility of given policy proposals. Because they need to act consensually, expert commissions are regarded as institutions that are unlikely to develop innovative policies (Klöti 1984: 322). The fact that expert commissions are formally meant to focus on the technical aspects of a bill makes them a tool for depoliticising debates (Katzenstein 1984: 119).

During the work of expert commissions, a constant concern is to avoid the prospect of an unsatisfied group calling a referendum against the bill that is being prepared. According to a survey carried out among expert commission members, the threat of a referendum is generally not mentioned explicitly, but it is constantly present (Germann 1982). This puts pressure on commission members to seek mutually acceptable solutions, and confirms the importance of the impact that referendums have on the whole policy process (Neidhart 1970; see above, 88).

The second stage in the consensus-building process is the consultation procedure. In this case a much wider number of organisations are consulted; they can comment and express their positions on draft legislation. In general, it is only bills which are likely to be controversial that go through both of these stages. A study by Poitry (1989) has shown that, between 1971 and 1975, 53 per cent of legislation went through some form of consultation. Some 16 per cent were subject to a simple consultation procedure; 11 per cent were drafted by an expert commission; and 26 per cent went through both mechanisms. Consensus-building procedures are used more often if a bill is seen as an important one, if it involves constitutional change or if it is in the area of social and economic policy (Kriesi 1995: 181).

When a bill is finalised, it is presented in parliament by the government; it is examined by the relevant parliamentary commission, which can propose amendments, and is then voted on. This procedure is repeated in each of the two chambers of parliament, until they can agree on a common text. In general, the impact of parliament is relatively limited, as usually the content of a bill is not changed substantially at this stage. This, however, was not the case with the 1995 pension reform, which was shaped mainly by a parliamentary commission of the National Council. After the acceptance of a bill by both chambers, there is a ninety-day period to call a referendum, which requires the collection of 50,000 signatures.

The existence of consensus-building procedures should not be seen as an opportunity given to all relevant groups in society to have some influence on a bill. For an interest group, the fact of being invited to join an expert commission largely depends on whether or not it is regarded as *Referendumsfähig*, able to call a referendum and to stand some chances of winning it (Klöti 1984; Kriesi 1995). It is relatively easy to call a referendum, as to collect 50,000 signatures costs on average around Sfr 250,000 (Kriesi 1995: 91), but the level of expenditure required on the campaign is far higher if the group wants to stand some chance of winning. The subordination of inclusion to *Referendumsfähigkeit* is an important limitation on the extent of minority integration. The interests of external groups are guaranteed with a virtual veto power only in so far as they can convince the government that they are capable of calling and winning a referendum if unsatisfied. This element might have played an important role in the 1995 pension reform, as the savings were targeted on women who are in the labour market between the age of sixty-two and sixty-four, a group less able than others to mobilise a majority in the electorate.

### The politics of oversized coalition government

In order to understand the way Swiss politics works, it is crucial to emphasise the difference between the notions of *majority* and *government*. While in most other democracies the two tend to overlap (most notably in the UK), this is not the case in Switzerland. In the areas of social and economic policy, there is a parliamentary right-wing majority, which includes the Liberal Democrats (PRD), the Christian Democrats (PDC) and the ex-farmers' party (UDC). These three parties, though they represent slightly different constituencies, share an overall pro-market orientation in economic and social policy, and together have consistently held majorities in both chambers of parliament. The governing coalition consists of these three parties and the Socialists (PSS), who, in contrast, have a more interventionist approach to social and economic policy. The result is a constant tension between these two entities, majority and government, because the two often take different views on social and economic issues. This was very clear in the 1995 pension reform, when the government decided not to increase women's retirement age, but the parliamentary majority overruled it and introduced this measure.

This is an inevitable feature of oversized coalition government, especially if the coalition includes parties representing conflicting interests. The practice of oversized coalition governments developed relatively early in Switzerland. Until 1891 the PRD, helped by a first-past-the-post electoral system,[5] ruled the country alone. Then it admitted the Conservative-Catholic Party in government in order to neutralise their

---

[5] The first-past-the-post electoral system was retained until 1919. Then, after a massive wave of strikes, it was decided to adopt proportional representation, in order to allow a fairer representation of minorities (in particular of the Socialists) in order to defuse social tensions and conflicts.

referendum-based obstructive strategy. Subsequently, in 1923, the UDC was included in the governing coalition, and finally, towards the end of 1943, the PSS was also admitted to the executive. The current composition of the Federal Council, described as the 'magic formula', was first adopted in 1959. The three big parties – PRD, PDC and PSS – have two ministers each, while the UDC has one.

As decisions within the Federal Council are taken through majority voting, the impact on policy of the two Socialist ministers is much smaller than that of their right-wing counterparts. According to Kriesi, the left has relatively little power in government. In general it can reject proposals that are seen as unacceptable, or initiate debates in the area of social policy, but has relatively little control on the overall government machine (1995). The marginality of the position of the PSS in government is clear when Federal Council members are elected. Members are elected individually by parliament and need the support of a majority. As a result, PSS candidates need the approval of other parties in order to get elected. In recent years, on two occasions, the right voted against the official candidate put forward by the PSS, and elected another candidate, who was on the right of the Socialist Party.

### Referendum politics

The Swiss constitution provides for different kinds of referendums. First, constitutional change always requires acceptance in a referendum. In this case an amendment must be accepted by a majority of voters both nationally and in a majority of cantons (double majority). The second kind, which is called 'popular initiative', is a proposal for constitutional change, has to be backed by 100,000 valid signatures and also requires a double majority in order to be successful. Third, on any piece of legislation a referendum can be called if backed by 50,000 valid signatures. Here a simple majority of voters nationally is sufficient for a referendum to be successful.

The political implications of the three instruments are different. For instance, constitutional referendums magnify the impact of the numerous but small rural cantons, as success in a majority of cantons is required in order to adopt change. The popular initiative allows marginal groups to raise their concerns to matters of national debate. The legislative referendum, finally, constitutes an additional veto point at which the adoption of a piece of legislation can be prevented if a suitable coalition is formed.

Referendum politics is substantially different from parliamentary politics, for two main reasons. First, referendum politics favours the formation of 'unholy' coalitions within the electorate, which are less likely in parliament and stand good chances of defeating a bill. Typically, a government-sponsored bill is supported by the centre of the political spectrum. It can happen that both the far right and the far left oppose the bill, as it is seen as being 'too little' for some and as being 'too much' for the others. A highly heterogeneous coalition is possible in a referendum, as it is a one-off event and it does not require agreement on the alternative to the bill, as is normally the case in parliament.

Second, and perhaps most importantly, party discipline among voters is not as strong as it is among MPs. Typically, political parties issue voting recommendations for each referendum. However, it has been estimated that, on average, 12.5 per cent of voters do not respect party recommendations in referendums (Papadopoulos 1996: 30). This figure might seem relatively low in relation to the fact the government coalition can count on the support of some 80 per cent of the electorate at general elections. Nevertheless, it should be noted than many referendums are relatively uncontroversial, which implies stronger compliance with party recommendations. On the other hand, of course, in the case of controversial decisions, non-respect of party guidelines is more widespread.

Referendum politics, thus, is characterised by a higher level of uncertainty than parliamentary politics. The government has only some limited instruments to try to influence the outcome of a referendum. For instance, it can decide the date for it to take place, and thus wait for the most favourable moment. It can also combine a radical popular initiative with a more moderate bill going in the same direction, thus reducing the chances of success of the initiative. Finally, like political parties, the government issues voting recommendations which are printed in the voting instructions that are mailed to every voter. These instruments allow the government to reduce the extent of uncertainty involved in referendum politics, which nevertheless remains important. In fact, defeats have become more frequent in recent years. The fact that government decisions are increasingly often challenged by unsatisfied minorities has prompted a number of commentators to argue that the 'consensus' model might be facing a crisis (Cattacin 1996; Church 1995; Kriesi 1995).

### Current challenges and consensus democracy

It has been argued that the consensual nature of the Swiss political system reduces adaptability and promptness of government action, and that, given the character of current challenges, it constitutes a burden for the country. This is for a number of reasons.

First, the complexity of these procedures requires much longer periods for the adoption of law than is the case in most other European countries. For instance, in the case of the 1995 pension reform, preliminary work started in 1979 and the law was passed sixteen years later. While this is long even by Swiss standards, it is by no means exceptional. Second, the existence of consensus-building mechanisms prevents policy-makers from developing innovative solutions, since compromise is generally easier to reach if close to the status quo. Third, new issues have emerged, on which it is extremely difficult to achieve a compromise. This is the case of the question of whether or not to join the European Union. As a yes/no question, this does not offer many opportunities for compromise (Church 1995).

The issue of the capacity of a consensual system to implement reform in the area of social policy has been addressed by Cattacin (1996). He argues that existing mechanisms are inadequate to deal with current challenges, because of the long time span they require to produce policy responses and because of the objective difficulty involved in reaching consensus in an unfavourable economic context. In general, the Federal Council, in order to be able to legitimise its intervention, must wait until there are strong economic pressures pushing for change. The federal government can de facto play only a reactive role. Cattacin argues that in recent years substantial change has come from the cantons, which have autonomously implemented legislation for an income support system; and from the voluntary sector, especially in the area of social services for HIV/AIDS sufferers. In these two cases, smaller units have been able to come up with innovative policies relatively quickly, which might in future be used to justify an intervention at the federal level.

Perhaps, however, the biggest strain on consensus politics is the impact of the recession. In the early 1990s, Switzerland went through the worst economic downturn since World War II, and is now facing the social and economic problems that its European neighbours have long known: rising budget deficits, mass unemployment, employers' pressures on the welfare state and on wages, and so forth. This new economic environment is making it more difficult to achieve consensual solutions to current problems.

The worsening of economic conditions in the 1990s has coincided with the emergence of a fairly controversial new debate on welfare retrenchment. Until the recession of the 1990s, there was an overall consensus on the desirability of maintaining the existing arrangements and structures. Given the low rate of unemployment and the overall good economic conditions, the financing of social programmes was not seen as problematic. With the recession and with rising government budget deficits, pressure to rethink much of the Swiss welfare state has built up. Between 1994 and

1995 three big reforms have been adopted, in the areas of pensions, health insurance and unemployment benefits. They are something rather new in the Swiss social policy landscape, as for the first time they include among their objectives the explicit aim of achieving savings. Unsurprisingly, these three reforms represented a big challenge for the consensus-building mechanism. Two of them were subjected to referendums, but eventually they were all adopted. Their common feature is the combination of retrenchment measures with elements of improvement and expansion (Bonoli 1997b). This strategy, which as will be shown was largely used in the 1995 pension reform, seems to be a new way round the referendum obstacle. While in the past the search for a consensus provided a means to keep the impact of referendums under relative control, now, consensus being more difficult to achieve, the majority seems to have adopted a 'combination strategy' which consists in the inclusion in a single piece of legislation of elements requested by different groups, in the hope that this will attract the support of a majority in the electorate. In the three reforms of 1994–5, this strategy worked, as all three, despite containing highly unpopular elements, are now law.

## 4.2    The Swiss pension system

The Swiss pension system is generally described as a three-pillar system, each pillar of which caters for a distinct level of provision. The first pillar (AVS, Assurance Vieillesse et Survivants) is meant to cover the basic needs of retirees. It is partly earnings-related and provides a means-tested pension supplement. The second pillar is meant to provide retirees with a standard of living close to the one they had while working and consists of a compulsory system of occupational pensions. Finally, the third pillar consists of non-compulsory private schemes which benefit from tax concessions. This functional division between three levels of pension provision is upheld by the federal constitution since 1972 (Article 34), and it is widely regarded as an important constraint with regard to policy change in the area of pensions. The 1995 pension reform, which is being analysed in this study, concerned only the first tier of provision (AVS).

Occupational pensions, the second tier, were first granted tax concessions in 1916. They developed substantially throughout the twentieth century, but coverage remained patchy. In 1970 some 50 per cent of employees were covered by an occupational pension, but only 25 per cent of women were (Switzerland, OFAS 1995: 4). Since 1985, however, occupational pension coverage is compulsory for all employees earning at least twice the amount of the minimum AVS pension (about 35 per cent of average salary). Coverage is virtually universal among male employees

but reaches only 80 per cent for female employees (ibid.: 10). A full occupational pension is granted to employees with an adequate contribution
record (currently thirty-seven years for women and forty for men, the
starting age being twenty-five). Those who were first covered by an occupational pension after the age of twenty-five are granted contribution
credits in order to compensate for shorter contribution periods. Benefits
vary according to the type of pension fund. As far as financing is concerned, occupational pensions are funded schemes. They are financed by
employer/employee contributions, the former contributing at least as
much as the latter. The sums involved in occupational pensions are quite
impressive: in 1992 occupational pension funds owned capital stock of
Sfr 257 billion, equal to 72 per cent of GDP; annual receipts amounted to
Sfr 43 billion and annual outlays to Sfr 19 billion.

The third tier of the pension system, private provision, consists mainly
of tax concessions on personal pension schemes. These can be more substantial for those who are not covered by an occupational pension (self-
employed, part-time or temporary workers). In 1994, some 1 million
people had personal pensions, with a total capital stock of Sfr 17 billion
(Switzerland, OFAS 1995: 15). Personal pensions, thus, play a relatively
minor role in the Swiss pension system, and the main providers of income
in old age are occupational pensions.

### The basic pension scheme (AVS)

The AVS pension scheme tends to be regarded as the most progressive
element of the Swiss welfare state. A trade unionist interviewed for this
study described it as a 'little miracle' as it is an unusually redistributive
scheme in the Swiss context. Even if compared to other Bismarckian
schemes (in France or Germany), the Swiss AVS fares rather well as far as
redistribution is concerned. In fact, while there is no ceiling on contributions, the amount of the benefit can vary between a floor and a ceiling, the
upper limit being twice the amount of the lower one. Within these limits,
the amount of the benefit is related to the contributions paid while in
work. In a way, the Swiss basic scheme is a compromise between the
Bismarckian tradition of earnings-related contributory pensions and the
Beveridgean flat-rate approach. Interestingly, in international comparisons the AVS is sometimes considered as a flat-rate pension scheme
(Schmähl 1991: 48).

The scheme was introduced in 1948.[6] A previous attempt had been
made in 1931, but on that occasion the government-sponsored proposal

---

[6] On the history of the AVS pension scheme, see Bernstein 1986 and Binswanger 1987.

Table 4.1 *Receipts and expenditure of the Swiss basic pension scheme (AVS), million Sfr*

|  | 1992 | 1993 | 1994 | 1995 | 1996 | 1997 |
|---|---|---|---|---|---|---|
| Receipts | 23,160 | 23,856 | 23,923 | 24,511 | 24,788 | 25,219 |
| Outlays | 21,206 | 23,046 | 23,363 | 24,503 | 24,817 | 25,803 |
| Balance | 1,954 | 810 | 560 | 8 | – 29 | –584 |

*Source:* Adapted from Switzerland, OFAS 1995: 7, tab. 12.1; *Sécurité sociale*, 1996, no. 2: 77 and 1999, no. 1: 54.

was defeated in a referendum. The legislation enacted in 1948, which in contrast was accepted by an overwhelming majority at the polls, provides the basis for the current system.

*Financing*

The AVS works almost on a pure pay-as-you-go basis, although it has a fund which corresponds to roughly one-year outlays. It is financed through contributions (4.2 per cent of salary each for employees and employers; up to 7.8 per cent for self-employed people), and receives a subsidy equal to 19 per cent of outlays.[7] Its coverage is universal, so that those who are not working (like students) are required to pay flat-rate contributions. Unemployed people pay contributions on their unemployment benefits, which are treated as a salary (the unemployment insurance fund contributing on their behalf 4.2 per cent of the unemployment benefit). As in Bismarckian systems, the AVS has a separate budget from the government. The social partners do take part in the management of the scheme at the local level, by running some branch-related funds. The central fund, however, is managed by the federal administration. The AVS budget was relatively healthy until the mid-1990s, but has since deteriorated (tab. 4.1). This came as a result of increases in the number of beneficiaries and of lower than expected revenues because of the recession.

*Benefits*

The replacement rate[8] varies, because of the existence of a lower and an upper limit on benefits, between 100 per cent (for someone on an

---

[7] The federal government provides a subsidy of 17 per cent of outlays, while the cantons jointly provide an additional 2 per cent.

[8] All replacement rates given in this section refer to gross average earnings in 1995.

Table 4.2 *Level of benefits of the Swiss AVS pension scheme (1995–6)*

| Average annual salary (adjusted for wage increases) | | Pension benefit (per month) | | Replacement rate |
|---|---|---|---|---|
| in Sfr | % av. earnings | in Sfr | % av. earnings | % av. earnings |
| up to 11,640 | 18 | 940 | 18 | 100 |
| 34,923 | 54 | 1,475 | 27 | 50 |
| 69,846 and more | 107 | 1,940 | 36 | 33 (or less) |

*Source:* Recalculation of data from *Sécurité sociale*, 1995, no. 2: 66 and 1994, no. 6: 250.

extremely low income, up to 18 per cent of average salary) to 40 per cent (for someone on a average earnings) and decreases for higher incomes (see tab. 4.2). The lower limit applies only to those who have a complete contribution record (currently forty-five years for men and forty-two for women, retirement age being sixty-five and sixty-two respectively); otherwise the pension is reduced correspondingly. Table 4.2 gives the level of benefit in relation to insured salary. Insured salary is the average of revalued (according to increases in average incomes) career earnings.

Benefits are adjusted according to a mixed index, i.e. the arithmetic average between changes in consumer prices and in gross earnings. This means that retirees receive a share of increases in productivity, but it also means that, in the long run, the replacement rate is going to deteriorate, albeit less fast than in the UK, where indexation of pensions is based on prices only. The indexation takes place every two years, unless consumer prices increase by more than 4 per cent, in which case benefits are increased when that threshold is reached.

According to the federal constitution as amended in 1972, the AVS pension scheme must cover the basic needs of retirees. This makes it a Beveridgean scheme in its orientation. Nevertheless, since it was introduced as a compromise between a Beveridgean and a Bismarckian scheme, it still includes elements of the latter, namely a partial relationship with former earnings. The tension between these two conceptions is present in the Swiss pension debate. Given current financial constraints, the fact that benefits remain partly earnings-related means that those at the bottom end do not receive enough to cover their basic needs. In fact, the introduction of a flat-rate benefit was considered during the debate leading to the 1995 reform, but plans going in that direction were eventually

Table 4.3 *Average amount of AVS benefits by gender and marital status in Switzerland (in Sfr per month, 1994), and percentage receiving means-tested pension supplement*

|            | Women | | Men | |
|            | Average benefit | Percentage receiving supplement | Average benefit | Percentage receiving supplement |
|------------|-----------------|---------------------------------|-----------------|---------------------------------|
| unmarried  | 1,371           | 24.1                            | 1,373           | 23.7                            |
| married    | 1,028           | 2.2                             | 1,644           | 4.1                             |
| separated  | 1,089           | N/A                             | 1,548           | N/A                             |
| widow(er)  | 1,701           | 18.4                            | 1,699           | 12.7                            |
| divorced   | 1,442           | 35.3                            | 1,601           | 24.5                            |

Source: *Sécurité sociale*, 1995, no. 2: 63.

dropped.[9] Because the minimum pension is regarded as insufficient to cover basic needs, a supplementary means-tested benefit was introduced in 1965. Initially the pension supplement was meant to be a temporary measure, but in fact it has now become part of the pension system. The pension supplement, depending on individual circumstances, can increase the AVS benefit to up to Sfr 27,768 per year (42 per cent of average earnings, 1995) and is applied also to those with incomplete contribution records. In 1993 there were some 160,000 recipients or 19 per cent of all pensioners (*Sécurité sociale*, 1995, no. 1: 13).

### Pressures for change

The main concern which prompted policy-makers in the late 1970s to start a debate on a new pension reform was the particularly discriminatory treatment of women in the AVS pension scheme. A married woman, unless she had a better contribution record than her husband, would lose her entitlement to a pension, this being replaced by a 50 per cent couple pension supplement paid to her husband. Contributions paid by married women were taken into account as far as earnings were concerned, but could not fill in an incomplete contribution record. In addition, there

[9] In 1993 the Council of States (upper chamber) asked the Federal Office of Social Insurance (OFAS) to produce a report on the impact of benefits and cost of the introduction (Switzerland, OFAS 1993). The proposal, however, was dropped because, if it were to be cost-neutral, it would mean a reduction in benefits for some 50 per cent of recipients; if it were to be at the level of the maximum benefit, it would have cost some Sfr 3 billion in 1993. Both options were regarded as politically unfeasible and thus abandoned.

were no contribution credits for years spent providing unpaid care. The result was that women in general, and most notably divorced or separated women, got a particularly bad deal out of the AVS. This was reflected by the impressive difference in the amount of average pensions according to marital status, as shown in table 4.3.

The most striking differences in benefit levels between men and women are in the cases of separated couples and divorcees.[10] Average pensions are lower for women, especially in the case of separated couples. Among divorcees, the reliance on the means-tested pension supplement is much higher among women than men (by more than 10 percentage points).

It was in response to pressures to remove discriminatory practices from the AVS and to correct its unequal outcomes that in 1979 the government requested the AVS Federal Commission, a permanent expert commission, to produce a reform proposal that would have improved the way women were treated by the scheme. The government was reacting to demands by women's organisations, and concern that had been expressed by some members of parliament (Binswanger 1987: 251). Pressure to remove all gender-based discrimination from the AVS pension scheme increased further in 1981, when the constitution was amended so as to include an article on gender equality (Article 4).

Progress on the reform was slow. A bill was presented in parliament only in 1990 and by the time it was being discussed the overall economic and political climate had changed quite dramatically. First, the recession caused a massive increase in the number of unemployed people, which had an impact on the balance of AVS budget (see tab. 4.1, 97). In addition, concern was growing with regard to the future financing prospects of the scheme because of the worsening contributors/beneficiaries ratio. According to the projections published by the Federal Office of Social Insurance in 1993, the ones which were used by policy-makers in the debate on the 1995 reform, the balance of the scheme would become negative from 1999 on, and, if nothing was done, the AVS would make losses of some Sfr 5 billion per year by 2015 (*Sécurité sociale*, 1994, no. 1: 7). In this context of sluggish economic performance and predicted imbalance in the fund's budget, the right-wing majority found relatively fertile ground for introducing an element of retrenchment in a pension reform which was initially meant to bring about an improvement in provision.

---

[10] The big difference between married men and women is due to the fact that women were not entitled to their own pension under 'standard' circumstances. This was unless the husband did not receive a pension (for example, because he worked abroad), a relatively infrequent event. The fact that only 2.2 per cent of married women receive a pension supplement suggests that in fact most of those belonging to this group have other sources of revenue as well.

## 4.3    The 1995 pension reform (tenth AVS revision)

*Pre-parliamentary work*

Following a series of interventions (*postulats*) made by a number of MPs, in 1979 the Federal Council asked the Federal Commission for the AVS to draft a reform proposal meant to improve the situation of women and eliminate the discriminatory practices in the way contributions are taken into account. The Federal Commission for the AVS is the equivalent of an expert commission, but has a permanent status, because the AVS requires virtually constant debate on reform. Its task, as for expert commissions, is to elaborate reform proposals which must be technically viable and, especially, politically feasible. The Federal Commission for the AVS includes representatives from a number of different organisations who have a stake in pensions and who can effectively oppose measures regarded as unsatisfactory.[11] It is essentially an instrument for pre-testing the political feasibility of reform proposals and thus, ultimately, for consensus building.

The AVS Federal Commission came up with a reform proposal in 1982 which included some minor improvements for women. However, since the government had requested the reform to be cost-neutral, these measures had to be financed by an increase in the age of retirement (for women only) from sixty-two to sixty-three. The reaction to these proposals was rather lukewarm, and even within the commission there was controversy with regard to the increased retirement age for women. The commission was asked by the government to reconsider its plans, but was nevertheless unable to produce a different proposal. According to Binswanger (1987: 250), it was the combination of cost-neutrality and the need to reach consensus that prevented the commission from producing a more satisfactory proposal.

Towards the end of the 1980s, after Flavio Cotti, a Christian Democrat, took office as interior minister,[12] the government decided to abandon the cost-neutrality requirement, which was blocking progress towards effective gender equality. In March 1990, the Federal Council was at last able to produce a bill for the reform of the AVS pension scheme (*Feuille Fédérale* 2, 1990: 1–231). The key element of the bill was the introduction of gender equality, without abandoning couple pensions for

---

[11] Typically, the AVS Commission includes representatives of the trade unions, employers, insurance companies, the cantons, organisations of retired persons, women's organisations, the federal government and the army.

[12] The Department of the Interior has responsibility for social insurance as well as for most social policy areas (including health care).

married people. Quite simply, contributions paid by the two spouses were to be combined and computed for a couple pension. This could have been split (half each) upon request. Basically, the proposed change was limited to the removal of all reference to gender in the calculation of the pension, making the law compatible with the constitutional requirement for gender equality. The bill, thus, did not introduce an individual right to a pension for married women as was being advocated by a number of influential organisations. The rationale of this decision was that, the married couple still being the predominant type of cohabitation, the introduction of a system of individual pensions for everyone regardless of marital status was premature.

In relation to the question of women's retirement age, the government argued that the constitutional requirement of gender equality would eventually have to be applied to retirement age as well as to other areas. However, given the fact that gender equality in the labour market (in terms of wages, career patterns, access to occupational pensions, etc.) was far from being achieved, it was thought that the existence of positive discrimination in favour of women was justified.

### The pension reform in parliament

The lack of an individual right to a pension regardless of gender and marital status in the 1990 pension bill became an important political issue. In the late 1980s, in all major political parties and the Federal Commission on Women's Issues (CFQF), a permanent expert commission like the one that exists for the AVS scheme, published documents in which they argued for the introduction of a system of individual pensions regardless of gender and marital status, calculated on the basis of a contribution sharing system. In general, it was suggested that contributions paid by the members of a couple be summed, divided by two and counted separately and individually for each of the two spouses, a system which became known by the term 'splitting'. Such plans were put forward by the Liberal Democrats (PRD 1988) and by the Socialist Party (PSS/USS 1987) which produced a joint document with the trade unions. The Christian Democratic Party did not produce a detailed proposal for a contribution sharing system, but in a document published in 1988 it argued in favour of a system which would guarantee full gender equality and an overall arrangement which would favour the family (PDC 1988: 6). This was not a clear-cut statement in favour of individual pensions. In fact the Christian Democrats were concerned that such a system might discriminate against married couples, which they regarded as unacceptable (Darbelley, in Télévision Suisse Romande 1995).

Because it maintained couple pensions, the 1990 pension reform bill was viewed by many with disappointment, especially by women's organisations and by women MPs in the Socialist and Liberal Democratic Parties. The bill was nevertheless adopted by the upper chamber of parliament, the Council of States, in March 1991. According to the standard procedure, it was subsequently examined by the Social Security Commission of the National Council (the lower chamber) in April 1991. Some members of the commission were clearly unsatisfied with the bill, as it did not include provision for individual pensions regardless of marital status or for contribution sharing between spouses. As a result, the commission requested the Federal Office for Social Insurance (OFAS) to produce a report which would explore the technical issues involved in the introduction of a contribution sharing system. The report was to be based on the three proposals made by the Federal Commission on Women's Issues (Switzerland, CFQF 1988), by the PRD (1988) and by the Socialist Party jointly with the Unions (PSS/USS 1987).

The report was published in August 1991 (Switzerland, OFAS 1991) and was debated by the commission in September of the same year. It did not make practical proposals but provided a comparison of the three documents published in 1987–8 and outlined a number of problems, such as provision for couples with one member abroad, which could not be treated satisfactorily by any of the three systems suggested. On that occasion, two members of the commission, Gret Haller (PSS) and Lily Nabholz (PRD), suggested setting up a working group with the task of elaborating a viable proposal for the introduction of a contribution sharing system. The working group included MPs of the main political parties[13] and convened seven times. It produced a final report that was published in March 1992 (Switzerland, Conseil National, Groupe de Travail 'Splitting' 1992).

This document was examined by the Social Security Commission of the National Council, which on that basis was going to draft a new version of the pension reform bill that would have been subsequently submitted to parliament. What happened within the Social Security Commission is not entirely clear since the proceedings of discussions taking place within parliamentary commissions are not disclosed. Nevertheless, by looking at the debates that took place in parliament afterwards (which, in contrast,

---

[13] The composition of the working group was a enlarged form of the 'magic formula' of the Federal Council. It included two PSS, two PDC, two PRD, one UDC, one Anneau des Indépendents (centre independent party), one Green Party and one Parti Libéral Suisse. The president was Heinz Allenspach (PRD) who was also president of the Social Security Commission, and the two MPs who initiated the debate on contribution sharing within the commission (Gret Haller and Lily Nabholz) were also members of the working group.

are transcribed and available for consultation), one can reconstruct the dynamics of decision-making within the commission with a fair degree of approximation. This is of great importance, since it was there that the proposals which subsequently became law were first elaborated.

The president of the Social Security Commission presented its final report in parliament in March 1993 (*Bulletin Officiel de l'Assemblée Fédérale. Conseil National* 103, 9 March 1993). The proposal relied heavily on the work of the Groupe de Travail 'Splitting' which had been published the previous year. The new version of the bill included the notion of an individual entitlement to a pension regardless of gender and of marital status. As suggested in the papers published by the main political parties in the late 1980s, the contribution records of two spouses while married was to be summed, divided by two and counted half each for the two spouses. In order not to penalise one-earner couples, a generous credit for couples with children was introduced. In addition, however, the report included provision for raising the retirement age for women from sixty-two to sixty-four.

There was substantial agreement among the main political parties on the introduction of a contribution sharing system for contributions paid by spouses. Only the Christian Democrats were somewhat sceptical initially, but by 1993 they came to accept the predominant view. The government, which in its 1990 bill argued that the introduction of contribution sharing and individual pensions was premature, rallied to the majority's view and accepted the substantial changes made by parliament. The position of the Federal Council on the changes adopted by parliament was expressed by Interior Minister Flavio Cotti as follows:

The Federal Council welcomes the changes introduced by the National Council, except some reservations with regard to the question of raising the age of retirement for women. However, if parliament decides to take this stance, the Federal Council is not going to oppose it. (*Bulletin Officiel de l'Assemblée Fédérale. Conseil National* 103, 6 March 1993)

A major problem which occurred as a result of the introduction of contribution sharing for married couples was that one-earner couples would end up with two individual pensions which, when combined, could be lower than a current couple pension.[14] However, in each of the three initial reports and subsequent proposals, provision was made to reduce the incidence of the abolition of a couple pension. There was an overall

---

[14] A couple pension corresponds to 150 per cent of a single-person pension. If the pension entitlement of only one spouse is split between two partners, they will receive a pension worth 50 per cent of a single-person pension each. As there is no supplement for being a couple, one-earner couples were disadvantaged.

agreement on the view that the best way to do that was through the introduction of a contribution credit for persons who are not engaged in paid
work in order to take care of children or relatives. The three initial
reports, however, came up with three different proposals as to how the
credit system should work. The joint report PSS/USS (1987) argued that
the contribution credit should correspond to at least the contribution
amount paid on a salary equal to three times the minimum pension (in
1992 Sfr 32,400 pa), as long as the couple has at least one child under the
age of sixteen. The Commission on Women's Issues, in contrast, suggested a 20 per cent increase in the retirement pension for people
who have taken care of children or relatives for at least fifteen years.
For shorter periods the amount would be reduced correspondingly
(Switzerland, CFQF 1988). Finally, the Liberal Democrats, although in
favour of the principle, suggested leaving to the Federal Council the task
of working out the details of the credit system. The Groupe de Travail
'Splitting' (1992: 9) supported the proposal made in the PSS/USS joint
report, which was carried through by the Social Security Commission,
accepted by parliament and is now law.

The most controversial issue, however, was certainly that of women's
retirement age. The overall aim of the pension reform was to achieve
compliance with the constitutional article on gender equality, which
theoretically applied to retirement age as well as to the other areas of
pension policy. However, when presenting the 1990 bill, the government
had argued that, given the persistence of substantial discrimination in the
labour market at the expense of women (wages, access to occupational
pensions and so forth), the difference in retirement age was justified for
the time being, and the issue would have been dealt with in the next (the
eleventh) revision of the AVS pension scheme (*Feuille Fédérale* 2, 1990:
1–231). Switzerland does not have a constitutional court, and the interpretation that the government makes of the constitution tends to be
regarded as the most legitimate. From the legal point of view, thus, parliament was not under pressure to equalise the age of retirement.

This view reflected to some extent the position of the Christian
Democrats, who also argued in favour of a common retirement age of
sixty-four to be phased in within the context of the eleventh AVS revision
(PDC 1988: 11). In contrast, the joint PSS/USS report (1987) suggested
the introduction of a flexible age of retirement between sixty-two and
sixty-five, for both sexes. Early retirement would be possible without
reductions in the level of the benefit, but conditional upon giving up work
(working at most half-time). Finally, the Liberal Democrats advocated a
common retirement age of sixty-five, with provision for early retirement
from the age of sixty-two, but with a reduction of 6.8 per cent in the level

of the benefit for each year of anticipation. The choice was justified with the need to achieve savings in the light of the expected increase in pension expenditure due to demographic ageing (PRD 1988). Finally, the Federal Commission on Women's Issues, which included members of all the above parties, suggested (by a weak majority) raising the age of retirement for women, but did not specify at what age, and introducing provision for early retirement from the age of sixty, with a reduction in the level of the benefit equal to 6.8 per cent per year of anticipation (Switzerland, CFQF 1988).

The Groupe de Travail 'Splitting' did not take a position on the issue of retirement age. This would not have been within its mandate. In fact, it was within the Social Security Commission of the National Council that the final arrangement (sixty-five/sixty-four) was adopted.[15] As mentioned above, it is not possible to have access to the proceedings of parliamentary commissions. However, by looking at the positions expressed before the examination of the proposals by the commission, and in the parliamentary debate which followed the presentation of the final report on 6 March 1993, it is possible to find out what the debates might have been like within the commission.

During the parliamentary debate, a number of right-wing MPs suggested that the bill be referred back to the commission (or to the Federal Council) for consideration of a flat-rate benefit. This would have eliminated the relationship between contributions and benefits and thus the need for a complex contribution sharing and credit system. The majority of the National Council, however, agreed to keep the commission's proposal as a basis for discussion.

The vote was carried out on an article-by-article basis, without encountering any serious problem, with the exception, of course, of the issue of whether or not to raise retirement age for women. The report adopted by the majority of the commission had argued that:

the constitutional article on gender equality requires that the age of retirement be the same for men and women [in addition], since the proposals made by this commission eliminate differences based on gender . . . one cannot deny the need for equalising the age of retirement for men and women . . . Finally, there is no doubt that because of demographic ageing a balanced budget for the AVS is not guaranteed in the long term. (*Bulletin Officiel de l'Assemblée Fédérale. Conseil National* 103, 9 March 1993, 222)

---

[15] The commission was composed of twenty-nine members of the National Council. Its president was Heinz Allenspach (PRD) who was also president of the umbrella organisation of Swiss employers (Union Centrale des Association Patronales Suisses). The commission accepted the final report with a majority of twenty-three to three (and three abstentions).

The commission gave basically two reasons for raising the age of retirement for women: to comply with the constitutional requirement of gender equality and to achieve some savings in view of the predicted worsening of the contributors/beneficiaries ratio within the state pension scheme. The decision to adopt a retirement age of sixty-four for women, however, was not taken unanimously. In fact, the National Council had to vote four different proposals on this issue. Besides the majority proposal which was included in the final report, there were three minority proposals. The first was supported by the Socialists and consisted of a flexible retirement age for men and women between sixty-two and sixty-five, without reduction in the level of benefit but conditional upon giving up work. It was the same proposal which had been presented in the joint document PSS/USS published in 1987. The second minority proposal was supported again by the Socialists and by a Christian Democrat. In case of the first minority proposal not being accepted, it requested that things should be left as they were, i.e. to have a differentiated age of retirement for men and women at sixty-five/sixty-two. There was a third minority proposal, which came from the right end of the political spectrum. It was supported by MPs of the UDC and by some right-wing MPs of smaller parties and intended to equalise the age of retirement at sixty-five. Unsurprisingly, the National Council chose the majority proposal, which in some respects, however, represents a compromise between the different options examined. It should be noted, in fact, that the then majority party, the PRD, initially supported a common retirement age of sixty-five, but within the commission it was decided to adopt a sixty-five/sixty-four arrangement. The bill was then examined by the upper chamber, the Council of States, where it was subject to some minor changes, and was subsequently debated a number of times in both chambers until the two could agree on a common version.

Since the presentation of the commission's proposal in the National Council, the largest federation of trade unions, the Union Syndicale Suisse (USS), made clear that it was going to call a referendum against the pension reform unless parliament decided to drop the increase in the age of retirement. As a result, both chambers tried to devise a new compromise which could have persuaded the trade unions not to call a referendum. First, in the Council of States, it was decided to adopt a longer transition period. For the first four years after the adoption of the new law, it was going to be possible to retire at sixty-two without reductions in the benefit, and for the next eight years, to take early retirement from sixty-two with a reduction of 3.4 per cent per year of anticipation. The full reduction rate of 6.8 per cent (actuarially determined) would be in force only twelve years after the adoption of the pension bill (*Bulletin Officiel de l'Assemblée Fédérale. Conseil des Etats* 104, 8 June 1994, 546–612). The compromise was also accepted by the National Council, but was not regarded as sufficient by the unions, who persisted in the idea of calling a referendum. A second attempt to avoid the referendum was made within the Social Security Commission of the National Council. A majority of commission members suggested differentiating the retirement age for women, according to whether one was still working in the five-year period before sixty-two or not. If that was the case, then retirement would have been possible at sixty-two without reduction until 2005, and thereafter at sixty-three, always without reduction. This last attempt to reach compromise, despite its complexity, did not manage to persuade the unions either. As a result, the PRD and the PDC, whose members had approved the proposal made by the commission, withdrew their support and the amendment was eventually abandoned.

The referendum represented a difficult issue for the left, because the new law included provision on gender equality that the left (both the PSS and the unions) had been backing for a long time. The introduction of a generous credit for taking care of a child or a relative was also seen as an important improvement, since it constituted a powerful recognition of the unpaid caring work carried out mainly by women. The other side of the coin was, of course, the increase in retirement age for women to sixty-four, which was seen as unacceptable by the trade unions and by the PSS. This was against what the left had been arguing recently, i.e. that there should be a tendency towards lowering the age of retirement, in order to free up jobs for the unemployed. The left, as seen above, was in favour of a flexible retirement age between sixty-two and sixty-five, regardless of sex and without reduction in the level of the pension. This combination of elements which were strongly supported and other elements which in contrast were powerfully opposed in a single bill resulted in a dilemma for the left. Referendums, in fact, can be called only on an entire bill, not on parts of it.

A last-minute attempt to find a way round was made in parliament in September 1994. The trade unionist and Socialist MP Christiane Brunner, speaking on behalf of a minority of the Social Security Commission, proposed to split the pension reform into two different acts. One included the articles on contribution credits and on contribution sharing for couples, while the second was only on the increase in retirement age. This would have made it possible to call a referendum only on retirement age, without taking the risk, in case of rejection, of postponing the introduction of gender equality, perhaps indefinitely. The proposal was rejected by the two other main parties (PDC and PRD) and was as a result defeated, although it managed to attract the votes of some Liberal

Democrats and Christian Democrats (*Bulletin Officiel de l'Assemblée Fédérale. Conseil National* 104, 21 September 1994, 1342–68).

The prospect of having to fight a referendum was a major pressure on parliament to adopt a consensual solution. Up to the last days before the final vote, concessions were made to convince the unions to drop their plan to call a referendum, though unsuccessfully. Even so, the final draft of the 1995 pension reform contains various elements of compromise between the different actors. The shape of final legislation was influenced mainly by the proposals made by the Socialists and the Liberal Democrats, with the exception, of course, of retirement age. The latter was imposed by the right-wing majority, and constituted, perhaps, a compromise between the PRD, which supported immediate equalisation at sixty-five, and the PDC, which advocated equalisation at sixty-four in the next reform. The fact that the new retirement age of sixty-five/sixty-four will be phased in over a twelve-year period supports this interpretation. The 1995 pension reform was not adopted consensually; nevertheless, the fact that each relevant actor had managed to get some of its priorities included in the proposed legislation would strengthen the bill *vis-à-vis* the referendum challenge.

### The referendum

The decision to call a referendum was taken jointly by the main federation of Swiss unions (USS) and by the Christian unions (CSC). For the USS, the inclusion of an increased retirement age for women could not be accepted. In fact, the general trend in USS pension policy was towards a reduction in retirement age. The USS (together with the PSS) had previously collected signatures for an initiative which proposed, among other things, the introduction of a flexible retirement age for men and women between sixty-two and sixty-five without reduction of benefit, but conditional upon giving up work.[16] For this reason it was not conceivable for the unions to accept an increase in women's retirement age. On the other hand, however, if the bill was to be defeated in a referendum, the improvements of provision for women would also have been rejected, and these had been long advocated by the unions. To avoid this dilemma, the USS and the CSC decided to collect the 50,000 signatures needed to call a referendum, but at the same time to call a second referendum (initiative) with the aim of introducing, after the possible defeat of the pension bill in the referendum, what they regarded as the 'good' elements of the 1995 pension reform, i.e. contribution sharing and credits.

[16] The vote on the PSS/USS initiative took place on the same day as the pension reform referendum (25 June 1996). The proposal was rejected by 72 per cent of voters.

A similar dilemma faced the leadership of the Socialist Party. They too were against raising retirement age for women, but this was not the point any longer, since the referendum was going to be on the whole bill. As a result, a division within the party emerged as to whether the good elements of the reform outweighed the bad ones, or vice versa (PSS 1995). The situation of the PSS was further complicated by the fact that the minister responsible for social security was now Ruth Dreyfuss, a Socialist, who had to comply with the majority view of the government, which was to favour the adoption of the reform. Her own opinion on the issue was the following:

It is most unfortunate that the issue of raising women's retirement age has been tied to the improvements of the pension reform . . . I continue to think that this measure was not needed in this reform. Nevertheless, my support for the reform is based on a conviction that the positive elements of the reform outweigh the negative ones. (Dreyfuss, in Télévision Suisse Romande 1995)

The leadership of the Socialist Party decided to deal with the dilemma by consulting party members. Some 30 per cent of them took part in a ballot, of whom 66 per cent were in favour of the reform (*Sécurité sociale*, 1995, no. 2: 59). The result was that the official voting recommendation of the PSS was to accept the 1995 pension reform.

For other parties and organisations the decision on whether to support or not the referendum was more straightforward one. All the other large parties had supported the reform in parliament, so that they were going to recommend backing the pension bill to their supporters. Similarly, the main employers' associations favoured the new pension bill. Women's organisations were divided, those more left-oriented being against and their right-wing counterparts being in favour of the pension bill. The overall picture before the referendum was one in which the unions were mainly alone in fighting the pension bill. Nevertheless there was some concern among federal authorities that the bill could be defeated in the referendum. It was feared that Conservative-Catholic voters might join the unions in rejecting the proposal, as the conception of the family on which the new law was based did not reflect traditional views on gender roles. Concern for the outcome of the referendum was also reflected by the important campaign launched by the Federal Office of Social Insurance through its periodical *Sécurité sociale*. Almost half of the February 1995 issue addressed the pension reform, and included articles by Ruth Dreyfuss and Walter Seiler, then director of the office, in support of the bill.

The vote took place on 25 June 1995. The turnout was of 40.4 per cent, which is in the norm[17] and saw a relatively clear prevalence of those in

Table 4.4 *Reasons for accepting or rejecting the Swiss 1995 pension reform in the referendum (spontaneous replies and multiple answers were possible)*

| Reasons for voting 'yes' | Percentage | Reasons for voting 'no' | Percentage |
|---|---|---|---|
| 1. It is a general improvement | 25 | 1. Higher retirement age for women | 59 |
| 2. Gender equality | 17 | 2. Unemployment | 20 |
| 3. Contribution credits | 15 | 3. It is a drawback | 10 |
| 4. Contribution sharing | 14 | 4. Was not necessary | 3 |
| 5. Higher retirement age for women | 10 | | |
| 6. Recommended by government | 8 | | |
| 7. Savings | 6 | | |

*Source:* Vox 1995.

favour of the bill (60.7 per cent). There were cantonal variations though, as the bill was accepted in all German-speaking cantons but was rejected in four out of six French-speaking cantons and in the Italian canton. According to an opinion poll carried out just after the vote, the best predictor of voters' behaviour was not language but party preference. Among those who said they supported one of the three right-wing government parties (PRD, PDC and UDC), the proportion of yes voters was some 10 percentage points higher than the average (Vox 1995). The survey also inquired about the reasons for voting yes or no in the referendum. The results are reported in table 4.4.

As table 4.4 shows, the main division in the electorate was between those who believed that the positive aspects outweighed the negative ones on the 'yes' side, and those who believed the opposite on the 'no' side. The reasons given by a clear majority of 'yes' voters concern the improvement side of the bill (items 1, 2, 3 and 4). According to the poll, only a minority would have supported the bill regardless of the presence of these improvements (items 5, 6 and 7). The bill would have encountered stronger opposition if it had not included elements which were widely regarded as improvements.

Conversely, among 'no' voters, the main reason for opposing the bill was, overwhelmingly, the increase in women's retirement age (59 per cent). Items 2 and 3 in fact refer to the same reason, as an increase in

---

[17] Depending on the year, the average turnout at referendums is between 35 per cent and 45 per cent (Kriesi 1995: 114).

retirement age is expected have an impact on unemployment. The 'unholy' alliance between the left and Conservative-Catholic voters, feared by federal authorities, did not take place. Only 3 per cent of 'no' voters rejected the bill on grounds that it was not needed, the only item which might imply a preference for the traditional vision of the married couple upheld by the pre-reform system.

Data from table 4.4 suggest that an increase in retirement age for women, adopted independently from the improvement side of the bill, would have been at a much higher risk of being defeated in a referendum. What made possible the only retrenchment element of the reform was its combination with a series of improvements. This conclusion must be taken carefully, though, because we have no guarantee that respondents replied with their genuine motives. Possibly, they might have followed the recommendation of their party or group of reference and subsequently rationalised their choice by backing it up with a sensible argument.[18] However, the fact that, always according to the same opinion polls, some 30 per cent of voters who said they identified with one of the three right-wing government parties voted against the bill lends support to the hypothesis that an increase in women's retirement age would not have been accepted if not accompanied by improvements.

## 4.4    Key elements of the 1995 pension reform

As anticipated in the previous sections, the 1995 pension reform includes three main elements: the introduction of a contribution sharing system for married couples, the institution of contribution credits for informal care providers and the increase in women's retirement age. In this section, I will look at the details of these measures.

### Contribution sharing system

This is perhaps the most innovative element of the 1995 pension reform. The basis of the sharing system is the introduction of an individual entitlement to a pension regardless of gender and marital status and the computation of half the contributions paid jointly by a married couple for each spouse individually. This implies the abolition of the couple pension,

---

[18] The validity of this interpretation depends also on the reliability of opinion poll results. Interestingly, the proportion of 'yes' voters found in the opinion poll (59.5 per cent) was very close to the actual referendum outcome (60.7 per cent). This is not always the case: differences of up to 10 percentage points can be found. This suggests that respondents had relatively strong views on how to vote and felt that their choice was legitimate, which arguably strengthens the findings of the opinion poll.

as with the new legislation each spouse is entitled to an individual pension. Contributions paid before marriage are not affected by the reform, and are counted 100 per cent for the person who paid them.

There were two main problems with the introduction of contribution sharing and the abolition of a couple pension. On the one hand, one-earner couples were going to be penalised because, instead of a couple pension worth 150 per cent of the husband's entitlement, they would receive two individual pensions, each based on 50 per cent of the earner's contribution record, which in any case was going to be lower than a former couple pension. On the other hand, the new system was going to favour two-earner couples, as again a couple pension of 150 per cent of the husband's entitlement was going to be replaced by two individual pensions worth up to 100 per cent of the main earner's entitlement (assuming similar career pattern and earnings between the two).

Two elements were introduced to deal with this issue. The situation of one-earner couples was improved with the introduction of a relatively generous contribution credit for those providing informal care, while it was decided to introduce a ceiling for couples with both spouses receiving a pension corresponding to 150 per cent of the maximum pension. Since the ceiling is based on the maximum pension, this measure affects mainly couples on high earnings. It should be noted that one-earner couples without children and who are not providing care are in fact disadvantaged by the contribution sharing system.

### Contribution credits

Contribution credits are granted to persons with children or providing other sorts of informal care (for instance to an elderly or a disabled relative). The amount credited corresponds to the contributions paid on a salary equal to three times the minimum pension, or 54 per cent of average gross earnings. The credit is granted irrespective of whether the carer gives up work. In the case of children, the credit is granted for as long as the household includes persons below the age of sixteen. Like actual contributions, the contribution credit is equally shared between the members of a couple.

It should be noted that the impact of the credit is higher for one-earner couples and for couples with low earnings. As earnings increase, its impact decreases. In the case of a couple in which both members earn 107 per cent of average gross earnings or more, contribution credits do not add anything to their pension entitlements, because both spouses receive the maximum pension anyway.

*Retirement age*

The retirement age for women was raised from sixty-two to sixty-four. This will be achieved over a relatively long transition period. The new pension legislation came into force in January 1997, but until 2000 women will be able to retire at sixty-two without any loss in the level of their benefit. Between 2001 and 2004 the standard retirement age for women will be sixty-three, but it will be possible to retire at sixty-two with a reduction of 3.4 per cent in the level of the benefit. Between 2005 and 2008 the standard retirement age for women will be sixty-four, though it will be possible to retire at sixty-two or at sixty-three, always with a 3.4 per cent reduction of the pension per year of anticipation. The transition period will end in 2009. Then the retirement age will be sixty-four, and early retirement will still be possible, but with a reduction of 6.8 per cent in the level of the benefit, which corresponds to the actuarially determined rate. Early retirement is possible for men as well, though with a reduction rate of 6.8 per cent per year of anticipation since the introduction of the new pension law.

The fact that the increase in women's retirement age is going to be phased in over a relatively long period of time means that the financial impact of the 1995 pension reform will be an increase in expenditure for the first few years. In fact, the improvements (contribution sharing and credits) come into force immediately. Nevertheless, by 2009, when the standard retirement age for women will have reached sixty-four, the overall impact of the reform will be to generate annual savings of Sfr 142 million (at 1993 prices), which corresponds to 0.6 per cent of 1993 outlays. In the long run, the overall impact of the reform is cost-neutral.

## 4.5    Consensus democracy and the politics of welfare retrenchment

The analysis of the Swiss case can shed light on the wider question of whether it is politically feasible to achieve retrenchment in pension policy in political systems characterised by a high density of veto points. As seen above, the extent and the degree of policy influence that institutions allow to external interests means that the Swiss political machine can function conveniently only if policy-makers are able to generate a generalised consensus on their policy proposals. In the past, during the expansion phase of the AVS pension scheme, it was easier to achieve consensus among the relevant actors. Between 1950 and 1979, the AVS scheme was reformed nine times. These reforms consisted mainly of improvements in the generosity of the scheme. Interestingly, out of nine reforms, only one (the ninth) was challenged by a referendum. The other reforms were adopted without serious controversy and in four cases by unanimous vote in both chambers of parliament.

The Swiss case provides support for the view that the politics of retrenchment is different from the politics of expansion (Pierson 1994: ch. 2), particularly with regard to the impact that this process has on broad coalition-formation patterns. In the past, the overall popularity of measures aimed at improving the coverage of social programmes constituted a powerful incentive for political actors to be part of the pro-expansion coalition. Policy-makers of different orientation had a clear interest in being associated with widely supported reforms, as this made electoral reward likely. In contrast, when policy change entails unpopular measures, it is rational for actors who want to maximise their public support to abandon the pro-retrenchment coalition. This mechanism, which certainly played a role in the process which led to the adoption of the 1995 pension reform, is of crucial importance in the Swiss context, where, because of political institutions, policy change requires the support of large coalitions of parties and interest groups.

As seen above, the Swiss inclination for consensual politics has been widely interpreted as the result of a particular institutional environment, which grants to minorities the opportunity to intervene at various stages of the law-making process. If this interpretation is correct, the inadequacy of the standard consensus-building procedure to deal with current issues in the area of social policy cannot be dealt with through the introduction of a majoritarian form of policy-making. Swiss institutions, in particular the referendum, do not allow a majority government to rule effectively. As a result, one needs to address the question of what will replace the consensual approach to policy-making when consensus simply cannot be reached. Its most widespread alternative, majoritarian policy-making, does not seem to be an available option for Switzerland.

The analysis of the process which led to the adoption of the 1995 pension reform is instructive in this respect. The standard decision-making procedures were unable to produce a compromise which could be regarded as satisfactory by all key actors. The 1990 pension bill, subsequently radically reviewed by parliament, constituted the minimum common denominator of the objectives of the main political actors. The government, because of its composition (ministers belonging to four different parties), and because of the well-established practice of taking decisions collegially, seems to have been unable to come up with anything more than the minimum amount of change required in order to comply with the constitutional article for gender equality. The result was that, while being acceptable to all relevant parts, the bill was widely regarded as unsatisfactory, as it did not include provision for individual pensions regardless of gender and marital status. After 1990, the pension bill came under the responsibility of parliament, which, in comparison to the government, is a much more majoritarian institution. There, within the Social Security Commission of the National Council, a more far-reaching version of the reform was elaborated, but consensus was lost. Change was brought about by a short-lived coalition between the Socialists and the Liberal Democrats, who agreed on the principle of introducing a contribution sharing and credit system. Nevertheless, they disagreed on whether or not additional costs should have been compensated by an increase in women's retirement age. The result was that, while the first part of the new pension bill, i.e. contribution sharing and credits, was supported by virtually all political parties, its second part, the increase in women's retirement age to sixty-four, was imposed by the right-wing majority.

The two measures, however, were included in a single piece of legislation. As a result, the left was unable to challenge the one element of retrenchment, the increase in women's retirement age, without taking the risk of undermining the parts of the bill it supported. The combination of elements of retrenchment and expansion in a single piece of legislation was imposed by the right-wing parliamentary majority against the will of the left. This strategy, of combining different components in a single act, can be regarded as a substitute for consensus. The bill, in fact, included a retrenchment element which satisfied the right-wing majority. At the same time, however, it also comprised widely supported expansion measures. The result was that, in the referendum, the combination of these two elements was likely to be supported more widely than the simple adoption of a higher retirement age for women.

The opinion poll carried out on the referendum (Vox 1995; see tab. 4.4, 111) indicates that only 10 per cent of those who voted 'yes' did so because they supported a higher retirement age for women. In contrast, at least 59 per cent of those who voted 'no' did so because they were against that measure. This suggests, quite powerfully, that it would have been much more difficult for the majority to obtain the acceptance in a referendum of an increase in retirement age alone. The combination of measures of different nature in a single reform contributed to widening its support basis, and thus to its success at the polls. In addition, this strategy proved an effective tool for blame avoidance for the right-wing majority, who were able to avoid being identified as retrenchers. In fact, media exposure of a bill is highest during the referendum campaign. At this stage, retrenchment advocates can focus their support on the popular parts of the bill, and do not need to argue openly in favour of the unpopular ones.

This is precisely what happened in the referendum on the 1995 pension reform. The right-wing majority was able to campaign in favour of the reform, without openly supporting the increase in women's retirement age. It is instructive to point out that the organisers of a televised debate on the pension reform referendum were unable to find a speaker who would argue in favour of raising retirement age for women *per se* (Télévision Suisse Romande 1995). Those who were responsible for the introduction of this measure in the bill were now arguing that perhaps a higher retirement age for women was not particularly desirable, but, as it was part of a wider reform, it had to be accepted since the remaining measures were highly positive and badly needed.

It seems, thus, that despite the change in the direction of policy institutions are still exerting a significant impact on Swiss policy-making. The pressures for consensus remain strong. This was shown by the several attempts made to avoid the referendum and, perhaps, also by the apparently odd decision to chose a retirement age of sixty-five/sixty-four, which still does not comply with gender equality. When the referendum became inevitable, then the right-wing majority had to maximise the chances of winning it – hence their refusal to go along with the proposal of dividing the reform into two different pieces of legislation and take separate votes. The combination of expansion and retrenchment within a single piece of legislation proved an effective strategy for the right-wing majority to deal with the uncertainty constituted by the referendum and to obtain the adoption of an element of retrenchment.

# 5    France: the search for an elusive consensus

As far as theory is concerned, France is probably the most interesting case among those covered by this study. Policy-makers unintentionally created ideal conditions for testing hypotheses concerning the determinants of pension policy and the factors that favour or hamper success in pension reform. In the space of only two years, two very similar plans for pension reform were put forward. The first concerned only private sector employees and was successfully transformed into law in summer 1993. The second, in 1995, consisted of the extension of the same measures to public sector employees. It generated a massive wave of strikes, mainly among rail workers, which forced the government to withdraw its plans. This chapter covers both events, and tries to answer the question of why two very similar plans for the reform of pensions generated such different public reactions.

## 5.1    Institutions and patterns of policy-making

Political scientists have generally considered France as a country where policy-making is characterised by a substantial degree of centralisation. Typically, public policy is decided at the top with little or no negotiation with external interests. In his comprehensive study of interest-group politics in France, Wilson points out that, albeit with some exceptions, the relationship between the state and organised interests in France is characterised by 'a power situation of a state capable of resisting interests and proceeding with its own ends regardless of group pressures' (Wilson 1987: 238). This view is reflected in the literature on corporatism, which typically views France as a counter-example. Lijphart and Crepaz, in their review of expert opinion on the degree of corporatism in various countries, found that France is most often considered as one of the least corporatist countries (1991: 240). Tripartite negotiations between employers, trade unions and the government in the areas of social and economic policy did not develop in France as they did in other European countries.

118

The absence of corporatist practices in France has been explained with reference to the asymmetry of power between the state and organised interests (Kriesi 1994; Merrien 1991). According to the literature on corporatism, a key precondition for inclusive policy-making is a relatively balanced power relationship between the various institutional and socio-economic actors which interact in the formulation of policy.[1] Such a balanced relationship cannot be found in France. Historically, the modern French state is the result of a long cumulative process of power concentration within the top level of the bureaucratic apparatus (Badie and Birnbaum 1983). Economic development was to a very large extent instigated by the state, during both the industrial revolution and the post-war boom. After World War II, planning was adopted as a standard instrument of economic policy and had, until the mid-1970s, an effective impact on the French economy (Shonfield 1965; Hall 1986: 140). In addition, the existence of a relatively large state-owned industrial and financial sector has further increased the grip of the state on society and on the economy. Finally, the creation in 1945 of a specialised school (ENA, Ecole Nationale d'Administration) where virtually all top civil servants are educated guarantees a community of background and views among bureaucrats.

It should be stressed that the use of the term 'state' instead of 'government' is not incidental. Power is not always concentrated in the hands of the government, as substantial influence is exerted by a few top layers of officials within the civil service. While carrying out the interviews needed for this study, I was struck by the ease with which high-ranking officials of the Ministry of Social Affairs were openly critical of current government policy. To some extent, the impression they gave was that they believed themselves to be the ones who knew what needed to be done in order to deal with the relevant issues. They considered themselves to be aware of the general interest, while all other actors, like trade unions, employers and politicians, were seen to be looking after their own interests.

On the other hand, organised interests cannot match the impressive level of power resources available to the state. First, with regard to labour, France has one of the lowest unionisation rates in the western world. While the exact number of unionised employees is not known, it is believed to be between 10 and 14 per cent of the workforce (Join-Lambert 1994: 110). In addition, the labour movement is divided along ideological lines. As a result, there are five major national federations of trade unions, which operate independently from each other. The divisions reflect the political spectrum. Starting from the left, the

---

[1] See for example Schmitter and Lehmbruch 1979; Lehmbruch and Schmitter 1982; Lehmbruch 1984; Regini 1984.

Confédération Générale du Travail (CGT) is of Communist inspiration. Force Ouvrière (FO) originated from a division within the CGT in 1947 and constitutes its non-communist component (it is sometimes referred to as CGT–FO). The Confédération Française des Travailleurs Chrétiens (CFTC) is a federation of Catholic unions. Finally, the Confédération Française Démocratique des Travailleurs (CFDT) emerged from a division of the CFTC and constitutes its non-religious component. In recent years it has been much more co-operative with the government than its counterparts have. Finally, there is also a federation representing managers (CFE–CGC, Confédération Française de l'Encadrement–Confédération Générale des Cadres).

On the employers' side, interest representation is more integrated, as the only division is between large companies belonging to the Conseil National du Patronnat Français (CNPF) and small and medium-sized firms (CGPME). The CNPF, however, because it represents companies with a wide range of different and possibly conflicting interests, is effective only in defending basic and common interests of French employers. This is why large firms rely more on individual lobbying rather than representation through the CNPF. The result is, of course, a substantial weakening of the institution (Kriesi 1994).

France thus, with a strong state and a weak and fragmented system of interest intermediation, lacks the preconditions needed in order to establish corporatist practices. Organised interests are consulted selectively, and their position is not seen as a basis for negotiation. Typically, policy is imposed by the central government. Among the consequences of this approach to policy-making is the inability of the government to exert any sort of control over the reactions of the public to its decisions. This, coupled with an extraordinary mobilising capacity of the trade unions, explains the relatively frequent occurrence of protest movements, which on occasions have been rather effective in forcing the government to abandon unpopular policies.

This analysis of French politics refers to broad and general trends, and it is accurate on that level. However, if one looks at the details of different areas of policy and of various combinations of political contingencies, one will find that this interpretation of the way French politics works needs to be amended somewhat. Next, I will argue that there are two particular instances, both relevant to the understanding of pension reform politics, in which the interpretation reviewed above does not seem to be entirely satisfactory. This is the case when the two key institutions of the French political system, the presidency and parliament, are controlled by different parties, as well as within the area of social security policy.

*The politics of cohabitation*

In the French political jargon, the word 'cohabitation' refers to a situation in which the president of the Republic and the prime minister belong to two different parties. The fact that parliament and the president are both elected directly and in two different polls makes this possible. The likelihood of having a majority in parliament and a president belonging to the opposition party is further increased by the fact that presidential and general elections do not occur at the same time and have different political cycles. Parliament is re-elected every five years while presidential elections are fought every seven years. The result is that between the two contests there may be substantial swings in public opinion, which can result in a situation of cohabitation.

Since the establishment of the Fifth Republic (1958), cohabitation has occurred three times: first, between 1986 and 1988 with Mitterrand as president and Chirac as prime minister; second, between 1993 and 1995 with President Mitterrand and Prime Minister Balladur; and finally, since May 1997 with Chirac as president and Jospin as prime minister. On all these occasions, the influence of the president on policy has been substantially reduced. When president and prime minister belong to the same party, it is the former who plays the key role in deciding policy. Prime ministers are chosen by the president and, since the latter is the key figure within his or her party, there are good chances that the person selected will be supported by parliament. In case of incompatibility emerging between the two figures, the president can always sack the prime minister. The result is that, in what is regarded as the 'normal' situation, the president is the one who decides the orientation of government policy.

The balance of power is reversed when parliament is dominated by a different party (or coalition) than the president's, in which case the president has little influence on the selection of a prime minister. Although formally it is always the president who appoints the head of government, in practice he or she is forced to choose the candidate supported by the majority of parliament. In this case, the president tends to play a role which is more akin to that of the ceremonial head of state known by most parliamentary systems. The overall orientation of government policy is decided by the prime minister (Duverger 1987). As a matter of fact, during the first cohabitation (1986–8), Prime Minister Jacques Chirac adopted a series of typically right-wing social and economic policies, such as privatisation of state-owned companies and welfare retrenchment, which had little in common with President Mitterrand's Socialist political orientation. During this period, the president was to a large extent excluded from the definition of policy.

Though sidelined in actual policy-making, however, Mitterrand did not restrain himself from taking part in public debates, particularly in response to the government's political mistakes. Some of Chirac's neo-liberal policies proved, in fact, extremely unpopular with the French public. Most notably this was the case in a 1986 attempt to impose a reform of the higher education system which would have allowed a bigger role for the private sector. The proposal was met with significant resistance by students' organisations, which managed to set up a strong protest movement, with strikes and demonstrations in the streets of Paris and other big cities, to which Chirac responded by sending in riot police. Mitterrand, after remaining silent for much of the crisis, took advantage of the situation and publicly intervened against the government. Chirac, deprived of presidential support, was forced to abandon his plans.

While Mitterrand had little formal power to prevent the government from carrying out unpopular policies, considerations of political convenience made it extremely unwise for Chirac to go ahead with his reform against not only public opinion, but also against a president who had been directly elected and who was going to be his rival in the upcoming 1988 presidential election. This episode showed that the president was not entirely deprived of his or her powers when in cohabitation. While unable to determine the content of policy, the president could still exert some sort of veto power. In this respect, cohabitation introduced a de facto veto point in the French policy-making process.

The first cohabitation ended in 1988, when Mitterrand won a second term in office and called a general election which gave the left a majority in parliament. France was back to united government, but only for five years, as in 1993 the right-wing coalition won that year's general election. This time, however, the right was going to be more cautious. When in April 1993 Edouard Balladur became the prime minister of the second cohabitation, there is little doubt that a key concern for him was to avoid a repetition of the mistakes committed by Chirac a few years earlier. In fact, being himself a presidential candidate for the 1995 election, Balladur could not afford to adopt unpopular measures and thus take the risk of alienating public support. His policy-making style was geared towards avoiding conflicts. As a French commentator put it:

The decision of Prime Minister [Balladur] to run for president in the 1995 election acted as a brake on the government's action . . . Edouard Balladur was in a position in which he could not upset too large sections of public opinion. He had to avoid a return to popularity of the Socialists and the loss of legitimacy of his candidature. (Bigaut 1995: 9)

During the two years he spent in office as prime minister, Balladur abandoned controversial policies on a number of occasions. For instance, when the government tried to reduce the level of the statutory minimum wage for young unemployed people, a trade union-led protest movement forced the withdrawal of the relevant bill. The same happened with a reform in the education system which would have expanded the private sector as well as with a plan to restructure the state-owned airline Air France. In sum, during his term in office, Balladur tried to avoid conflict as much as possible, and seemingly renounced the centralised approach to policy-making that is typical of France. As will be seen below, this particular situation, cohabitation coupled with the upcoming presidential election, played an important role also in determining the government's approach to pension reform.

### The politics of Sécurité sociale

The political debate on pension policy and, more generally, on welfare reforms is strongly influenced by the institutional structure of the French social security system. The position of the different actors within the system determines what their interests are, and creates opportunities for negotiation that may not exist in other countries. A key element in this context is the fact that social insurance in France is managed jointly by the social partners. This affects in a significant way the trade unions–government relationship in matters of social insurance reform. While in most other countries the controversy between government and trade unions concerns mainly the level of provision, in France the issue of who controls the system is also one of paramount importance. Here I will concentrate on the implications of this particular institutional feature on the politics of social security. A more detailed description of the French pension system is provided in the next section.

The French welfare state can be described as a dual social protection system. Its main component is a wide-ranging social insurance system, referred to as Sécurité sociale.[2] It is almost entirely financed through employment-related contributions and provides earnings-related benefits. Sécurité sociale, in theory at least, works according to the principles of social insurance, which imply a relatively strong connection between what one pays into the system (contributions) and what one gets

---

[2] Sécurité sociale provides coverage for health care, basic pensions and family benefits. Unemployment insurance was set up at a later stage (1959) and is not part of social security. Its organisational structure, however, is very similar to that of the main system, as it is also managed jointly by the social partners, is contribution-financed and grants contributory benefits.

out of it (benefits).[3] Its second component, referred to as *solidarité nationale*, consists of non-contributory schemes, generally designed to cater for
those who have been unable to build up an adequate contribution record.

The political relevance of this dichotomy refers to the fact that the
social insurance system (*Sécurité sociale*) is managed jointly by employees'
and employers' representatives. This is what was agreed in 1945, when
the existing system was set up. At that time, it was the trade unions (particularly the CGT, which was dominant) which insisted on this type of
arrangement (Guillemard 1986). Since then, the trade unions have
always shown a strong attachment to joint management by employers and
employees. This is understandable. First, taking part in the management
of social security gives the unions an important degree of visibility and of
legitimacy in the eyes of public opinion. It has been argued, in fact, that
the managerial role played by the unions in social insurance somewhat
compensates for their relatively low unionisation rates (Rosanvallon
1995: 81). Second, and not unimportantly, social insurance schemes constitute an important source of employment for trade union members. In
contrast, the non-insurance component of the French welfare state (*solidarité nationale*) is considered to be the responsibility of the government.

The two components are regarded as two coherent and independent
sets of elements. For instance, social insurance has to be strictly contributory, grants earnings related-benefits and is to be managed by the social
partners. *Solidarité nationale*, in contrast, is financed through general taxation, is managed by the government and grants non-contributory
benefits. The two systems are generally seen as two different sets of policies, which have to be kept separate. The extent of this normative perception is well captured by Rosanvallon:

Social insurance should be distinguished from *solidarité nationale* [non-contribu-
tory element]: this cry is becoming one of the most widespread platitudes of the
end of this century. Everything, from administrative constraints to philosophical
uncertainties, is pulling in that direction. (Rosanvallon 1995: 82)

In fact, however, the distinction between the two systems is more theoretical and normative than real. Social insurance schemes have been
amended numerous times since 1945, and currently contain elements of
both components. This is especially the case with health insurance, where
coverage is granted on a non-contributory basis to a number of disadvantaged categories (such as long-term unemployed people), and with the
family benefits scheme, which since 1978 has lost its insurance character
and now grants universal and means-tested benefits only. The same is

---

[3] For an informed discussion on the principles of social insurance, see Clasen 1997a.

true for pensions. While the bulk of pension expenditure is used to pay for contributory benefits, insurance-based schemes contain a number of exceptions to the social insurance principle. For instance, older people who do not have a sufficient contribution record to be entitled to what is regarded as an adequate pension are eligible for an income-tested minimum pension (*minimum vieillesse*). In addition, there are measures such as contribution credits granted to unemployed persons and parents raising children which are also considered to be alien to social insurance.

In sum, over the last few decades, governments faced with rising social problems have tended to use the social insurance system to achieve their social policy objectives. Instead of duplicating social insurance schemes for those unable to build up a sufficient contribution record, it was decided to extend social insurance entitlements beyond the core of actual contributors. This move, however, did not find favour with the trade unions, who viewed the use of the social insurance system to achieve social policy objectives such as poverty prevention in old age as an aberration. French trade unions, in fact, tend to regard the social insurance system as an insurance plan covering all salaried employees. Its use as a social policy instrument is bound to be resisted.

Differences in views between the government and the unions on the appropriate role of social insurance have been a constant source of tension between the two actors (Bonoli and Palier 1997). Governments of different political persuasions have tried to increase their control over the social insurance system. Increased state control over the social insurance is seen by the government as a precondition for the adoption of successful cost-containment measures. Needless to say, such moves are strenuously resisted by the trade unions, which might risk losing their influence in the management of the system, and all the benefits that go with it. The issue of control over social security has become a major source of confrontation between the government and the union movement.

The participation of the trade unions in the management of social insurance and the political repercussions of it have some important implications for the politics of pension reform. First, since social insurance is widely seen as something belonging to the realm of employment (as opposed to a state policy), trade unions find it easier to mobilise public opinion on matters relating to social insurance than is the case in other areas of public policy. This undoubtedly puts considerable pressure on the government to adopt a more co-operative approach to reform in the area of social insurance than is the case in other areas of public policy. Second, and most importantly, trade unions have a clear set of demands with regard to the control and the management of social insurance. This allows some additional scope for negotiation and creates the opportunity for non-zero sum games to take place. For instance, the government can trade retrenchment in the level of provision with concessions on the management side of social insurance. As will be seen below, this is precisely what happened in the 1993 pension reform, and arguably what made it politically feasible. A similar *quid pro quo* was not sought in 1995: hence the failure of Juppé's attempt to reform public sector pensions.

### Policy-making patterns and pension reform

The analysis of pension reform in France put forward in this chapter is based on the hypothesis that two institutional factors played a substantial role in determining the government's approach to change and the fortunes of government policy. First, cohabitation, coupled with the upcoming presidential election, persuaded the right-wing Balladur government to adopt a relatively co-operative stance in the 1993 reform as far as the unions were concerned. Second, the fact that social security is managed by the unions (jointly with employers) gave the government the opportunity to trade cutbacks in provision with guarantees concerning the control of the system.

The situation was reversed in 1995 when the Juppé government tried to extend the measures adopted in the 1993 reform to the public sector. The right-wing majority then controlled both the presidency and parliament. With the next general election scheduled for 1998, the government was under no pressure to negotiate with the social partners over the content of pension reform, and it did not. The result, however, was a massive protest movement that eventually forced the government to renounce its plans for public sector pension reform.

### 5.2    The French pension system

The current structure of the French pension system is characterised by an impressive degree of fragmentation along occupational lines.[4] Its origins go back to 1945, when French social reformers, under the influence of the Beveridge report, set out to create a comprehensive and universal social security system (Kerschen 1995). Their explicit intention was to develop a scheme which would have incorporated all the existing ones, thereby achieving the goal of universality. This proved, however, to be overambi-

---

[4] The following description refers only to basic pensions. In addition, however, most French workers are covered by a second tier of provision known as *régimes complémentaires*. Since pension reform affected only basic pensions, these are not treated here. For a good presentation of second-tier pension in France, see Reynaud 1994.

tious. A separate scheme for farmers was accepted from the beginning, given the different socio-economic profile of this group.[5] In addition, immediately after the introduction of the *régime général*, it became clear that groups already covered by pension arrangements, mainly public sector employees, had no intention of joining the new social security system, and were allowed to maintain their own. Similarly, various groups of self-employed people who felt economically secure enough on their own declined to join the general scheme (Baldwin 1990: 252–87).

As a result France has a pension system which distinguishes between four large collectivities: waged employees in industry and commerce who are covered by the *régime général* (65 per cent); farmers (3 per cent); public sector employees (20 per cent); and the self-employed (12 per cent). The last two groups, moreover, are further fragmented according to employer or profession. Within the public sector, for instance, there are separate schemes for civil servants; local government employees; miners; rail workers; and electricity and gas employees. In general, public sector employees enjoy more generous treatment than their counterparts.

In order to avoid excessive inequalities between pensioners covered by different schemes, a system of 'inter-regime compensation' was introduced in 1974. This consists of actuarially determined cash transfers from schemes with a favourable demographic profile towards those which are worse off. In practice the *régime général* subsidises schemes such as the ones for farmers or for miners, which currently have among their members more retirees than contributors. These cash transfers are supplemented by government subsidies for schemes which have been particularly disadvantaged by socio-economic developments, particularly by low wage growth (Chatagner 1993: 53; Reynaud 1994: 12).

### The régime général (general scheme)

All private sector employees (except in agriculture) are covered by the *régime général*. The scheme is financed through employers' and employees' contributions and provides earnings-related benefits. Contributions are 14.75 per cent (employer: 8.2 per cent; employee: 6.55 per cent) of gross salary, with a ceiling;[6] and an additional contribution of 1.6 per cent

---

[5] According to Dupeyroux and Prétot (1993: 113), among the key reasons for having a separate scheme for farmers were the unfavourable demographic profile; the individual quality of farming; and the slower growth rate of incomes relative to industry and services, which implies that farmers are unable to contribute to a social insurance system on the same basis as other professions. The scheme, in fact, is heavily subsidised.

[6] The ceiling is set at around 120 per cent of the average net wage (Join-Lambert 1994: 301).

of gross salary without ceiling payable by the employer only. With regard to benefits, before the 1993 reform, a full pension of 50 per cent of reference salary was granted to those who had paid contributions for 37.5 years. For shorter contribution records the pension is reduced correspondingly. The reference salary was calculated on the basis of earnings over the final ten years before retirement.

The retirement age is sixty for both men and women. However, someone with an inadequate contribution record can go on working until he or she fulfils the qualifying conditions for a full pension, or reaches sixty-five. Those who retire at sixty-five are entitled to a full pension regardless of their contribution record. For shorter contribution periods, the pension is reduced by 5 percentage points for each missing year. Longer contribution periods, however, are not compensated with higher pensions since the 50 per cent replacement rate is considered as the maximum level (Dupeyroux and Prétot 1993: 50).

In addition to contributory pensions, the *régime général* provides means-tested coverage for older persons whose income is below around 55 per cent of an average net wage (Join-Lambert 1994: 365). The means-tested pension, known as the *minimum vieillesse*, is a key source of income for the very old (over eighty) and for lone elderly women. Although it is managed by the *régime général*, the minimum pension is granted regardless of the former occupation of the recipient. Means-tested pensions are used mainly by workers who, because of the late introduction of old age insurance, were unable to build up an adequate contribution record. As younger generations have started reaching retirement age, the number of beneficiaries of the *minimum vieillesse* has fallen dramatically from 2.5 million in 1960 to 1.3 million in 1990 (France, CGP 1991: 62).

### The régimes spéciaux (separate schemes)

As seen above, the existence of separate schemes goes back to 1945 when the current social security system was set up and a number of occupational groups who already had pension coverage declined to be part of it. These schemes, which constitute the legacy of the first efforts in the area of provision for retirement, now provide pension coverage for public sector employees. As in other industrial countries among the first groups covered by a pension arrangement were the civil service workers, seamen, rail workers, gas and electricity workers and so forth. At the end of World War II there were some 160 separate schemes. Currently there are about 100, of which only fifteen accept new members. Altogether, separate schemes have 4.4 million members and provide pension coverage for some 3 million retirees (Reynaud 1994: 12).

Pension formulas and qualifying conditions vary according to the different schemes, but they are generally more generous than is the case in the general scheme. For instance, the scheme for civil servants uses the final salary as a reference salary, and the pension is calculated as 2 per cent of reference salary per year of contribution. The full pension, granted after 37.5 contribution years, corresponds thus to 75 per cent of the last salary, well above the 50 per cent granted by the general scheme (Reynaud 1994: 12).[7] Retirement age can also be lower than in the general scheme. For instance, train drivers of the national railways company (SNCF) and of the Parisian underground (RATP) retire at fifty; some employees of the national electricity and gas companies at fifty-five (Dupeyroux and Prétot 1993: 106).

### Pressures for change

Concern for the medium- and long-term financing of pensions emerged as a political issue in the mid-1980s. This came as a result of recurrent deficits in the social security budget but also in response to the publication of long-term demographic projections produced by the government's statistical service in 1986. By the mid-1980s, the deficit of the *régime général* basic pension scheme had reached worrying proportions (see tab. 5.1). This was at a time when the demographic structure of the scheme's members was still rather favourable. Things were already bad, and were going to get worse.

A budget deficit in a social security scheme is seen as a short-term problem which has to be solved rapidly. Social security schemes, which are not included in the general government budget, cannot borrow to finance current expenditure. The difference between receipts and outlays is temporarily made up with government money, but the deficit is transferred to the following year's budget (Hirsch 1993: 52). For some time, the main approach to dealing with budget deficits had been to increase contribution rates. For instance, in 1986, the employee contribution to the basic pension scheme was raised by 0.7 percentage points; a year later by another 0.2 percentage points. In 1990, the ceiling on employers' contribution was removed for 1.6 per cent of salary, though compensated by a reduction in their payment to the family benefits scheme (Oudin 1992: 146–54). The strategy of raising contribution rates to keep the pension scheme budget balanced, however, could not be used indefinitely. As was being done in other areas of the welfare state (most notably health care), policy needed to contain expenditure as well (Palier 1999: 305–66).

---

[7] It should be noted that public sector employees are not covered by a second-tier pension arrangement. The combined replacement rate of first- and second-tier provision for private sector employees is around 70 per cent for a full contribution record.

Table 5.1 *Balance of the French basic pension scheme,*
régime général *(1978–95), in FF billion*

| 1978 | −8.0 | 1984 | −1.7 | 1990 | −6.6 |
|------|------|------|------|------|------|
| 1979 | −0.9 | 1985 | −7.9 | 1991 | −18.7 |
| 1980 | +1.1 | 1986 | −15.6 | 1992 | −17.9 |
| 1981 | −0.7 | 1987 | −10.3 | 1993 | −39.5 |
| 1982 | −1.1 | 1988 | −17.1 | 1994 | −12.7 |
| 1983 | −8.8 | 1989 | −4.6 | 1995 | +10.1 |

Source: Palier 1999: 309.

Table 5.2 *Contribution rates needed to finance
French pension expenditure, based on pre-1993
legislation (percentage of gross salary, combined rate
for employers and employees)*

|      | Best-case scenario | Worst-case scenario |
|------|--------------------|---------------------|
| 1990 | 18.9 | 18.9 |
| 2000 | 20.7 | 21.1 |
| 2010 | 24.3 | 26.2 |
| 2020 | 28.9 | 33.4 |
| 2030 | 31.4 | 39.9 |
| 2040 | 30.9 | 41.9 |

*Assumptions:*
   *Best-case scenario* assumes: fertility rate of 2.1 on average
between 2005 and 2030; labour force participation rate for
the fifty-five to sixty-four age group to reach 54 per cent in
2040; unemployment at 4.5 per cent between 2005 and
2010 and 3 per cent after 2030.
   *Worst-case scenario* assumes: fertility rate of 1.8 on average
between 2005 and 2030; labour force participation rate for
the fifty-five to sixty-four age group to remain stable at 39.2
per cent; unemployment at 8 per cent between 2005 and
2010 and 6 per cent after 2030.
*Source:* France, CGP 1991: 96.

On the top of that, in the mid-1980s additional pressure to reform the
basic pension scheme came as the government published its long-term
projections of pension expenditure in 1986. For the first time, these projections looked at the expected impact of ageing on pension expenditure
until 2025. Their conclusion was rather bleak: in 2025, in order to keep
the scheme balanced, contributions had to be increased by 170 per cent

or, alternatively, benefits had to be halved (Ruellan 1993: 911–12). This event marked the beginning of a long pension debate, characterised by a series of studies and official reports, mandated by governments of different political orientation, all of which emphasised the non-sustainability of current pension arrangements in the long term.

The White Paper on pensions, published by the government in 1991, provides a review of projections based on a number of different assumptions with regard to fertility, LFPRs in the fifty-five to sixty-four age group, and unemployment (France, CGP 1991). For each scenario, the paper gives the contribution rate needed in order to keep the budget balanced, if pension legislation remains unchanged. The projections refer to a hypothetical universal pension scheme. The data, reproduced in table 5.2, can also be read as the weighted average of contribution rates of the different basic schemes.

Table 5.2 shows a rather bleak picture for the future of pensions in France. Even in the best-case scenario the combined employer/employee contribution rate to finance basic pensions would be somewhere in the region of 30 per cent of gross salary. The model does not take into account increases in productivity because, being based on pre-1993 legislation, it assumes that increases in wages will be offset by corresponding increases on the benefits side (according to pre-1993 legislation, benefits were indexed according to gross wages).

Since the mid-1980s, and particularly in the early 1990s, financial pressures to reform the basic pension scheme have become rather strong. In comparison to other countries, and particularly the ones reviewed in this study, what is striking is the fact that in France pension reform did not anticipate an expected deficit in a pay-as-you-go pension scheme. In contrast, reform came after more than a decade of recurrent budget deficits. To some extent, this is due to the fact that, unlike in Britain or Switzerland, in France the basic pension is virtually entirely financed through contributions and does not receive substantial government subsidies. Under such circumstances it is more difficult to have a balanced budget, especially during a recession. However, in order to appreciate the reasons behind French procrastination in dealing with the pension issue, one needs to turn to the political dimension of pension policy.

## 5.3    The pension debate in the 1980s and early 1990s

There is an apparent contradiction in French pension policy-making from the mid-1980s onwards. On the one hand, there is an agreement among all major political parties (with the exception of the Communists) that cuts are needed in order to restore the financial equilibrium of the basic scheme, let alone to guarantee the viability of the system in future. On the other hand, no saving measure was adopted until 1993. In contrast, contribution rates were increased regularly. The reasons behind this contradiction arise from two different but related areas.

First, governments of different political persuasions have been equally afraid of the public's reaction to a pension reform (Ruellan 1993). Opinion polls show the comparatively high level of popularity of public pensions in France (Ferrera 1993a: 34), and the attitude of the general public towards the social security system has been characterised as one of strong emotional attachment (Palier 1991). In addition, it is well known that French trade unions, despite the low degree of unionisation, can have a substantial mobilising capacity. Like public opinion – and perhaps more so – trade unions are likely to oppose cutbacks in the area of pensions. In this context, it is understandable that a pension reform is considered to be an extremely sensitive political issue. Of course, pension reforms are politically dangerous exercises everywhere, but given the proven vehemence of France's informal protests, governments were perhaps less inclined to risk political capital on a pension reform than some of their counterparts in other countries.

Second, politicians willing to embark on a pension reform are likely to wait for the most appropriate timing. Like all potentially unpopular policies, cutbacks in pensions are easier to implement when there is no upcoming important election. While this is a feature common to all democracies, France has the specificity of having a double electoral cycle: as seen above, general elections take place every five years whereas presidential ones are fought every seven years. The result is a narrowing down of the size of these 'windows' in which pension reforms can be forced through with reduced political risk. Between 1985 and 1995, French voters were asked to elect a parliament three times, in 1986, 1988 and 1993, and a president twice, in 1988 and 1995. The two-year lag between the two political cycles means a reduction in the period of time available to 'safely' implement unpopular measures.

The result is that, between 1985 and 1993, one can count at least seven official reports on pensions, all of which give policy recommendations, which, incidentally, are surprisingly similar. In fact, it seems that these reports, produced by various commissions, have a double objective. To some extent, they have to test the political feasibility of given options for reform. On the other hand, however, they create the impression that the government is actually doing something to guarantee the current and long-term viability of the pension system, without putting much political capital at stake. Interestingly, over the same period, the employee contribution rate rose from 4.7 per cent in 1984 to the current 6.55 per cent, and an additional employer's contribution of 1.6 per cent without ceiling was introduced in 1990.

### The emergence of pension reform as a political issue

According to Ruellan (1993: 912), it is a report commissioned by the Socialist prime minister Laurent Fabius in 1985 that marks the beginning of the official debate on basic pensions reform. The report (France, CGP 1986), published in June 1986, took a fairly pessimistic view of the future financial problems of French pensions. Its main conclusion was that an increase in retirement age was inevitable. With regard to other possible measures, the report rejected as impractical proposals to move from a pay-as-you-go system to a funded one. In contrast, an extension of the period over which the reference salary is calculated was viewed more positively. Similarly, the removal of non-contributory provision from the insurance-based scheme was also given some consideration, as this would ease the financial pressure on it. Some of these suggestions were going to be extremely influential in the upcoming debate on the reform of basic pensions.

After the change of government in 1986, the newly appointed minister of social affairs, the Gaullist Philippe Seguin, followed his predecessor and mandated another study, with very similar terms of reference, i.e. 'to make suggestions so as to ensure a satisfactory equilibrium of the general scheme's basic pension in 2000–2005' (Ruellan 1993: 912). One of the objectives of this second report (Schopflin 1987) was to test the political feasibility of various proposals, including those suggested in the previous one. The task of writing it, in fact, was given to a commission which included representatives of both employers' and employees' organisations. The result was a watered-down version of the first report. The increase of retirement age was seen as something that could be done, but in a flexible way. With regard to a possible extension of the period over which the reference salary is calculated, the commission could not reach an agreement. Concerning benefit indexation, a mixed index was suggested, combining changes in earnings and prices.

### The Etats Généraux of social security

The pension issue was brought up again at the 'Etats Généraux de la sécurité sociale', a major convention on the future of social security organised by the Chirac government in 1987. The declared objective of this exercise was to initiate a national debate on the options for reform of the social security system. The debate was led by a 'Committee of Wise

Men', appointed by the prime minister, who had the task of consulting a wide range of relevant interest groups and, through postal submissions of evidence, the public at large. Much emphasis was placed on the government's intention to develop a reform process based on the inclusion of the various interests and of the population. In the words of the then prime minister, 'It belongs to the French people to get the information and to express views on a problem that affects them all . . . Together they will have to suggest the direction for the future. It is only through the concertation of all of us that we will succeed in saving our social security' (Chirac 1987). At that time, the government discourse was characterised by a strong emphasis on the need for consensus. The unilateral imposition of what were nevertheless seen as necessary measures was ruled out both by the prime minister and by the minister of social affairs on various occasions (Palier 1991: 46).

A number of reasons explain the choice of a non-confrontational strategy by the Chirac government, some of which have been anticipated above. First, there was a general preoccupation with the possible reaction of the trade unions and of the public to a reduction in pension entitlements. Perhaps most crucially, however, the convention was only a few months away from the 1988 presidential election in which Chirac intended to run. Obviously, the time was not particularly favourable for the adoption of unpopular policies, and Chirac had already suffered two important setbacks in trying to implement neo-liberal policies: in the face of public opposition he had to withdraw plans for higher education and civil service reform.

Among the consequences of these setbacks was a change in the government's attitude to policy-making. In the official discourse, much emphasis was placed on the notion of *décider autrement* (to decide in a different way), which referred precisely to a consensual approach to policy-making. The *Etats Généraux* of social security provided an excellent opportunity for the government to improve its image just one year before the presidential election. According to Palier, 'The prime minister hoped that, thanks to this wide-ranging debate, he could avoid new social conflicts as he could not afford to be seen as the only responsible person for unpopular measures in the area of social security' (1991: 50).

The final report produced in autumn 1987 by the 'Committee of Wise Men' included a section on pensions (France, Comité des sages 1987). Despite the solemnity of the exercise, however, the proposals made were not significantly different from what had been suggested on previous occasions. As far as retirement age was concerned, it was argued that an increase was inevitable. A shift towards a defined-contribution system was seen positively as was an extension of the qualifying period for a full pension. Finally, with regard to indexation, the 'wise men' argued in favour of net wages. Nevertheless, with a presidential election only a few months away, the prime minister and presidential candidate Jacques Chirac had more pressing things to worry about than a risky pension reform. As a result no action was taken on that occasion.

### The Socialist approach to pension reform (1988–92)

The first consequence of Mitterrand's victory in the 1988 presidential election was to call an early general election which gave a relative majority to the Socialists. With the external support of the Communist Party, the left was able to govern France for another five-year term. With regard to pension policy and more in general to social protection, the task of producing a framework for reform was given to the Commissariat Général au Plan.[8] A report was published in June 1989 which picked up many of the measures suggested by its predecessors. More specifically, it argued in favour of benefit indexation based on net wages; to extend the reference period for the calculation of a pension from the ten to the twenty-five best years; to extend the qualifying period for a full pension from 37.5 to 41.25 years; and, finally, it suggested changing the pension formula from 50 per cent of gross wage to 60 per cent of net wage. The removal of non-contributory benefits from the old age insurance scheme was considered but discarded because it was seen as impractical (France, CGP 1989).

The report met with mixed reactions. First, as far as the trade unions were concerned, the moderate CFDT, in its official response, did not comment on individual proposals but argued against raising retirement age, even if this was to be done through an extension of the qualifying period for a full pension. It suggested that the purchasing power of retirees should evolve in parallel to that of the working population, and 'express[ed] regret that the commission decided to drop proposals for removing non-contributory elements from the old age insurance scheme' (CFDT 1989). More solid opposition to the CGP report came from the radical FO. In its official response it argued against each saving measure suggested. It concluded that 'It is absolutely unacceptable for Force Ouvrière to reduce the pension entitlements of salaried workers and

---

[8] The Commissariat Général au Plan (General Planning Commission) is a peculiar French institution. It was set up in 1946 and had the task of producing a five-year plan which would guide the government's actions in the broad area of economic policy. The plan was seen as an important institution in the period immediately after World War II, but has lost influence in more recent years. Currently, the documents produced by the Planning Commission are little more than contributions to a general debate (Jobert 1981; Hall 1986: 140).

retired people, as suggested in the CGP report' (FO 1989). Total dissatisfaction with the CGP report was expressed also by the Communist CGT,
which 'reject[ed it] and call[ed] on salaried employees and retired people
to fight the proposals with determination' (CGT 1989). In contrast, the
report was welcomed by the employers' association (CNPF 1989).
Nevertheless, the approval of employers was of little use to a Socialist
minority government, who needed the votes of the Communists and did
not receive support from within the labour movement. In these conditions, a successful pension reform was almost unthinkable. On the other
hand, the financial pressures on the social security budget were growing,
and the pension scheme accounted for a substantial part of it.

The following step was the publication of a White Paper (France, CGP
1991) on the reform of pensions, which again reiterated the suggestions
made in the previous reports. In particular, it argued for the extension of
the qualifying period for a full pension to forty-two years and the reference salary to be calculated on the basis of the best twenty-five years.
Benefit indexation, it was suggested, should be made on the basis of
inflation. At the same time, however, the report argued that pensioners
should profit from economic growth, although it did not specify how.

The task of testing the political feasibility of the proposals mentioned in
the White Paper was given to a commission set up by the Ministry of
Social Affairs. After consultation with the relevant interests, mainly
employers' and employees' organisations, the commission produced a
report which rejected much of what had been argued in the White Paper.
The extension of the period over which the reference salary is calculated
to twenty-five years was rejected, and instead of prices the report suggested net wages as a basis for the indexation of pensions. Only the extension of the qualifying period was accepted, but to forty years instead of
forty-two. The report (Mission Cottave 1992) mentioned again the sug-
gestion of removing non-contributory elements from the insurance
scheme. In addition, for the first time, there were suggestions of modifying the scheme for private sector employees only (*régime général*), and
leaving the public sector for a later reform. The reactions of the trade
unions this time were fairly positive, as the report was based to a large
extent on their requirements (*Le Monde* 16 January 1992, 15).

On the basis of this last set of proposals, the minister of social affairs set
up a second consultation in early 1992 (Mission Bruhnes). Basically the
results of the first consultation were confirmed. In addition it suggested
devolving the task of setting contribution and indexation rates to the
administration board of the basic pension scheme, composed of representatives of the trade unions and employers. This indicates that there might
have been some scope for compromise between the government and the

unions. The latter were prepared to accept reductions in the generosity of pension entitlements if these were compensated by more autonomy for the social partners in the management of basic pensions and by the removal of non-contributory benefits from the insurance scheme (which would reduce the financial pressure on it). However, the two actors were still far apart with regard to the size of such reductions and to the issue of indexation.

At that stage, the only element of the reform which seemed able to attract a sufficient level of support was the removal of non-contributory elements from the old age insurance scheme. For the government, it had the advantage of reducing the deficit that appears every year in the social security budget, though the cost would simply be transferred to the general government budget. For the trade unions this measure had the advantage of transforming the basic pension in a pure social insurance scheme. This removed state money from the scheme and by the same token state influence on it. The result was the prospect of increased autonomy and legitimacy for the management of old age insurance by the social partners, which was clearly in the interest of the trade unions.

A bill setting up a tax-financed fund designed to pay for non-contributory benefits was presented in parliament in November 1992, as a first step towards a pension reform. The bill was nevertheless defeated at the first reading: the right rejected the proposal as 'cosmetic accounting' since it did not produce actual savings, but only shifted some pension expenditure from the social security to the general government budget. Similarly the Parti Communiste Français declined its support since 'the new measure could open the way to a two-tiered system in retirement' (*Le Monde* 12 December 1992, 1). Alone, the Socialists, who did not have a majority in parliament, were unable to pass legislation. As a result, and with a general election scheduled for early 1993, the pension reform issue was again dropped from the government's agenda.

## 5.4    The Balladur government and the 1993 pension reform

The 1993 general election gave an overwhelming majority to the right-of-centre coalition. A controversial pension reform could easily have been pushed through in parliament. Nevertheless, the upcoming presidential election made this prospect unlikely. The French Gaullist party (Rassemblement pour la République) leadership was extremely wary not to repeat the mistakes of 1986–8. Then, the attempted imposition of controversial measures resulted in a loss of popularity of the Chirac government and ultimately contributed to his defeat in the 1988 presidential election. In fact, between 1993 and 1995, the Balladur government abandoned controversial measures on a number of occasions (Bigaut 1995: 9). In the area of pensions, however, the government managed to push through a reform which had been in the offing for almost a decade, and which all its predecessors failed to implement. In fact, to the surprise of French commentators (*Le Monde* 30 August 1993, 1; Ruellan 1993), the 1993 reform went through relatively smoothly, both in parliament and as far as the trade unions' and public opinion's reactions were concerned.

To some extent, this came as a result of the impressive electoral victory of the right-wing coalition, which, at least, guaranteed the compliance of parliament to the government proposals. By contrast, the previous Socialist government, having to rely on the external support of the Communists, was in a much less powerful position. In addition, the fresh landslide victory gave the right-wing coalition strong legitimacy in the eyes of the public, which made the organisation of an informal protest certainly more difficult. In July 1993, when the reform was announced, Balladur was still in his honeymoon period with the French electorate.

Besides these contingent factors, what certainly played a role in explaining the unexpected success of Balladur's pension reform is the style he adopted in policy-making. The government took a deliberately, and unusual, non-confrontational stance with the trade unions and the final content of the reform was decided only after intense negotiations with the trade unions (author interview, Ministry of Social Affairs, 20 December 1996). The fact that at the time France was in a situation of cohabitation, with executive power was shared between Prime Minister Balladur and President Mitterrand, helps to account for the adoption of such a non-confrontational approach.

The proposal put forward by the government reflected to a large extent the suggestions made in the White Paper, which had been heavily criticised by various trade unions. In addition, however, the government was prepared to include elements that were likely to be more acceptable to the unions. In particular, it was planned to set up a tax-financed fund run by the government, which would finance all non-contributory benefits in the area of old age pensions.

The impact of the fund is twofold. First, by removing non-contributory elements from the insurance scheme, it relieves the financial pressure on it. Second, it marks a clear distinction between social insurance and non-contributory provision. As seen above, this had been a key demand of some trade unions. The separation of these two components of pension provision, in fact, meant the recognition and acceptance by the government of the managing role played by the social partners in social insurance. This measure had been advocated by the CFDT (1989) and was also likely to be acceptable to the FO. In fact, according to a civil servant who took part in the negotiations with the social partners, these two confederations were a privileged target in the government's effort for concertation. In his own words:

It was important for us to gain the approval of the CFDT because we knew that the FO and the CGT would be hostile anyway . . . We needed at least the neutrality of the other confederations. It was also important to avoid the FO adopting too violent a position. In fact they were against, but did not react as they did in 1995 against the Juppé plan. They did not mobilise their members saying that the new legislation was shameful. (Author interview, Ministry of Social Affairs, 20 December 1996)

The government proposal was subjected to a vote at the administration board of the basic pension scheme, the Caisse Nationale d'Assurance Vieillesse (CNAV), which is composed of representatives of employees and employers. The two elements of the reform, cutbacks and the creation of a tax-financed fund for non-contributory benefits, were dealt with separately. With regard to the saving measures, only employers and the Catholic union CFTC were in favour. In contrast, the creation of a solidarity fund was approved by the CFDT, FO, CFTC and employers (France, CNAV 1993). This vote did not have any legal consequence, but gave a clear indication to the government as to the likely reaction of the various unions to the new legislation. On this basis, the government decided to go ahead, and the pension reform was adopted on 22 July 1993 (law) and on 27 August (decrees). The new pension legislation came into force at the beginning of 1994, albeit with a transition period for some of the measures.

### The content of the 1993 reform

The changes adopted in 1993 fall under two categories.[9] First a 'Fonds de solidarité vieillesse' was created, which has the task of funding non-contributory benefits. Second, in line with the proposals made in the White Paper, the qualifying period for a full pension is extended from thirty-seven and a half to forty years; the period over which the reference salary is calculated is extended from the best ten years to the best twenty-five. These measures, which affect the *régime général* only, are being introduced gradually over a ten-year transition period. Finally the indexation of benefits is based on prices (as opposed to earnings) for a five-year period.

[9] The relevant pieces of legislation are: law No. 93–936 of 22 July 1993; and decrees No. 93–1022 and No. 93–1023 of 27 August 1993. The law sets up the new 'Fonds de Solidarité Vieillesse' (see main text) and makes provision for allowing decisions concerning the indexation of pension to be made by decree. The two decrees change the pension formula and the indexation mechanism.

The Fonds de Solidarité Vieillesse (FSV) is a new institution which has the task of financing non-contributory benefits. It provides pensions for retired people with an inadequate contribution record, but it also compensates social insurance schemes for the contribution credits they grant to unemployed people and other groups of people who are not engaged in paid employment. In addition, the FSV has the task of repaying the debt accumulated by the social security system. It is financed by an earmarked tax,[10] which was raised by 1.3 percentage points on that occasion and by duties on alcoholic and non-alcoholic drinks (Chadelat 1994).

With regard to the indexation mechanism, the law has been modified so that it is now possible for the government to fix the amount of indexation by decree. Under previous legislation this decision had to go through parliament. At the same time, the government has adopted a decree that for a five-year period links the indexation of pensions to consumer prices. In fact, this had been the case before, since 1987 pensions had been indexed according to prices, with *ad hoc* legislation being passed by parliament every year (Ruellan 1993: 919). In 1998 the measure was extended by the Socialist government (Palier 1999: 352).

In the long term, the impact of the reform on pension expenditure could be quite substantial. According to projections by the administration of old age insurance scheme (CNAV), without the 1993 reform, contribution rates in 2010 would have had to be increased by around 10 percentage points. With the reform, if indexation according to prices is maintained, this figure could be between 2.73 and 7.26 percentage points (see tab. 5.3).

The 1993 reform will have an impact on the amount of pensions as well as on the actual age of retirement. Because of the extension to forty years of the qualifying period, it is expected that some employees will delay their retirement in order to receive a full pension despite the reform. The extension of the period over which the reference salary is calculated will have an impact on the level of pensions. The impact of this measure is a reduction in benefits by 7–8 per cent for high salaries, but does not affect those on the minimum wage, as they receive the minimum pension, which has not been modified by the reform (Ruellan 1993: 922).

---

[10] The FSV is financed through a tax called 'Contribution sociale généralisée' (CSG). The CSG is a new form of tax that was introduced in 1990 at a rate of 1.1 per cent and is earmarked for non-contributory benefits. It is levied on all sorts of income (not only wages) and is proportional. Despite the use of the term 'contribution', the CSG is considered to be a tax rather than a social insurance contribution (the French equivalent of contribution is 'cotisation').

Table 5.3 *The impact of the 1993 French reform on pension expenditure (increase in contribution rates needed to cover current expenditure, percentage points)*

|  | Scenario 1: expansion | | Scenario 2: contraction | |
|---|---|---|---|---|
|  | Pre-1993 legislation | Post-1993 legislation | Pre-1993 legislation | Post-1993 legislation |
| 2000 | 3.95 | 2.02 | 5.19 | 3.64 |
| 2005 | 5.39 | 2.00 | 7.89 | 4.87 |
| 2010 | 8.23 | 2.73 | 12.45 | 7.26 |

*Assumptions*: scenario 1 assumes that the number of salaried employees will grow by 1 per cent until 2010 and that average yearly real wage growth will be 1.5 per cent. Scenario 2 assumes no growth in the size of the workforce and a 1 per cent real increase in wages.
*Source:* Ruellan 1993: 921.

## 5.5    The reform of public sector pensions: the Juppé plan

The measures adopted in the 1993 pension reform affected only the *régime général*, which covers employees in industry and commerce. Given the differences in entitlement rules, and the particular socio-demographic profile and working conditions of some categories within the public sector (miners, rail workers), it was decided to deal with the two issues separately as early as 1991 (Mission Cottave 1992). Perhaps the real reason, which was nevertheless absent from the official discourse, was that politicians were afraid of the possible consequences of such a move. At 26 per cent, the rate of unionisation is considerably higher in the public than in the private sector. In addition, public sector employees had been shown on more than one occasion to be particularly effective in generating protest movements.

Financial pressures on separate schemes, however, are quite substantial. For instance, in the pension scheme for rail workers, employment-related contributions cover only about a third of expenditure. The rest is made up of transfers from other schemes and of government subsidies (*Le Monde* 2 December 1995, 8). Financial problems, coupled with the more favourable conditions enjoyed by members of this scheme, were the key reasons put forward in order to justify a reform of the rail workers scheme, as well as of other public sector schemes. The debate on reforming public sector pensions, however, did not come to the fore until after the 1995 presidential election, presumably for the reasons mentioned above.

In May 1995, the newly elected president Jacques Chirac appointed as prime minister Alain Juppé, the former foreign affairs minister and most senior figure in the Chirac camp. Chirac's electoral campaign was regarded as surprisingly left-wing. He spent considerable time emphasising notions of social cohesion and, with regard to the financing of social protection, his position was that economic growth would have solved that problem, and thus that cuts were not needed. He also favoured wage increases, which would have 'painlessly' increased social protection receipts (see, for instance, *Le Monde* 25 March 1995, 7). The fact that his main opponent, Edouard Balladur, was preaching austerity measures to restore sound state finances certainly played a role in Chirac's choice of a campaign strategy.

Initially, electoral promises were honoured. In June 1995, the statutory minimum wage was increased by 4 per cent and the minimum pension by 2.8 per cent, well above the rate of inflation of 1.8 per cent in 1995 (*Le Monde* 24 June 1995, 6). Towards the end of the summer, however, there were signs of a change of direction in government policy. Prime Minister Juppé announced a major reform of the social security system, the details of which still had to be worked out (*Le Monde* 31 August 1995, 5). Both Juppé and Chirac made clear that they intended to deal with the structural deficit of the social security budget and not to act through minor adjustments in order to secure a balanced budget for the current year only. This came up in the description of the sort of questions that, according to Alain Juppé, had to guide the debate. As he put it:

I intend to ask a number of 'strong' questions on the future of social protection, which is expensive and unjust . . . Are all French people equal in the face of retirement? No, they aren't. There are 600,000 French men and women who are not covered by health insurance . . . 75 per cent of social protection receipts come from employment-related contributions. It is a unique situation in Europe and the result is that our firms are truly disadvantaged. (Juppé, quoted in *Le Monde* 31 August 1995, 5)

This quotation makes reference to a number of notoriously politically sensitive issues. Inequality in the face of retirement refers precisely to the more generous conditions enjoyed by public sector employees, especially after the 1993 reform that affected only those working in the private sector. Moreover, the quotation shows concern with the basic structure of the French welfare state, which relies to a large extent on contributory social insurance and is managed by the social partners. As seen above, the shift from the present arrangement towards a state-managed and tax-financed one is a major source of disagreement between the government and the unions. The inclusion of such controversial proposals in its agenda had the effect of reducing the scope for a concerted solution.

This time, however, the government was not looking for consensus. The political situation was certainly favourable to a major reform, if not ideal. The government had an overwhelming majority in parliament. The next general election was almost three years away and the presidential one was scheduled for 2002. In addition, the adoption of austerity measures could be justified by the need to comply with the requirements for monetary union.[11] This was an additional asset in the hands of the government, since European integration remains widely supported by the French public. Against such a favourable background, the government might well have decided that it was strong enough to take on the unions. This, at least, is what appears from the analysis of the policy-making process.

The preparation of a reform plan for social security continued until November 1995. During that period there were contacts with trade union officials and political parties both at the national and at the regional level. The content of the plan, however, was kept secret until the day it was presented to parliament. The issue of reforming public sector pensions was seen as an extremely sensitive exercise. According to press reports, the minister responsible for public sector employment, Jean Puech, concerned with the possible consequences of such a move had managed to convince the prime minister to drop plans for public sector pension reform. In fact, trade unions were informed, on a non-official basis, that this controversial item was not going to be part of the final version of the plan. The change of direction by the government was apparently decided on the night before the publication of the report. Alain Juppé needed the support of his predecessor and fellow party member, Edouard Balladur, who had criticised the government for its lack of commitment to sound state finances. In order to secure the support of the Balladur camp, Juppé included plans to set up a commission which would have made proposals as to how to restore the financial viability of public sector pension schemes (*Le Monde* 21 December 1995, 2).

The 'Plan for the Reform of Social Protection', or the Juppé plan for short, was presented in parliament on 15 November 1995. It was a declaration of intentions covering all areas of social security. It did not include actual legislative proposals, but provided an agenda for the implementation of a number of measures, some of which were already specified in their details. These are its main points:
• Introduction of a universal health insurance scheme;
• the reform of public sector pension schemes (*régimes spéciaux*), through the establishment of a commission that within four months would make

---

[11] Among the Maastricht criteria for monetary union, it was the 3 per cent of GDP limit on government budget deficit that constituted a problem for France. According to the government, in order to comply with this requirement, cuts were needed in various areas of social protection.

proposals so as to ensure the financial equilibrium of these schemes, such as the extension on the qualifying period for a full pension to forty years;
- family benefits to be frozen in 1996 and taxable after 1997;
- partial shift of health insurance financing from contributions to taxation (CSG; see n. 10);
- increase of health insurance contributions for unemployed and retired people by 1.2 per cent in 1996 and in 1997 (at that time at 1.4 per cent, or 5.4 percentage points below the standard contribution rate for those in work);
- introduction of a new tax, levied at a rate of 0.5 per cent on all revenues, earmarked for the repayment of the debt accumulated by the social security system;
- a constitutional amendment which allows parliament to vote on a social security budget.

(Source: France, Gouvernement Français 1995).

The plan was viewed by French and international commentators as a major restructuring of the social security system. It did in fact contain a number of measures that were bound to be extremely controversial. Obviously, the reform of public sector pension was one of these. In addition, however, there were a number of structural changes that did not directly affect the level of protection, but that were geared towards removing, in part at least, the control of the social partners over the system. This was the case, for instance, of the proposing of a constitutional amendment allowing more power to parliament; the increase in the use of taxation in financing, as opposed to employment-related contributions; and the introduction of a universal health care scheme. What these measures have in common is that they contribute to the change of the original Bismarckian nature of the French social security system. This was regarded as unacceptable by the trade unions, who had forcefully opposed similar measures in the past.

Unsurprisingly, the reactions to the Juppé plan were mixed. First, among the unions, the CGT and FO condemned the whole programme, and called a one-day strike in the public sector. Other trade unions took a less radical position. The CFDT agreed with much of what was said in the plan, with the exception of public sector pension reform. In contrast, employers were satisfied with the proposed measures. The Socialists, initially, were divided. Through their official spokesperson, they condemned the plan, though it was not entirely clear on what grounds, since it included proposals that had been put forward by them only a few years earlier. In fact, some of the more outspoken party members took a different stance. A former health care minister, Bernard Kouchner, commented that: 'it is an ambitious and courageous plan, which picks up on many of our proposals' (*Le Monde* 17 November 1995, 12). The Socialist leader, Lionel Jospin, was able to unite the party only a few days later. The line adopted was to attack the method of the government's approach, imposition without concertation, rather than the content of the plan, which in fact was not too distant from what the Socialists had been arguing for in the past.

The protest movement started a few days later, on 24 November. Initially it was mainly employees of the national rail company (SNCF) and of the Paris underground (RATP) who went on strike. The level of participation, however, was rather impressive. The strikers were able to literally bring the country to a halt. The rail and underground workers' strike lasted for some three weeks, and during that period it was virtually impossible to reach central Paris from the suburbs in less than four to five hours. Obviously, losses for the French economy were substantial. In the following days, other groups of public sector employees joined the transport workers in the strike, mainly the post office employees and teachers. In parallel, students took to the streets as well, not against the Juppé plan, but in order to ask for more financial resources in education. The result was a gigantic, incoherent but growing protest movement, perfectly in line with the French tradition of unorthodox political actions. The protest reached its climax on 12 December, when some 2 million people were reported to have taken the streets in various French cities (*Le Monde* 21 December 1995, 6).

The national leadership of the main trade union federations were obviously quick to join and to encourage the protest movement against the Juppé plan. What they regarded as unacceptable, however, was not only the presence of cuts in public sector pension schemes, but the explicit intention of the government to increase its grip on social security, and by the same token to reduce the unions' influence on it. This motive was particularly strong in the case of Force Ouvrière. As its leader, Marc Blondel, put it:

[The Juppé plan] is the biggest theft in the history of the French Republic. It is the end of the *Sécurité sociale*. By deciding that parliament is going to direct social protection, it robs the FF 2,200 billion made up of contributions paid by employers and employees. We were told that we needed to act in order to save social security, but they are taking it away from us. (*Le Monde* 17 November 1995, 12)

This interpretation of the Juppé plan must be seen in the context of the ongoing struggle for the control of social security between the government and the unions discussed above. The inclusion in the plan of measures aimed at removing the control of the unions over the system certainly contributed to their determination to oppose it. The Juppé plan attacked a number of different interests, mainly public sector employees and trade unions, which made possible the formation of a strong coalition against it. The result was that the government was forced to retreat on some of the measures. On 10 December, Juppé announced the withdrawal of plans for public sector pension reform, though the remainder of the plan was maintained. In addition, plans to restructure the SNCF were renegotiated with rail worker unions, so as to allow a longer period to restore a balanced budget in the company. The protest movement gradually faded away, leaving the national trade union leadership unsatisfied since the measures aiming at increasing the government's control were maintained.

## 5.6    Institutions and the politics of pension reform in France

This chapter has described the processes that led to the adoption of the 1993 pension reform and to the presentation of the Juppé plan to the French parliament. The two initiatives share a number of similar features, as they both include potentially controversial elements of retrenchment in pension provision. The part of the Juppé plan concerned with public sector pensions, in fact, envisaged the implementation of some of the measures adopted in 1993 for the private sector, namely the extension of the qualifying period for a full pension to forty years. Given the similarity of the two exercises, what is striking is the very different way in which these two reforms were met by the unions and by public opinion at large. Why was there no reaction to the 1993 reform and a massive protest movement against 1995 plan? There are a number of possible ways to answer that question.

First, union density within the public sector is significantly higher than among private sector employees. The rate of unionisation of the French workforce is somewhere between 10 per cent and 14 per cent, but it reaches 26 per cent within the state sector (Join-Lambert 1994: 110). The difference in unionisation rates might explain the success of the 1995 protest movement, even though 26 per cent is still a comparatively low rate by European standards. Nevertheless, this explanation is of little use if one needs to account for the different reactions of interest groups, rather than for the outcome of informal protest, and even less useful if one wants to explain why the government acted in different ways on the two occasions. A stronger labour movement in the public sector, if anything, should have pushed the government to seek agreement with the unions.

A second explanation relates the vehemence of the protest movement generated by the Juppé plan to the fact that it came at a time when the management of the SNCF was engaged in difficult negotiations with the unions for restructuring the loss-making national railway company. The conjunction of this event with the prospect of seeing pension entitlements reduced created a climate of general dissatisfaction among rail workers, who were thus more determined to take on the government (*Le Monde* 21 December 1995, 3). Considering the fact that the rail strike was the centrepiece of the protest movement, this explanation certainly has some relevance.

A third possible interpretation refers to the fact that the public saw the Juppé plan as a betrayal of the electoral promises made by Jacques Chirac just a few months earlier. During the presidential campaign, in fact, Chirac denied that retrenchment measures were needed in the area of social security, arguing that economic growth alone would have sufficed to restore the financial viability of the various schemes. The Juppé plan, which envisaged substantial cuts in family benefits and public sector pensions, was seen by many as a complete reversal of Chirac's policy in the area of social security. According to an opinion poll commissioned by the newspaper *Le Monde* on the day the Juppé plan was announced, 68 per cent of those interviewed felt that 'this reform of social security did not comply with the promises made by Jacques Chirac during the presidential campaign' (*Le Monde* 17 November 1996, 8).

All these factors contribute to explaining the different reactions provoked by the 1993 pension reform and by the 1995 Juppé plan. However, what seems to have been crucial is that fact the two events were characterised by very different patterns of policy-making. In line with the theoretical approach adopted in this study, it can be argued that this difference in policy-making patterns relates to the different power configurations at the time when the reform was decided. The division within the executive in 1993 constituted a veto point which put pressure on the government to negotiate with the unions. In contrast, two years later, the high level of power concentration which resulted from the same camp controlling both the presidency and parliament did not create the conditions favourable to negotiation. In 1995 the government felt strong enough and thought it could act without the approval of the labour movement.

Differences in policy-making were matched by differences in content. The 1993 reform, in fact, combined some retrenchment measures with the creation of a new solidarity fund. This fund did not affect the overall level of provision, but resulted in the transfer of expenditure on non-contributory pensions from the old age insurance scheme to the general government budget. This move was seen positively by the unions, since it meant that the insurance scheme was going to be under less financial pressure and that the risk of seeing their managerial role questioned was reduced. To some extent, it can be argued that the Balladur government in 1993 traded a reduction in pension entitlements with a concession on the management side of social insurance. According to an official of the CNAV (old age insurance scheme):

The introduction of the Fonds de Solidarité Vieillesse was a skilful move, because it reduced the deficit of the old age insurance budget in a way that was acceptable to the trade unions. It showed that the state was making an effort. In fact the FSV had been carefully designed in order to be able to attract the approval of the social partners. (Author interview, CNAV, 19 December 1996)

The 1993 pension reform cannot be seen as a case of concertation between the government and the unions. The latter, with the exception of the Catholic CFTC, maintained their rejection to the cuts introduced by the new legislation. A fully concerted solution, in fact, would have been extremely unusual in the French context. Nevertheless, the government did, as mentioned in the above quotation, make an effort in the direction of what was demanded by the unions. That effort arguably played a role in securing if not their approval, at least their acquiescence.

In contrast, the 1995 Juppé plan included nothing that could be seen as a move towards the unions' requests. In addition, it represented a clear attack against the FO union, who had been among the keenest supporters of a health insurance system managed by the social partners and with little state intervention, not least because it had traditionally presided over the national health insurance fund. As a civil servant put it, 'the Juppé plan was a slap in the face for the FO, who had been claiming a strict separation between insurance and non-contributory provision' (author interview, Ministry of Social Affairs, 19 December 1996). The Juppé plan – by envisaging the creation of a universal health insurance scheme, the parliamentary vote on the social security budget, and the introduction of taxation as a means to finance health insurance – took a series of measures that contributed to undermining the traditional role of the social partners in social insurance management. All theses measures, many of which have been introduced in subsequent years, tend to increase the state's control over the health insurance system.

The Juppé plan, thus, not only failed to include provision that was at least acceptable to the unions, but it also put forward a number of other measures that were against what large sections of the labour movement had been arguing throughout the previous decade. However, to receive the unions' approval was not a priority for the government. The Juppé plan, in fact, was drafted in total secrecy. There was no consultation with the relevant interests, and trade unionists purportedly learned about the contents of the plan together with the rest of the nation, when Juppé presented it in parliament (interview, FO, 20 December 1996). Arguably, the government did not want to engage in lengthy negotiations, which carried the risk of failure as had happened to many of their predecessors. The balance of power in parliament, the unity of the executive (president and prime minister belonging to the same party) and the fact that the next election was some three years away wrongly persuaded the government that it could afford not to negotiate.

The analysis of pension reform in France points out the existence of two different sorts of institutions which can affect policy outcomes: pension scheme design and political institutions. With regard to the first, a crucial feature of the French basic pension scheme, and more in general the whole social security system, is the fact that it is managed jointly by representatives of employers and employees. As seen above, this has been the source of a long-standing conflict over the control of social insurance between the trade unions, which largely benefit from their managerial role, and governments of different political persuasions. At the same time, however, this particular institutional feature created an opportunity for a *quid pro quo* which was exploited in the 1993 reform. The unions accepted a reduction in pension entitlements also because they received a guarantee that their managerial role in the area of pensions would not be questioned. In a state-run system, such as exists in Britain, such an opportunity would not have been available.

Political institutions played a role too. The existence of two distinct and non-coordinated electoral cycles and the division of the executive power between a president and a prime minister produced different configurations of power which were more or less propitious for negotiated policy change. In 1993, cohabitation between a Socialist president and a Gaullist prime minister, coupled with concern for the upcoming presidential election, put pressure on the government to negotiate the content of reform with the unions. In contrast, in 1995 that pressure was absent, hence the attempt of Juppé to impose the reform of public sector pensions. Because of these different approaches and despite being very similar in their content, the two initiatives generated opposite responses among the labour movement and public opinion, which made the difference between success and failure.

In this respect, the French case highlights the dynamic character of the influence of institutions on policy-making. Depending on electoral results and on the stage of the electoral cycle at a given time, the very same set of political institutions produced two opposite effects on pension policy-making, as it encouraged negotiation in 1993 and confrontation in 1995. This finding has important implications for theory, as it suggests that institutional effects are highly contingent. A given set of political institutions will not always exert the same sort of influence on policy-making. Its impact depends on a range of factors that need to be identified on a case-by-case basis.

# 6    Institutions, power concentration and pension reform

The most striking element that emerges from the analysis of the pension reforms presented in the previous three chapters is perhaps the fact that policy change has occurred in each of the three countries covered. This is in spite of a generalised concern among commentators about the alleged inability of continental European countries to undertake structural reform in the broad areas of social and economic policy. Even countries like France and Switzerland, which are generally depicted as some of the most reluctant to adapt their post-war welfare states to new international and domestic constraints, have managed to secure the adoption of unpopular retrenchment measures. These, although limited, can be seen as a first step towards a more comprehensive recasting of their respective pension systems. Perhaps, after all, the continental European welfare states are not as frozen as is generally thought (see also Taylor-Gooby 1996).

Policy change has occurred in the three countries covered by this study. Their governments, however, have used different strategies to secure the adoption of typically unpopular pension reforms. In particular, in Switzerland and on one occasion in France (1993), governments have dealt with the political difficulties associated with retrenchment by designing reform packages which included elements that had been previously demanded by key potential opponents of reform. To some extent, through the inclusion of these *quid pro quos*, they have managed to neutralise the effect of those veto points that exist in their political systems. In contrast, in the two other instances reviewed, the 1986 British reform and the 1995 failed attempt in France, legislation did not include similar concessions targeted on pro-welfare groups. While all countries succeeded in adopting some policy change, the overall content of the reforms varied significantly. Governments enjoyed different degrees of control over policy outcomes, and on one occasion, in the French 1995 initiative, plans for reform had to be withdrawn.

This chapter, by comparing the information presented in the country chapters, will try to account for this variation and to examine whether such differences in patterns of pension policy-making have an impact on the path to pension system adaptation which is followed by any given welfare state. This study has shown that, despite the controversial character of welfare retrenchment, an inclusive approach to it is possible and has occurred in some continental European countries. The question, then, is whether this process will be qualitatively different from the Anglo-Saxon variety of retrenchment which was characterised by the exclusion of external groups from decision-making and by the imposition of controversial measures. In the first part of the chapter, I will deal with the question of what accounts for different patterns of policy-making in pension reform. The argument presented is that a key determinant are political institutions, although their impact on policy-making is highly contingent upon other factors, such as electoral results and the position in the electoral cycle at the time of reform. In the second part, I will turn to the more difficult issue of whether these different patterns of policy-making lead to a qualitatively different process of pension system adaptation. I will argue that it is not possible to make specific predictions by looking only at political institutions as an independent variable. However, if this factor is seen as interacting with other ones, such as pension scheme design, then one can identify some regularities in the cases covered by this study.

## 6.1    Policy-making strategies in pension reform

The accounts of pension reforms presented in the country chapters have shown that governments were generally well aware of the potential for controversy embodied in the pension reform issue. In all three cases, the adoption of measures that, for various reasons, were seen as needed by the respective governments was accompanied by other measures that in contrast were not particularly in line with their priorities, but were nevertheless adopted with the objective of increasing the political feasibility of the reform or to minimise its potential electoral damage. These measures were more or less targeted at groups likely to oppose reform, or to electorally punish the government. Among the four instances reviewed, the attempted reform of French public sector pensions in 1995 is possibly the only one in which cuts were not coupled with measures aimed at reducing their negative impact. This might help to account for the fact that the French government was eventually forced to withdraw its plans as a result of a massive protest movement. In contrast, on the three other occasions reviewed here, governments did adopt a policy-making strategy which was clearly aimed at increasing the political feasibility or at minimising the electoral consequences of generally unpopular reforms.

*Britain*

The 1986 British reform did not rely on inclusion as a means to reduce the political cost of reform. As seen in chapter 3, the policy-making process was dominated by the government, and more particularly by the secretary of state for social services, and very few concessions were made to external interests. The only exception was the decision to drop plans for the abolition of the state scheme SERPS. On this issue, however, there was a division within the Cabinet, the Treasury being fiercely opposed to the scrapping of the programme. As a result, one cannot say for certain whether the government's change of direction constituted a concession to external interests or was simply the result of internal divisions. To some extent, the disagreement between the Department of Health and Social Security and the Treasury highlighted the existence of a de facto veto point in the British political system: the Treasury (Hall 1986: 62).

One crucial feature of the 1986 British pension reform is the fact that it did not affect the whole population, which is unusual for a pension reform. A division in the British pension system, between those who are covered by the state scheme and those who are members of occupational pension plans, allowed the government to target its saving measures on a given section of the population only. Many British employees, mainly middle class, who have access to occupational provision, were unaffected by the changes adopted in 1986. The saving measures and the transfer from the state to the market concerned only the part of the population covered by SERPS. As a result, the government was able to achieve substantial long-term savings; to make some progress towards its vision of popular capitalism; and at the same time to reduce the risk of electoral punishment, since a large section of the population was not directly affected by the change (about 50 per cent of employees). Moreover, the decision to introduce an additional fiscal encouragement, the so called 2 per cent bribe,[1] reduced the potential for dissatisfaction among those who, in contrast, were directly affected by the changes. The result was that the new personal pensions proved rather popular and, despite the opposition generated by the 1986 reform, the Conservatives were able to win the general election the next year. The strategy adopted by the Thatcher government, which exploited a division in provision for retirement, proved successful in avoiding the possible negative electoral impact of cutbacks in pensions.

---

[1]    This was an additional rebate in social security contributions for employees who took out a personal pension between 1988 and 1993 (see ch. 3).

### Switzerland

In the Swiss case the cuts affected a universal scheme, the basic pension, which made it impossible to use a policy-making strategy based on divisions in pension coverage. Moreover, the main concern for Swiss policymakers was not electoral punishment, but the ability to get the new legislation accepted in a referendum. As a result, the right-wing parliamentary majority decided to combine within a single piece of legislation an increase in retirement age for women together with other measures likely to improve the position of women in the basic pension. The latter, which included the introduction of contribution credits for years spent taking care of a child or a relative and the sharing of contributions between spouses, had long been a key demand of the left and of the trade unions. By combining these two types of measures within a single piece of legislation, the right-wing majority was able to generate support for the 1995 pension reform from various sections of the political spectrum, including the left, who would otherwise have opposed plans to increase retirement age. As seen in chapter 4, the inclusion of expansion and retrenchment measures within a single piece of legislation proved instrumental in making the changes acceptable to the electorate. The reform, in fact, was supported by the main political parties including the Socialists, which facilitated its acceptance in the referendum of June 1995.

### France

In France, the attachment of the general public to existing pension arrangements and the absence of a tradition of co-operation between the state and the labour movement made pension reform a particularly thorny issue. The former prime minister, Socialist Michel Rocard, was quoted as saying that pension reform was an issue capable of bringing down more than one government. In this respect, a consensual reform, possibly negotiated with the trade unions, would have been extremely difficult. As seen in chapter 5, such a solution was in fact well beyond the ambitions of the Ministry of Social Affairs negotiators who had to prepare the 1993 reform. Instead, their priority was to avoid the sort of informal protest that the French trade unions have repeatedly shown themselves to be capable of. In sum, the Balladur government in 1993 was not seeking the approval of the labour movement. The acquiescence of its more radical sections was the most it could hope for.

As a result, the 1993 pension reform, which included cuts in the main basic pension scheme (the *régime général*, covering private sector employees), was adopted together with a new 'old age solidarity fund', which in fact constituted a significant step towards meeting the unions' demands in the areas of financing and management of the basic pension scheme. The new fund, which is tax-financed, is intended to pay for the non-contributory elements (such as means-tested pensions) provided by the insurance-based scheme. By taking responsibility for this sort of provision, the government de facto recognised the social partners as the legitimate actors for the management of the contributory elements of the insurance scheme. This had been one of the key demands of the most radical sections of the labour movement, and proved crucial in securing their acquiescence.

In contrast, the 1995 attempt at reforming public sector pensions did not include elements aimed at generating support for it or at appeasing opposition. In fact, cuts in pension provision for public sector employees were combined with other measures which constituted an attack on the trade unions' position within the social security system. These consisted mainly of an increased role for the state in the management of health insurance. In addition, plans for public sector pension reform were published at a time when a restructuring package for the national railway company (SNCF) was being negotiated. The outcome was concentration of dissatisfaction among rail workers and trade unionists in general, which resulted in one of the most impressive protest movements France has seen since 1968. The government was thus forced to drop its plans for the reform of public sector pensions. The lack of an inclusive strategy such as the one used in France two years earlier or in the Swiss pension reform certainly helps to account for the government's failure on this occasion.

With one exception, thus, the pension reforms analysed in this study have been accompanied by a policy-making strategy clearly aimed at making them more acceptable to the public or to key political actors, such as the French trade unions or the Swiss left. In France and in Switzerland, the objective of these strategies was to increase the political feasibility of reform. In Britain, where the control over policy-making was such that feasibility was not a seen as a problem, the main concern was to avoid electoral punishment. Political institutions, electoral considerations and pension system design seem to be the key factors that affect the choice of a given strategy by a government willing to retrench pensions. The question of what explains the adoption of a course of policy, however, will be dealt with after the next section, which introduces three additional cases into the discussion.

## 6.2    Developments in other countries

The 1990s have seen the pension issue high on the agenda in virtually all European countries, and pension reforms, understood as changes in legislation which aim at containing or reducing pension expenditure, have been adopted in a majority of them. This section briefly looks at what has happened in Italy, Sweden and Germany, three countries that are not covered by the present study but that, because of their size or distinctiveness in terms of welfare state institutions, are generally considered as relevant to research on pension policy. The inclusion of three more cases in the analysis provides additional empirical material to test the hypotheses discussed in the rest of this chapter.

### Italy

Until the early 1990s, Italy had one of the most generous and costly pension systems in Europe. The state scheme provided pensions equal to 70 per cent of the last five working years' average salary from the age of fifty-five or sixty for women and men respectively. Financial pressures on the scheme intensified in the late 1980s, when the government budget deficit reached worrying proportions. A first attempt at containing pension expenditure was made in 1992. On that occasion the statutory age of retirement was increased to sixty for women and sixty-five for men and the reference salary was changed from the average of the last five years to that of the last ten years. Considering the unusual generosity of previous legislation and the fact that the changes adopted in 1992 were not enforced immediately, but were meant to be phased in over a fairly long period, the 1992 reform constituted only a very limited attempt to deal with a very serious problem in financing pensions (Ferrera 1997).

That is why, towards the mid-1990s, pension reform came back on to the political agenda. First, in 1994 a right-of-centre government headed by Silvio Berlusconi tried to adopt a series of cuts in pensions without seeking external support. The response of the trade unions was to call a general strike, which persuaded the government to abandon its plans. In contrast, in 1995, a 'technical' government (composed of non-politicians) which had the support of the left in parliament managed to push through a more fundamental reform. The key modification was a shift from a defined-benefit system, where benefits are expressed as a proportion of earnings over a given number of years, to a defined-contribution system. Benefits now depend on the total amount of contributions paid by workers, which upon retirement is converted into an annuity the value of which depends on the age of the person, on how the country's economy is performing and on the number of pensioners. The last two parameters are meant to allow the government to keep pension expenditure under control. The reform will most likely result in lower benefits (Ferrera 1997; Artoni and Zanardi 1997).

From the first stages of the preparatory work for the 1995 reform, it was clear that for the government it was essential to obtain the support, or at least the acquiescence, of the labour movement. Berlusconi's failure to retrench pensions unilaterally and the weakness of the 'technical' government which did not have its own majority in parliament (but was supported externally by a small number of centre-left parties) provided powerful incentives to seek consensus. As a matter of fact, the starting point of the negotiations was a document drafted by trade union experts. The 1995 reform was adopted with the support of the trade unions who, in return for their approval, obtained a fairly long phasing-in period for the new system, which will become fully effective for people retiring from 2013 onwards. The key constituencies of the Italian trade union movement, current pensioners and older workers were not affected by the reform (Regini and Regalia 1997: 215–17).

### Sweden

A reform based on a shift from a defined-benefit to a defined-contribution system was also adopted in Sweden. The earnings-related component of the Swedish pension system was modified in 1994. Under the new legislation, the pension is to be based on lifetime contributions revalued according to changes in real wages, and calculated on the basis of the life expectancy of the relevant cohort. These measures are supposed to mitigate the impact of ageing on pension expenditure. As a result of the change, the amount of the standard pension is expected to decline from 65 per cent to 60 per cent of gross earnings. The reform, however, has also introduced a funded element in the system. Contributions, which amount to 18.5 per cent of gross earnings, are split between the pay-as-you-go scheme (16.5 per cent) and a new funded scheme (2 per cent). According to current projections, the funded element should compensate employees for the reduction of the standard benefit (Stahlberg 1997; Palme and Wennemo 1997).

Many of the parameters that will determine the value of pension benefits in future – like life expectancy, wage growth and returns on capital for the 2 per cent contribution to a funded scheme – are not known at present. As a result it is not possible to ascertain whether the Swedish reform constitutes an instance of retrenchment, expansion or simply continuity. The new scheme was designed to deliver the same benefits that are paid today, if demographic and economic developments follow the central government projections. In case of departures from it, future benefits could be lower as well as higher than present ones, while contribution rates will remain stable. The overall effect of the reform was to shift the burden of uncertainty associated with pension provision from the state to the individual: if the impact of demographics and the economy are going to be worse than expected, the resulting additional costs will be borne by pensioners through lower benefits, and not by the state.

The Swedish reform obtained cross-party consensus and overall union approval (Pierson 1996: 172; Stephens 1996: 46). Without it, contribution rates might have had to be increased from 17 per cent to 24–40 per cent over the next few decades (Myles and Pierson 1998). The new pension legislation allows the stabilisation of contribution rates (at 18.5 per cent), without necessarily reducing benefits. In this respect, it had clear political appeal.

### Germany

Germany has reformed its pension system twice in the 1990s. The first reform, the *Rentenreform* 1992 (designated by the year it came into force), was explicitly designed to respond to the expected increase in pension expenditure due to population ageing. The main changes were a shift in the indexation of pensions from gross to net earnings and an increase in the cost of early retirement for workers. The change in indexation was seen as introducing an element of self-regulation in pension expenditure: under the post-1992 system, if contributions are increased to finance increased pension expenditure, this will reduce net earnings and as a result pension payments. The goal is to achieve an equitable share between workers and retirees in bearing the cost of population ageing (Schmähl 1993).

The 1992 reform was adopted by the Christian Democrat government with the support of the Social Democrats and of the trade unions. At that time it was felt that the pension problem had been dealt with, for a few years at least. However, towards the mid-1990s, amidst concern about rising rates of unemployment, an ambitious reform programme was launched, with the intention of creating a more favourable environment for job creation, particularly by reducing social insurance contributions. Initially, this programme was to be carried out in a characteristically German consensual manner: negotiating change with the Social Democrats, the trade unions and employers. However, after the left, worried by the overall direction of reform, abandoned the negotiations, the government decided to go ahead on its own. As part of the first set of measures, adopted in 1996, the phasing-in of the retrenchment measures agreed in the 1992 pension reform was accelerated: instead of 2012, the transition will be completed by 2004.

The most significant changes, however, were passed in 1997, as part of the *Rentenreform* 1999. Among the most important, and controversial, of these was the introduction of 'demographic weighting' of pension benefits. If life expectancy increases, benefits are reduced to counter the effect of demographic pressures. On the basis of current demographic projections, it is expected that the standard replacement rate will be gradually lowered from 70 to 64 per cent of average earnings.

The reform was adopted despite the efforts of the Social Democrats, then in opposition.[2] Besides demographic weighting, however, it included measures that were likely to be more in line with the demands of the left and of the trade unions. These included an increase in the federal subsidy to the pension scheme (paid for by a 1 percentage point increase in VAT), and the improvement of contribution credits paid to those with caring responsibilities. The earnings basis of the credit was increased from 75 to 100 percent of the average salary, and the credit will not be reduced if the carer is involved in paid work (Hinrichs 1998).

Italian, Swedish and German reforms highlight some of the themes that have already been observed in the three countries covered by this study. Pension reform appears to be such a thorny issue that it can persuade policy-makers to proceed cautiously and seek consensus. The result has been that, in most cases, governments have tended to combine cuts with concessions to pro-welfare actors, such as the trade unions. When they have failed to do so, they have exposed themselves to enormous political risks, as, for example, did Berlusconi with his 1994 unsuccessful attempt at cutting Italian pensions. The existence of a strong political dimension in pension policy-making in the 1990s seems to be confirmed by the developments in these other countries.

From the point of view of theory, however, these cases provide additional empirical evidence against which to test hypotheses concerning the determinants of pension reform policy. The combination of independent variables here is not as well suited for studying the impact of political institutions on pension policy as that of the original sample (see 29), but can help us test alternative hypotheses concerning the impact of corporatism on pension policy and the dynamics of institutional effects. The

---

[2] After coming to power in October 1998, the Social Democrats signalled their intention to repeal some of the changes introduced by their predecessors, such as demographic weighting of pensions.

new sample includes two countries with a strong corporatist tradition (Sweden, Germany) and a country, Italy, which has dealt with the pension issue at different times and with different power configurations. These cases are referred to in the following discussion.

## 6.3    Political institutions and policy-making strategies

Political institutions are a key determinant of the strategy adopted by governments to secure the adoption of potentially controversial policy change. Pension reforms adopted in political systems characterised by a high density of veto points have tended to include concessions targeted on key opponents to a significant extent (Switzerland). In contrast, reform adopted in a political system with few veto points and high power concentration has reflected the government's priorities to a larger extent and has been imposed in the face of strong external opposition (Britain). While this finding is not particularly surprising, the analysis of the French case adds some interesting insights into the relationship between political institutions and retrenchment strategies in pension policy. In France, depending on electoral results and on the position of the country in the electoral cycle, political institutions have had opposite effects on patterns of pension policy-making: in 1993 they favoured an inclusive approach, whereas in 1995 they encouraged confrontation. This suggests that the impact of political institutions on patterns of policy-making is contingent upon political factors. The relevance of this aspect is not necessarily limited to France, although that is where it was observed most clearly among the countries covered by this study.

### The dynamics of institutional effects

The impact of political institutions on policy depends to a large extent on electoral results.[3] A set of formal institutions which concentrates power within the executive might have a different impact on policy-making patterns if no party obtains a majority. Between 1988 and 1993 the Socialist minority government of France, committed to adopting a pension reform, was unable to find allies to get its legislation approved by parliament. Of course, electoral results are to some extent related to electoral

---

[3] This view reflects the findings of Immergut: 'to understand how these institutions work in practice, we must add the de facto rules that arise from electoral results and party systems . . . The effective power of a political executive and the dynamics of executive–legislative relations depend on the partisan composition of the various houses of parliament, on whether the executive enjoys a stable parliamentary majority, and on whether party discipline is in force' (1992: 27).

laws, and thus to political institutions. The British first-past-the-post electoral system favours the party with a relative majority and by the same token makes coalition or minority government a relatively infrequent event. In contrast, in countries with proportional representation like Switzerland, or with a two-round plurality system (France), coalition governments are virtually the rule. Electoral results, however, are not determined by electoral laws only, and thus deserve to be treated as an independent variable in their own right.

Nevertheless, whether electoral results will affect the impact of political institutions on policy-making is likely to depend upon these very same institutions. In particular, the effect of electoral results is likely to be greatest in political systems in which incongruently elected bodies have similar levels of influence over policy-making. This is the case of countries with incongruent, balanced bicameral parliaments, like Germany, where the two chambers can be dominated by different majorities. It is also the case in France, but in relation to the division of executive power between a president and a prime minister. In 1993, the presidency was controlled by the Socialists, while it was the right-wing that dominated parliament. In contrast, in 1995 both institutions were controlled by the right-wing coalition. As seen in chapter 5, these two different patterns of power configuration were associated with different approaches to policy-making: more inclusive in 1993 and more exclusive in 1995.

While formally the person responsible for deciding the course of policy in France is the prime minister, the president enjoys an important degree of legitimacy in the eyes of public opinion. If he or she disagrees with actions taken by the government, the president can sack the prime minister or call an early election. With these constraints, prime ministers are likely to be reluctant to embark on a politically risky action such as enforcing a pension reform against the unions' will, unless they are sure of the president's approval. In 1995, Prime Minister Juppé was publicly supported by President Chirac, and managed to resist to unions' demands for some three weeks, as well as maintaining most of his plan. If all this had occurred when Mitterrand was president, it is difficult to imagine that the latter would not have intervened in one way or another against his political opponents in government, as he had done in the past (see 121–3). As seen in chapter 5, the sharing of executive power between two different camps constituted a pressure for the Balladur government to seek trade unions' acquiescence to its pension reform. It seems thus that, when different parties, or coalitions of parties, control the various key democratic institutions, governments are more inclined to adopt concerted solutions.

A second factor which contributes to the dynamic character of the impact of political institutions on policy-making is the electoral cycle. In the French case, on various occasions the proximity of an important election delayed the adoption of a pension reform. The fact that France has two parallel electoral cycles, for presidential and parliamentary elections, has reduced the amount of time available to policy-makers to 'safely' implement unpopular policies. In 1993, the proximity of the 1995 presidential election acted as a deterrent on the government in the adoption of a confrontational stance *vis-à-vis* the unions. The requirement not to upset public opinion or influential actors prior to a crucial election provided an incentive for the government not to seek confrontation with the unions.

Interestingly, in 1997 French commentators (*Le Monde* 14 May 1997) explained the decision of President Chirac to call an early general election with reference to electoral cycles. Since he was committed to joining the EMU and as a result to reducing public spending, Chirac intended to adopt a series of unpopular measures, possibly including cuts in social programmes. By calling an early election, Chirac hoped to avoid the political risk involved in the adoption of unpopular measures in the year preceding a general election. For this strategy to work, however, the right-wing coalition had to win the 1997 election, which it failed to do. Electoral cycles, thus, seem to be playing an important role in the reform of the French welfare state. To some extent, this is related to the existence of the double electoral cycle in that country, though increases in politicians' sensitivity to the public mood when an important election approaches are a basic feature of representative democracy.

Political considerations of convenience induced by electoral cycles might have played a role in the British reform of 1986, adopted just one year before a general election. In this situation the government had to contain the risks associated with the accountability effect. To the losers of the British reform, it was clear who was to blame for the damage they were going to suffer, and they were going to have the opportunity to sanction them in a few months' time. However, as the cuts affected only a section of the population, those in SERPS, the potential for electoral punishment was not particularly strong. In addition, even among this group, some did rather well in transferring their pension to a private provider, not least because of the various tax concessions available. In the British case the preconditions for a strong accountability effect were all there – a FPTP electoral system, an upcoming election (1987) and bipartism – yet the government was successful at neutralising it.

*Corporatist traditions*

This study has concentrated on state institutions. However, the political mechanisms it has looked at are also influenced by the structure of organised interests. Their access to policy-making depends on state structures as much as on their own. Of particular interest in this respect is the literature on corporatism, which highlights particular patterns of inclusion of organised interests into policy-making. Corporatism is understood as a system of interest intermediation in which groups supporting different (and often conflicting) interests are included in policy-making. According to Lehmbruch, corporatism 'involves . . . a plurality of organisations usually representing antagonistic interests [which] . . . manage their conflicts and co-ordinate their action with that of government expressly in regard to the . . . systemic requirements of the economy' (1984: 62). Typically, corporatist practices are associated with strong and well-integrated labour movements and employers' associations. According to Schmitter (1982: 264), among the preconditions for corporatist concertation to take place are a system of interest organisation based on centralisation and monopoly of representation. These features are important because they affect interest groups' threat potential (such as the ability to call and sustain strike activities) and as a result constitute a powerful pressure on governments to adopt negotiated solutions in the relevant areas of public policy.

In this respect, the existence of a corporatist tradition in a country can be expected to encourage inclusive policy-making in the area of pensions, as well as in other areas of social and economic policy. This is for two reasons. First, the conditions that have been identified as favourable to the establishment of corporatist practices are likely to put pressure on governments to seek external support for planned legislation. In countries with strong and well-integrated labour movements, governments will be more inclined to adopt a consensual approach to welfare retrenchment, since there the trade unions can credibly threaten to prevent the adoption of controversial legislation, through mass protest or by exploiting the veto points provided by political institutions. Second, countries with a strong corporatist tradition have developed standard procedures in policy-making which include the concertation of policy with external interests. Organised interests, in turn, having been used to negotiate between themselves and with the government, are less likely to adopt an uncompromising stance on reform. Corporatist countries, in fact are often characterised by what Katzenstein (1985: 32–3) has termed 'the ideology of social partnership', a notion referring to labour movements and employers' associations which are sensitive to the needs of the national economy rather than concentrated on simply defending the interests of their members.

The existence of a tradition in public policy-making that values compromise and consensus can be seen as an element favouring a negotiated solution to a pension reform. As a matter of fact, countries with a strong corporatist tradition have sought to reach consensus on retrenchment measures in the area of pensions. This was the case in Switzerland, as seen in chapter 4, but also in the German 1992 reform, which was supported by the main political parties (both by the ruling coalition and by the Social Democratic opposition), and was to a large extent influenced by the proposals made jointly by the trade unions and employer organisations. Similarly, the Swedish 1994 pension reform was adopted with union support. The exception here seems to be the German 1999 reform, which was not endorsed by the unions. However, the inclusion of measures such as improved contribution credits for carers and increased state subsidies for pensions might help to account for the overall acquiescence of the labour movement.

In fact, it is not surprising that countries with well-established corporatist practices tend to deal with the pension issue in a more consensual way. What is more striking, instead, is the fact that countries which lack a corporatist tradition have also been able to follow an inclusive approach to pension reform. This was the case, for instance, with the 1995 Italian pension reform, which reflected to a large extent the proposals made by the trade unions (Regini and Regalia 1997), and with the French 1993 reform. As argued in chapter 5, the French reform, though it was not officially approved by a large section of the labour movement, included elements that were clearly geared at gaining its acquiescence. In both countries, governments were admittedly afraid of the possible confrontational reaction of the trade unions, so that they opted for a negotiated solution.

This observation on the emergence of corporatist-like practices in non-corporatist countries leads to two different conclusions. First, it suggests that the strong attachment of the population to existing pension arrangements, which makes union-led mobilisation easier, compensates for the weakness and poor integration of labour movements in these countries. In both countries, attempts to deal with pensions in a confrontational way failed as a result of impressive trade union-led protest movements. In 1994, the Italian government had to drop plans for a pension reform after a general strike had been called, while in France the attempt to impose pension cuts on public sector employees in 1995 generated a major protest movement and forced the government to withdraw its plans. Standard indicators of trade union density, thus, do not seem to reflect accurately the extent to which labour movements are able to challenge the adoption of pension reform legislation. The case of France, in particular, shows that even numerically weak trade unions are able to set up and sustain massive protest movements, which can ultimately succeed in preventing the adoption of controversial reforms.

Second, the instances of corporatist-like practices of policy-making reviewed above can also be explained with reference to the dynamic character of the impact of political institutions on policy. Both the Italian and the French (successful) reforms were adopted at particular moments, in which the level of power concentration with the respective governments was exceptionally low. As seen in chapter 5, in the case of France it was a combination of a divided executive with the upcoming presidential election that put pressure on the government to adopt a negotiated solution. In Italy, the 1995 pension reform was adopted by a 'technical' government which did not have direct control of a majority in parliament. As a result, the government needed to generate the broadest possible support for its measures, as it could not rely on automatic political backing (Regini and Regalia 1997).

The structure of organised interests is certainly an important factor which helps to account for patterns of inclusion in and exclusion from policy-making in the area of pensions as well as in other areas of social and economic policy. Nevertheless, the emergence of inclusive patterns of policy-making in non-corporatist countries suggests that a tradition of co-operation between the state and external interests is not a necessary condition for inclusive policy-making to occur. The specific character of pension reform, and particularly its potential for controversy, together with changes in the impact of political institutions on power concentration, can generate similar types of policy responses.

### 6.4     The impact of policy-making patterns on pension reform

Having looked at the link between political institutions and patterns of policy-making, we can now turn to the second element of the causal chain explored by this study: the impact of such patterns on actual policy outcomes. The analysis of pension reform in three countries presented here points in some given directions with regard to the dimensions which are likely to be most significantly affected by policy-making patterns. First, it appears that the reforms studied did not occur at the same stage in the evolution of the 'pension problem'. In some instances reform tended to anticipate predicted demographic change, on other occasions, instead, it came as a response to recurrent budget deficits. Second, the scale of the various reforms appears to vary as well. Although, as will be seen below, to measure the extent of welfare retrenchment is not a straightforward task, it seems appropriate to distinguish reforms according to their significance. Third, sometimes reforms have included demands formulated by the left or the unions, and in such instances the overall direction of reform has been affected. These three dimensions seem to be related to the policy-making patterns which have characterised the adoption of given pension reforms. The following discussion will show how for each of them.

### Timing

The notion of 'timing' of a pension reform refers to when, in the development of the pension problem, a reform is adopted. British and Swiss reforms have introduced cuts with a view to anticipating an expected financial problem. In contrast France intervened after various years of deficits in the basic pension scheme budget. To some extent, this difference is related to the different patterns of pensions financing in the three countries. In France, the basic scheme is financed almost exclusively through employment-related contributions; in Switzerland it receives also a substantial subsidy from the federal government; in the UK, in contrast, the borderline between the pension scheme and the general government budgets is not well defined, so that it is not possible to identify a 'pension scheme budget deficit' as is the case in France.

Theoretically, one can expect countries which can afford to exclude external interests to be better able to anticipate predicted financial imbalances. Conversely, governments which tend to include minorities are more likely to react to financial imbalances rather than to anticipate them. The rationale of this hypothesis lies with the different credibility status granted to predicted and actual budget deficits. If the socio-economic pressure for reform is an expenditure projection, it will be more difficult to convince actors who support current pension arrangements that cuts are needed. In contrast, when a pension reform is put forward by the government after a few years of recurring deficits, it will be easier for it to persuade external interests that such a reform is inevitable.

In relation to this hypothesis the evidence presented in chapters 3 to 5 is inconclusive. Swiss and British reforms, both of which anticipated predicted budget imbalances, were adopted with different policy-making patterns. In the case of Switzerland, however, the inclusion of the trade unions and of the Socialists in pension policy-making did not concern the increase in retirement age (the only element of retrenchment in the Swiss reform). On that point, as seen in chapter 4, the left was in disagreement with the right-wing majority, which suggests a link between anticipation and exclusion of external interests.

In the case of France, in contrast, the fact that the 1993 reform came after various years of recurrent budget deficits did not manage to convince the most radical sections of the labour movement (the CGT and FO) that a pension reform such as the one put forward by the government was needed. As seen in chapter 5, although these two federations of trade unions did not take on the government through informal protest, they did not support cuts either. The Italian case is perhaps more telling in this respect. There, the 1995 pension reform was adopted with the support of the trade unions which agreed on a series of saving measures, which they regarded as inevitable because of the current (and not just predicted) financial difficulties of the pension scheme budget.

While the relationship between reform timing and policy-making patterns might need to be explored more systematically, it seems that, when governments intend to act in anticipation of a predicted worsening of pension schemes finances, they are likely to have difficulties in convincing external interests of the inevitability of pension reform, and as a result to include them in policy-making. This is likely to constitute a problem for governments operating in political systems which provide veto points because they need the approval or acquiescence of external interests in order to be able to legislate. In this respect, political institutions which generate power concentration might constitute an asset in the hands of governments wishing to anticipate a predicted financing problem in their pension systems.

### Scale

Patterns of policy-making can have an impact on the scale of pension reform. If external interests are included, retrenchment-oriented governments are more likely to show moderation in their approach. In contrast, if they can afford to act without the support or acquiescence of external interests, their reforming ambitions can be fulfilled to a larger extent. To measure the scale of welfare retrenchment, however, is just as problematic as is measuring the size of welfare states. After a few decades of comparative studies of welfare state development, there is a relatively widespread agreement on the fact that a purely quantitative approach is simply inadequate to account for the diversity found among welfare states (see, for example, Esping-Andersen 1990; Ferrera 1993b). Similarly, in order to assess the size of welfare retrenchment in a country or in a scheme, one cannot rely on a purely quantitative approach, such as looking at changes in expenditure (Pierson 1994: 15).

In order to test the 'scale' hypothesis, however, it is essential to identify one or more criteria which allow us to discriminate between reforms according to their significance. As I have argued elsewhere (Bonoli and Palier 1998), it seems appropriate to distinguish between welfare reforms that reduce expenditure through localised cuts and those that, by creating new constituencies or destabilising existing ones, affect the politics surrounding a given scheme. This distinction is of crucial importance for the medium- and long-term implications of welfare reforms. In the first case, localised cuts such as changes in the benefit formula or in the indexation method, though they can generate substantial savings, can be reversed and do not necessarily have an impact on the long-term developments of a given scheme. In contrast, structural change that modifies the politics of a scheme is more difficult to reverse and can open up the way to further retrenchment.

The British 1986 Social Security Act constitutes a clear example of reform which affected the politics of pension policy. First, it created a new and fairly large constituency, i.e. private pension holders, who have a set of given stakes in the new pension system. Since their pensions will depend on the returns to their invested capital, they are likely to oppose legislation which might have a negative impact on capital gains (such as increased taxation, or, more in general, policies which are not appreciated by investors). Second, the changes have removed a relatively important number of contributors, many of whom were relatively young, from a pay-as-you-go system. This, in future, is likely to exacerbate possible financial difficulties in that scheme and thus make further retrenchment more likely. Third, the devolution from the state to the private sector of responsibility for the retirement pensions of some 5 million people has substantially reinforced the stake that insurance companies and financial institutions have in the pension system. As a result, these actors are likely to oppose any measure which might reduce their ability to achieve substantial profits in the area of pensions.

Swiss and French (1993) reforms, in contrast, did not have a substantial impact on the politics of pensions. Changes in retirement age (Switzerland) and in the indexation and benefit formulas (France) created some disappointment, but did not affect the power relationship between the various actors and constituencies that structure the politics of pensions. The failed 1995 French public sector pension reform would not have modified political equilibria either, since the measures planned were the same as those adopted in 1993 for private sector employees. However, as seen in chapter 5, on that occasion, together with cuts in pensions, the government adopted a series of measures aimed at reducing the extent of control of the social partners on the health insurance scheme. This second series of measures, in contrast, did modify political equilibria, by strengthening the influence of the state and reducing that of the trade unions on future decisions concerning health insurance. This was one of the key factors that prompted the unions' hostile reaction.

Interestingly, of the four reforms reviewed here, the two which included elements likely to affect the politics of the relevant schemes were decided without concertation with external interests (UK and France 1995). In contrast the Swiss and French 1993 reforms, which were adopted after negotiations with the unions and included elements geared towards meeting some of their demands, did not significantly influence political equilibria. It seems thus that reforms which alter the fundamental structure of a scheme, and thereby modify the politics surrounding it, are more likely to be implemented by governments which can afford to exclude external interests from policy-making.

This result could have some important implications for the future of the welfare state. First, since structural change is more likely in countries with a strong concentration of power in the executive, it seems plausible to assume that, even if current socio-economic conditions persist, we are unlikely to see convergence among welfare states. Instead, what this hypothesis would suggest is the persistence of the basic features of current welfare arrangements in countries where power is fragmented (such as Switzerland, possibly Germany) and their possible abandonment in countries where power is concentrated with the government (UK).

### Quid pro quos

Besides timing and scale of policy change, the analysis of four pension reforms in three countries has pointed out that, when policy-making is inclusive, policy outcomes tend to combine saving measures with either elements of expansion (Switzerland) or elements which meet the demands of key actors (the trade unions in the 1993 French reform). To some extent this observation is rather obvious. In fact, the inclusion of external interests in policy-making is often achieved by making concessions to those actors who favour existing arrangements. Nevertheless, *quid pro quos* are not the only possible way to include external interests. An alternative strategy could be that of reducing the amount of cuts planned after negotiations with the trade unions. However, this second approach was not used in either of the two relevant instances covered by this study. While moderation in cuts might be an effective strategy for governments wishing to reform their pension systems without upsetting public opinion or key political actors, there are a number of reasons to believe that the inclusion of *quid pro quos* is a more effective tool to reach the same goal. In the cases of both Switzerland and France 1993, the concessions made to the left and to the unions concerned a long-lasting request of the latter.

In the Swiss case, the unions and the Socialist Party had been arguing for an improvement in the situation of women in the basic pension scheme for more than a decade. In such a context, to oppose reform, and thus to reduce the chances of the new pension legislation to be adopted, would have put the left in a difficult situation with public opinion, with the risk of being held responsible for the possible failure to improve women's situation in retirement. Through its strategy of combining elements of retrenchment and expansion within a single piece of legislation, the right-wing majority managed to secure sufficient support for its reform plans and to win the referendum.

In the French case, the 1993 reform also included an element which was known to be palatable to the trade unions. The creation of a new 'old age solidarity fund' intended to finance non-contributory pensions was de facto a recognition of the division of tasks between the social partners and the state, the former being responsible for social insurance and the latter for non-contributory provision. Such a distinction had been one of the key demands of the labour movement in the previous years, since it provided a guarantee that they would continue to fulfil their managing role in the old age branch of social insurance. To oppose this legislation would have been against the self-interest of the unions' leadership.

In this respect, the inclusion in pension reforms of carefully selected elements able to attract the approval of key actors (France 1993), or the combination of elements of expansion and of retrenchment within a single piece of legislation (Switzerland), has certainly contributed to strengthen the potential support of otherwise politically difficult reforms. Possibly, given the impressive level of controversy generated by the pension reform issue, the combination of retrenchment with *quid pro quos* might be a pattern for the future of pension policy in countries which lack the level of power concentration needed to impose new legislation without the support or acquiescence of external groups.

The sort of *quid pro quos* that are likely to be adopted in different countries seems to be related, among other things, to the institutional design of the scheme that is being reformed. Different institutional structures are likely to provide different opportunities for *quid pro quos*. For example, the trading of cuts with guarantees on the management side of the pension scheme which occurred in the 1993 French reform would not be an available option in countries where the labour movement is not involved in social insurance management. The next stage of the present discussion, thus, is to identify what sort of institutional opportunities for *quid pro quos* exist in different pension systems.

## 6.5     Pension scheme design and opportunities for *quid pro quos*

There are at least two reasons which suggest that the institutional design of a pension scheme has an impact on the sort of *quid pro quos* that are available to policy-makers to gain trade unions' support or acquiescence for their pension reform plans. First, the interests and the stakes that the various relevant actors have in a scheme depend to a large extent on the role they play within that scheme. As seen in chapter 5, the French trade unions, which are involved in the management of the whole social security system, have consistently shown a strong attachment to their role. Second, depending on the structure of the scheme, some groups are likely to fare better than others. As a result those who are disadvantaged can be convinced to support retrenchment if they see their position improved.

In this respect, it seems that the distinction between pension schemes of Bismarckian and Beveridgean inspiration (see chs. 1 and 2) might bear some relevance with regard to what sort of *quid pro quos* are likely to be demanded by the trade unions, or by other relevant pressure groups, and conceded by governments. The sample selected for this study includes countries which reflect the principles of each model. France reflects many features of the Bismarckian model. Switzerland, because it has a ceiling on benefits, does not exactly respect the Bismarckian principle of equivalence between contributions and benefits, but comes nevertheless nearer to the Bismarckian end of the spectrum in so far as entitlement and financing are concerned. Britain comes closer to the Beveridgean model.

Because in the British case the government did not include elements aimed at meeting the demands of the unions (nor of other external interests), it is difficult on the basis of this study to identify opportunities for *quid pro quos* in Beveridgean countries. In contrast, the presence of two Bismarckian-leaning countries in the sample makes possible the identification of likely patterns of *quid pro quos* in such countries.

### Quid pro quos *in Bismarckian countries*

As pointed out elsewhere (Bonoli *et al.* 1996), trade unions in Bismarckian countries tend to view insurance-based pension schemes as some sort of collective insurance plan covering all salaried employees (and the self-employed if included). As a result they generally disagree with governments when they use insurance-based schemes for general social policy purposes, such as poverty alleviation in old age. This is not only the case in France (see ch. 6) but also in countries like Germany and Italy. For instance, the German trade unions opposed their government's decision to apply a non-contributory eligibility criterion to social insurance benefits in the former East Germany after the unification (ibid.: 8). Similarly, in Italy, in the negotiations which led to the 1995 pension reform, a key demand of the labour movement was that the state take financial responsibility for the non-contributory elements of the insurance-based pension scheme (*La Repubblica* 14 March 1995).

There are two possible reasons behind this common position of trade unions in Bismarckian countries. First, the exclusion of non-contributory elements from the main scheme means a stricter correspondence between the contribution-payer community and the beneficiaries. This reduces the size of the transfer of resources from workers to other categories and increases the financial capacity of insurance-based schemes. Second, since in Bismarckian countries the trade unions are generally involved in the management of social insurance, a strict separation between non-contributory and insurance-based provision constitutes a de facto acceptance of their role. This second factor is especially strong in France (see also Myles and Pierson 1998).

In this respect, the institutional design of pension schemes of Bismarckian inspiration offers governments the opportunity to trade concessions on the separation between insurance-based and non-contributory provision with a reduction in the generosity of pension provision. This combination of measures aiming in different directions can attract the support or the acquiescence of the labour movement. The compromise is likely to satisfy both governments and unions. The former, without additional spending (expenditure is simply transferred from the social insurance to general government budget), is able to secure at least the acquiescence of the labour movement; the latter see financial pressure on insurance-based schemes reduced and as a result further retrenchment less likely. This sort of *quid pro quo*, however, has the disadvantage of being available only once. When the separation between insurance-based and non-contributory provision has been fully achieved, scope for such compromises is exhausted.

The Swiss case points in another possible direction for *quid pro quos* in Bismarckian countries. Since in these systems entitlement to benefits is based on the payment of work-related contributions, groups with discontinuous employment patterns fare generally less well than those with 'standard' careers. This is particularly the case for women. The situation of women in retirement, however, can be improved through the introduction of contribution credits and/or contribution sharing between spouses/partners. Both measures take into account the peculiarity of women's career patterns, by compensating for periods of inactivity.

Bismarckian pension schemes, although they were designed with the male breadwinner model in mind, can be corrected and made more responsive to women's needs.

Progress towards gender equality in retirement can be also be used by governments to obtain support or acquiescence of progressive groups to their plan for pension reform. Generally, left-wing parties and trade unions are particularly sensitive to the issue of gender equality. If given the opportunity to achieve this objective in provision for retirement, these groups might accept cuts in the overall generosity of a pension scheme which they would otherwise oppose. This is precisely what happened in Switzerland in the 1995 pension reform. The Swiss case, however, is rather peculiar because the level of gender inequality before the reform was particularly strong and seen as unacceptable by large sections of the population. Possibly, the sort of *quid pro quo* seen in the Swiss case is more likely to occur when discrimination against women is strong. Countries which have already taken steps towards gender equality are obviously less likely to reach a compromise on pension reform in this way.

### 6.6    Political institutions and the future of retirement

This study has emphasised the potential for policy change embodied in different political systems. In particular, it has argued that the view of a frozen welfare landscape in much of continental Europe is inaccurate. Despite having to overcome significant political obstacles, governments enjoying low levels of power concentration and reforming pension schemes with high degrees of middle-class integration have been able to achieve some change. This might be good news for the welfare state, as the inability to adapt to new international and domestic contexts might in the long term lead to a collapse of the whole welfare system (Taylor-Gooby 1996; Ferrera 1998). This view contrasts with the pessimism suggested by the pension expenditure projections presented in chapter 1. Although it is true that the levels of spending expected around the year 2020 seem unsustainable, there are good reasons to believe that these projections are a purely theoretical exercise, as the various countries will never get to that point.

The adaptation process, however, is likely to follow slightly different paths, depending on the degree of power concentration enjoyed by governments. In particular, radical and unilateral reforms may not be 'politically feasible' in countries in which constitutional arrangements encourage power-sharing. This could simply mean that in these countries the adaptation process of welfare states will take longer, but will eventually produce the same results obtained in countries with strong power concentration. However, the fact that power-fragmented systems tend to combine retrenchment with *quid pro quos* could result in an alternative path to adaptation, which combines the requirements of economic competitiveness with responses to emerging needs. Trading cuts in provision with an improvement of women's treatment (as happened in the Swiss reform) could be an example. If this pattern of *quid pro quos* is to be reproduced elsewhere, the adaptation process of pension policy might include a dimension of modernisation, which implies that the new needs and aspirations of citizens are taken into account.

A negotiated approach to pension reform might also constitute a safeguard against overreaction in dealing with the pension problem. Overreaction is arguably what happened in the 1986 British reform, and that is why the Labour government of the late 1990s has been forced to intervene again in pension policy. While the Thatcher government managed to deal with the financial side of the pension issue, it created new problems in relation to coverage, especially for people on low income and with discontinuous career patterns. Although many did point to this issue during the debate that preceded the adoption of the 1986 Social Security Act, they had little opportunity to influence the course of policy. If this had happened in a country in which political institutions provide veto points, their impact on legislation could have been substantial.

If consensus does produce results qualitatively different from those of confrontation, perhaps the expected convergence in pension policy due to common socio-economic pressures will not materialise. While in the past the main obstacle to convergence has been politics, there are strong reasons to believe that in the current and future phase of welfare restructuring this key role will be played by formal institutions. As socio-economic pressures due to ageing and globalisation intensify, the room for manoeuvre allowed to left-wing parties in government diminishes. As a result, although in the late 1990s the left has been very successful in a large number of European countries, the sort of policies adopted when in government are not significantly different from those enacted by their right-wing predecessors. The result is a change in the configuration of welfare politics: the classical opposition left–right is being replaced by a confrontation between governments (regardless of political persuasion) and a pro-welfare coalition, generally led by the labour movement. This pattern of political confrontation has long been the case in France, which has been ruled by the left for most of the 1980s, and has become clear in Italy and Britain as left-of-centre governments have been voted into power in these countries. As the political orientation of governments loses relevance as a determinant of the direction of policy, the role played by formal institutions is likely to become more visible.

# References

Abel-Smith, B. and Townsend, P. (1984) 'Introduction: Challenging Government Assumptions', in *Social Security: The Real Agenda*, London, Fabian Society Tract No. 498.

Age Concern (1982) 'Submission of Evidence to the Social Service Committee, Third Report, Age of Retirement', in United Kingdom, Social Services Select Committee 1982, HC 26–2.

(1984) *Submission of Evidence to the Inquiry into Provision for Retirement*, London, Age Concern.

(1985) *Green Paper Will Not Solve Pensioner Poverty*, press release, 3 June.

(1986) *SERPS Changes Cause Deep Concern*, press release, 28 January.

Alber, J. (1986) 'Germany', in P. Flora (ed.) *Growth to Limits*, vol. II, Florence, European University Institute, 4–149.

Artoni, R. and Zanardi, A. (1997) 'The Evolution of the Italian Pension System', in Mission de Recherche et Experimentation (ed.) *Comparing Welfare States in Southern Europe*, Paris, Mission de Recherche et Experimentation, 243–66.

Atkinson, T. (1994) *State Pensions for Today and Tomorrow*, London, Welfare State Programme Discussion Paper No. 104.

Badie, B. and Birnbaum, P. (1983) *The Sociology of the State*, Chicago, University of Chicago Press.

Baldwin, P. (1990) *The Politics of Social Solidarity*, Cambridge, Cambridge University Press.

Banting, K. and Boadway, R. (eds.) *Reform of Retirement Income Policy: International and Canadian Perspectives*, Kingston (Ontario), Queen's University, School of Policy Studies.

BBC (1996) *Consequences: Personal Pensions*, Radio 4, broadcast 27 January.

Bernstein, A. (1986) *L'assurance-vieillesse suisse, son elaboration et son évolution*, Lausanne, Réalités Sociales.

Beveridge, W. (1942) *Social Security and Allied Services*, London, HMSO.

Bigaut, C. (1995) 'Les cohabitations institutionnelles de 1986–1988 et 1993–1995', *Regards sur l'actualité*, 211, 3–30.

Binswanger, P. (1987) *Histoire de l'AVS*, Zurich, Pro Senectute.

Bonoli, G. (1997a) 'Classifying Welfare States: A Two-Dimension Approach', *Journal of Social Policy*, 26, 3, 351–72.

(1997b) 'Switzerland: The Politics of Consensual Retrenchment', in Clasen 1997b, 107–29.

Bonoli, G., George, V. and Taylor-Gooby, P. (1996) 'Politics Against Convergence?: Current Trends in European Social Policy', *Swiss Political Science Review*, 2, 3, 1–17.

Bonoli, G. and Palier, B. (1997) 'Reclaiming Welfare: The Politics of Social Protection Reform in France', in M. Rhodes (ed.) *Southern European Welfare States: Between Crisis and Reform*, London, Francis Cass, 240–59.

(1998) 'Changing the Politics of Social Programmes: Innovative Change in British and French Welfare Reforms', *Journal of European Social Policy*, 8, 4, 317–30.

Brown, J. (1990) *Social Security for Retirement*, York, Joseph Rowntree Foundation.

Budge, I. (1996) 'Great Britain and Ireland: Variations on Dominant Party Government', in Colomer 1996, 18–61.

Bull, M. and Rhodes, M. (eds.) *Crisis and Transition in Italian Politics*, London, Frank Cass.

Calot, G. and Sardon, J.-P. (1996) 'Etonnante fécondité suédoise', *Futuribles*, 127, 5–15.

Castles, F. (ed.) (1982) *The Impact of Parties*, London, Sage.

Cattacin, S. (1996) 'Die Transformation des schweizer Sozialstaates', *Swiss Political Science Review*, 2, 1, 89–102.

Chadelat, J.-F. (1994) 'Le Fonds de solidarité vieillesse', *Droit social*, 7–8, 727–33.

Chassard, Y. and Quintin, O. (1992) 'Social Protection in the European Community: Towards a Convergence of Policies', *International Social Security Review*, 45, 1–2, 91–108.

Chatagner, F. (1993) *La protection sociale*, Paris, Editions le Monde.

Chirac, J. (1987) Letter to the members of the Committee of Wise Men of the *Etats Généraux* of Social Security, 17 April.

Church, C. (1995) 'The Crisis of Konkordanz Democracy in Switzerland', paper presented at workshop on 'Consociationalism, Parties and Party Systems', European Consortium for Political Research, Bordeaux.

Clasen, J. (1997a) 'Social Insurance: An Outdated Policy Design?', in Clasen 1997b, 1–13.

(1997b) (ed.) *Social Insurance in Europe*, Bristol, Policy Press.

Colomer, J. (1996) (ed.) *Political Institutions in Europe*, London, Routledge.

Confédération Française Démocratique des Travailleurs (CFDT) (1989) 'Position de la CFDT sur le rapport de la Commission Protection sociale du Xème plan', in France, CGP 1989.

Confédération Générale du Travail (CGT) (1989) 'Positions de la CGT sur le Xème plan', in France, CGP 1989.

Confederation of British Industry (CBI) (1984) *CBI Evidence to the Government's Special Inquiry into Pension Provision*, London (unpublished document).

(1985) *CBI Response to the Green Paper*, London (unpublished document).

(1986) *CBI Response to the Social Security Bill*, London (unpublished document).

Conseil National du Patronnat Français (CNPF) (1989) 'Lettre de M. Pierre Guillen, Président de la Commission sociale du CNPF à M. René Teulade, President de la Commission Protection sociale en date du 23 juin 1989', in France, CGP 1989.

Conservative Party (1983) *The Conservative Manifesto 1983*, Conservative Central Office, London.

Cutright, P. (1965) 'Political Structure, Economic Development, and National Social Security Programs', *American Journal of Sociology*, 70, 537–50.

Davis, E. P. (1997) *Private Pensions in OECD Countries: The United Kingdom*, Paris, OECD, Labour Market and Social Policy Occasional Paper No. 21.

Desai, R. (1994) 'Second-Hand Dealers in Ideas: Think-Tanks and Thatcherite Hegemony', *New Left Review*, 203, 27–64.

Dilnot, A. (1997) 'Public and Private Roles in the Provision of Retirement Income', in Banting and Boadway 1997, 49–61.

Dupeyroux, J.-J. and Prétot, X. (1993) *Droit de la sécurité sociale*, Paris, Dalloz.

Duverger, M. (1963) *Political Parties: Their Organization and Activity in the Modern State*, New York, Wiley.

(1987) *La cohabitation des Français*, Paris, Presses Universitaires de France.

Ermisch, J. (1983) *The Political Economy of Demographic Change*, London, Heinemann.

(1990) *Fewer Babies, Longer Lives*, York, Rowntree Foundation.

Esping-Andersen, G. (1985) *Politics Against Markets*, Princeton, Princeton University Press.

(1990) *The Three Worlds of Welfare Capitalism*, Cambridge, Polity.

(1996a) (ed.) *Welfare States in Transition: National Adaptations in Global Economies*, London, Sage.

(1996b) 'Welfare States Without Work: The Impasse of Labour Shedding and Familialism in Continental European Social Policy', in Esping-Andersen 1996a, 66–87.

European Commission (1995) *Social Protection in Europe 1995*, Brussels, European Commission.

Ferrera, M. (1993a) *EU Citizens and Social Protection*, Brussels, European Commission.

(1993b) *Modelli di solidarietà*, Bologna, Il Mulino.

(1996a) 'Modèles de solidarité, divergences, convergences: perspectives pour l'Europe', *Swiss Political Science Review*, 2, 1, 55–72.

(1996b) 'The Southern Model of Welfare in Social Europe', *Journal of European Social Policy*, 6, 1, 17–37.

(1997) 'The Uncertain Future of the Italian Welfare State', in Bull and Rhodes 1997, 231–49.

(1998) *Le trappole del welfare: uno stato sociale sostenibile per l'Europa del XXI secolo*, Bologna, Il Mulino.

Field, F. (1996) *Stakeholder Welfare*, London, Institute of Economic Affairs.

Force Ouvrière (FO) (1989) 'Position de la Confédération Générale du Travail Force Ouvrière', in France, CGP 1989.

Foucault, J.-B. de (1994) 'Document de travail du Commissaire au Plan: pistes de reflection sur le financement de la protection sociale', *Liaisons sociales*, Supplément No. 119.

France, Caisse Nationale d'Assurance Vieillesse (CNAV) (1993) 'Internal memorandum' dated 18 May.

France, Comité des sages (1987) *Rapport du Comité des sages des Etats Généraux de la sécurité sociale*, Paris, La Documentation Française.

France, Commissariat Général au Plan (CGP) (1986) *Vieillir solidaires*, Paris, La Documentation Française.

(1989) *Protection sociale: rapport de la commission présidée par M. René Teulade*, Paris, La Documentation Française.

(1991) *Livre blanc sur les retraites*, Rapports officiels, Paris, La Documentation Française.

France, Gouvernement Français (1995) 'Plan pour la réforme de la protection sociale (Plan Juppé)', press release, 15 November.

George, V. (1998) 'Political Ideology, Globalisation and Welfare Futures in Europe', *Journal of Social Policy*, 17, 1, 17–36.

George, V., Taylor-Gooby, P. and Bonoli, G. (1995) *Squaring the Welfare Circle in Europe: The Working Papers*, Canterbury, University of Kent (mimeo).

Germann, R. (1982) *Ausserparlamentarische Kommissionen: Die Milizverwaltung des Bundes*, Berne, Haupt.

Gilliand, P. (1988) *Politique sociale en Suisse*, Lausanne, Réalités Sociales.

Goldthorpe, J. (1984) (ed.) *Order and Conflict in Contemporary Capitalism*, Oxford, Clarendon Press.

Gough, I. (1996) 'Social Welfare and Competitiveness', *New Political Economy*, 1, 2, 210–32.

Gough, O. and Shackleton, J. R. (1996) 'The Pensions Act 1995: Unfinished Business?', *Public Money and Management*, 16, 3, 41–8.

Guillemard, A.-M. (1986) *Le declin du social*, Paris, Presses Universitaires de France.

Hall, P. (1986) *Governing the Economy: The Politics of State Intervention in Britain and France*, Cambridge, Polity Press.

(1989) (ed.) *The Political Power of Economic Ideas: Keynesianism Across Nations*, Princeton, Princeton University Press.

(1992) 'The Movement from Keynesianism to Monetarism: Institutional Analysis and British Economic Policy in the 1970s', in Steinmo et al. 1992, 90–113.

Hall, P. and Taylor, R. (1996) 'Political Science and the Three New Institutionalisms', *Political Studies*, 44, 5, 936–57.

Hannah, L. (1986) *Inventing Retirement*, Cambridge, Cambridge University Press.

Hayward, J. and Klein, R. (1994) 'Grande Bretagne: de la gestion publique à la gestion privée du déclin économique', in Jobert 1994, 87–122.

Heclo, H. (1974) *Modern Social Politics in Britain and Sweden*, New Haven, Yale University Press.

Hinrichs, K. (1998) *Reforming the Public Pension Scheme in Germany: The End of the Traditional Consensus?*, Bremen, Zes-Arbeitspapier No. 11/98.

Hirsch, M. (1993) *Les enjeux de la protection sociale*, Paris, Montchrestien.

Huber, E., Ragin, C. and Stephens, J. (1993) 'Social Democracy, Christian Democracy, Constitutional Structure and the Welfare State', *American Journal of Sociology*, 99, 3, 711–49.

Immergut, E. (1992) *Health Politics: Interests and Institutions in Western Europe*, Cambridge, Cambridge University Press.

Jessop, B., Bonnet, K., Bromley, S. and Ling, T. (1988) *Thatcherism: A Tale of Two Nations*, Cambridge, Polity Press.

Jobert, B. (1981) *Le social en plan*, Paris, Editions Ouvrières.

(1994) (ed.) *Le tournant néo-liberal en Europe*, Paris, L'Harmattan.

Johnson, P. and Falkingham, J. (1992) *Ageing and Economic Welfare*, London, Sage.

Join-Lambert, M.-T. (1994) *Politiques sociales*, Paris, Dalloz.

Kato, J. (1996) 'Review Article: Institutions and Rationality in Politics – Three Varieties of Neo-Institutionalism', *British Journal of Political Science*, 26, 4, 553–82.

Katzenstein, P. (1984) *Corporatism and Change: Austria, Switzerland, and the Politics of Industry*, Ithaca, Cornell University Press.

(1985) *Small States in World Markets: Industrial Policy in Europe*, Ithaca, Cornell University Press.

Kavanagh, D. (1990) *Thatcherism and British Politics: The End of Consensus?* (2nd edn), Oxford, Oxford University Press.

Kerschen, N. (1995) 'L'influence de rapport Beveridge sur le plan français de sécurité sociale de 1945', *Revue française de science politique*, 45, 4, 570–95.

King, D. (1995) *Actively Seeking Work?: The Politics of Unemployment and Welfare Policy in the United States and Great Britain*, Chicago, University of Chicago Press.

Klöti, U. (1984) *Handbuch politisches System der Schweiz: Strukturen und Prozesse*, Berne and Stuttgart, P. Haupt.

Kobach, K. (1993) *The Referendum: Direct Democracy in Switzerland*, Aldershot, Dartmouth.

Korpi, W. (1983) *The Democratic Class Struggle*, London, Routledge & Kegan.

Kosonen, P. (1994) *European Integration: A Welfare State Perspective*, Helsinki, University of Helsinki.

Kriesi, H.-P. (1994) *Les démocraties occidentales*, Paris, Economica.

(1995) *Le système politique suisse*, Paris, Economica.

Labour Party (1983) *The Labour Party Manifesto: New Hope for Britain*, London, Labour Party.

(1985) *Report of the Annual Conference of the Labour Party*, London, Labour Party.

(1987) *Labour Manifesto: Britain Will Win*, London, Labour Party.

Lehmbruch, G. (1979) 'Consociational Democracy, Class Conflict and the New Corporatism', in Schmitter and Lehmbruch 1979, 53–61.

(1984) 'Concertation and the Structure of Corporatist Networks', in Goldthorpe 1984, 60–80.

(1993) 'Consociational Democracy and Corporatism in Switzerland', *Publius: The Journal of Federalism*, 23, 43–60.

Lehmbruch, G. and Schmitter, P. (1982) (eds.) *Patterns of Corporatist Policy-Making*, London, Sage.

Lehner, F. (1984) 'Consociational Democracy in Switzerland: Political-Economic Explanation and Some Empirical Evidence', *European Journal of Political Research*, 12, 25–42.

Leibfried, S. (1992) 'Towards a European Welfare State?: On Integrating Poverty Regimes into the European Community', in Z. Ferge and J. Kolberg (eds.) *Social Policy in a Changing Europe*, Frankfurt, Campus Verlag, 245–79.

Lijphart, A. (1984) *Democracies: Pattern of Majoritarian and Consensus Government in Twenty-One Countries*, New Haven and London, Yale University Press.

Lijphart, A. and Crepaz, L. (1991) 'Corporatism and Consensus Democracy in Eighteen Countries: Conceptual and Empirical Linkages', *British Journal of Political Science*, 21, 235–56.

Longman, P. (1987) *Born to Pay: The New Politics of Ageing in America*, Boston, Houghton Mifflin.

Lusenti, G. (1989), *Les institutions de prevoyance en Suisse, au Royaume Uni et en Allemagne Federale*, Geneva, Georg.

March, J. and Olsen, J. (1984) 'The New Institutionalism: Organizational Factors in Political Life', *American Political Science Review*, 78, 4, 734–49.

(1989) *Rediscovering Institutions: The Organizational Basis of Politics*, New York, Free Press.

Meacher, M. (1991) 'Speech to the Association of Pension Lawyers', 9 May.

Merrien, F.-X. (1991) 'L'état par défaut', in J.-P. Durand and F.-X. Merrien (eds.) *Sortie de siècle: La France en mutation*, Paris, Vigot, 274–93.

Mission Cottave (1992) 'Rapport de la Mission Retraites', reproduced in *Droit social*, 2, 165–73.

Mitchell, D. (1991) *Income Transfers in Ten Welfare States*, Aldershot, Avebury.

Morgan, E. (1984) *Choice in Pensions: The Political Economy of Saving for Retirement*, London, Institute of Economic Affairs.

Myles, J. (1984) *Old Age in the Welfare State*, Boston, Little Brown & Co.

Myles, J. and Pierson, P. (1998) 'The Political Economy of Pension Reform', paper presented at the workshop 'The New Politics of the Welfare State', Center for European Studies, Harvard University, Cambridge, MA, 30 October–1 November.

Myles, J. and Quadagno, J. (1997) 'Recent Trends in Public Pension Reform: A Comparative View', in Banting and Boadway 1997, 247–72.

National Association of Pension Funds (NAPF) (1984) 'NAPF Evidence on Personal Portable Pensions', reproduced in *Pensions World*, 13, 2, 65–8.

(1985) 'NAPF Response to the Green Paper' (abstract), reproduced in *Pensions World*, 14, 11, 696–9.

Neidhart, L. (1970) *Plebiszit und pluralitäre Democratie: Eine Analyse der Funktionen des schweizerischen Gesetzreferendums*, Berne, Francke.

Nesbitt, S. (1995) *British Pension Policy Making in the 1980s: The Rise and Fall of a Policy Community*, Aldershot, Avebury.

Niemelä, H. and Salminen, K. (1995) *How to Define a Pension Scheme*, Helsinki, Social Insurance Institution, Social Security and Health Reports No. 3.

North, D. (1990) *Institutions, Institutional Change, and Economic Performance*, Cambridge, Cambridge University Press.

Occupational Pensions Board (OPB) (1981) *Improved Protection for the Occupational Pension Rights and Expectations of Early Leavers*, London, HMSO, Cmnd 8271.

Organisation for Economic Co-operation and Development (OECD) (1988a) *Ageing Populations: The Social Policy Implications*, Paris, OECD.

(1988b) *Reforming Public Pensions*, Paris, OECD.

(1994) *New Orientations for Social Policy*, Paris, OECD.

(1995) 'Effect of Ageing Populations on Government Budgets', *Economic Outlook*, 57, 33–42.

Oudin, J. (1992) *Rapport d'information sur les aspects financiers de la protection sociale*, Paris, French Government.

Overbye, E. (1996a) 'The New Zealand Pension System in an International Context: An Outsider's View', *Social Policy Journal of New Zealand*, 6, 23–42.

(1996b) 'Pension Politics in the Nordic Countries: A Case Study', *International Political Science Review*, 17, 1, 67–90.

Palier, B. (1991) *La baleine et les sages*, unpublished DEA thesis, Paris, Institut d'Etudes Politiques.

(1999) *Réformer la sécurité sociale: les interventions gouvernementales en matière de protection sociale depuis 1945, la France en perspective comparative*, Paris, Institut d'études politiques, Ph.D dissertation.

Palme, J. (1990) *Pension Rights in Welfare Capitalism*, Stockholm, Swedish Institute for Social Research.

Palme, J. and Wennemo, I. (1997) *Swedish Social Security in the 1990s: Reform and Retrenchment*, Stockholm, Swedish Institute for Social Research (mimeo).

Papadopoulos, Y. (1996) 'Les mécanismes du vote référendaire en Suisse: l'impact de l'offre politique', *Revue française de sociologie*, 37, 5–35.

Parti Démocrate-Chrétien (PDC) (1988) 'Thèses sur la 10e révision de l'AVS', *Le point de vue du PDC*, No. 38, Berne.

Parti Radical Démocratique (PRD) (1988) 'Avenir de l'AVS: rapport final d'un groupe de travail du Parti radical-démocratique suisse', *Revue politique*, 67, 2, 34–45.

Parti Socialiste Suisse (PSS) (1995) *Presse Dienst. Sonderausgabe: 10. AHV-Revision*, No. 406/407, Berne.

Parti Socialiste Suisse/Union Syndicale Suisse (PSS/USS) (1987) *Droits égaux dans l'AVS: propositions du Parti socialiste suisse et de l'Union syndicale suisse pour la révision de l'AVS*, PSS/USS, Berne.

Pierson, P. (1994) *Dismantling the Welfare State?: Reagan, Thatcher and the Politics of Retrenchment*, Cambridge, Cambridge University Press.

(1996) 'The New Politics of the Welfare State', *World Politics*, 48, 2, 143–79.

(1997a) *Increasing Returns, Path Dependence and the Study of Politics*, Florence, European University Institute, Jean Monnet Chair Paper No. 44.

(1997b) 'The Politics of Pension Reform', in Banting and Boadway 1997, 273–94.

Pierson, P. and Weaver, K. (1993) 'Imposing Losses in Pension Policy', in Weaver and Rockman 1993b, 110–50.

Poitry, A.-V. (1989) *La fonction d'ordre de l'état: analyse des mécanismes et des déterminants sélectifs dans le processus législatif suisse*, Berne, Lang.

Quadagno, J. (1989) 'Generational Equity and the Politics of the Welfare State', *Politics and Society*, 17, 3, 353–76.

Rake, K. (1996) 'Ageing and Inequality: How Older Women and Men Fare in Britain, France and Germany', paper presented at the Social Policy Association annual conference, Sheffield Hallam University, Sheffield, 16–18 July.

Randall's Parliamentary Services (1986) *Comparison of Party Policies: Pension Policies*, n.p.

Reddin, M. (1985) *Can We Afford Our Future?*, London, Age Concern.

Regini, M. (1984) 'The Conditions for Political Exchange: How Concertation Emerged and Collapsed in Italy and Great Britain', in Goldthorpe 1984, 124–42.

Regini, M. and Regalia, I. (1997) 'Employers, Unions and the State: The Resurgence of Concertation in Italy?', in Bull and Rhodes 1997, 210–30.

Reynaud, E. (1994) *Les retraites complémentaires en France*, Paris, La Documentation Française.

Rhodes, M. (1996) 'Globalization and West European Welfare States: A Critical Review of Recent Debates', *Journal of European Social Policy*, 6, 4, 305–27.

Riddel, P. (1989) *The Thatcher Decade: How Britain Has Changed During the 1980s*, London, Blackwell.

Rosanvallon, P. (1995) *La nouvelle question sociale: repenser l'Etat-Providence*, Paris, Seuil.

Roseveare, P., Leibfritz, W., Fore, D. and Wurzel, E. (1996) *Ageing Populations, Pension Systems and Government Budgets: Simulation for 20 OECD Countries*, Paris, OECD, Economic Department Working Papers No. 168.

Ruellan, R. (1993) 'Retraites: l'impossible réforme est-elle achevée?', *Droit social*, 12, 911–29.

Saint-Jours, Y. (1982) 'France', in P. Koehler and H. Zacher (eds.) *The Evolution of Social Insurance, 1881–1981*, London, Frances Pinter, 93–148.

Salminen, K. (1993) *Pension Schemes in the Making: A Comparative Study of Scandinavian Countries*, Helsinki, Central Pension Security Institute.

Saunders, P. (1995) 'Privatization, Share Ownership and Voting', *British Journal of Political Science*, 25, 131–43.

Scharpf, F. (1997a) 'Economic Integration, Democracy and the Welfare State', *Journal of European Public Policy*, 4, 1, 18–36.

(1997b) *Games Real Actors Play: Actor Centered Institutionalism in Policy Research*, Oxford, Westview Press.

Schmähl, W. (1990) 'Demographic Change and Social Security: Some Elements of a Complex Relationship', *Journal of Population Economics*, 3, 159–77.

(1991) (ed.) *The Future of Basic and Supplementary Pensions Schemes in the European Community – 1992 and Beyond*, Baden-Baden, Nomos, 1991.

(1993) 'The 1992 Reform of Public Pensions in Germany: Main Elements and Some Effects', *Journal of European Social Policy*, 3, 1, 39–52.

Schmidt, M. (1996) 'Germany: The Grand Coalition State', in Colomer 1996, 62–98.

Schmitter, P. (1982) 'Reflections on Where the Theory of Neo-corporatism Has Gone and Where the Praxis of Neo-corporatism May Be Going', in Lehmbruch and Schmitter 1982.

Schmitter, P. and Lehmbruch, G. (1979) (eds.) *Trends Toward Corporatist Intermediation*, London, Sage.

Schopflin, P. (1987) *Rapport de la commission d'évaluation et de sauvegarde de l'assurance vieillesse*, Paris, La Documentation Française.

Shonfield, A. (1965) *Modern Capitalism: The Changing Balance of Public and Private Power*, Oxford, Oxford University Press.

Silburn, R. (1995) 'Beveridge', in V. George and R. Page (eds.) *Modern Thinkers on Welfare*, Hemel Hempstead, Harvester and Wheatsheaf, 84–101.

Skocpol, T. (1985) 'Bringing the State back in', in P. Evans, D. Rueschemeyer, and T. Skocpol (eds.) *Bringing the State back in*, Cambridge, Cambridge University Press, 3–43.

(1995) *Social Policy in the United States*, Princeton, Princeton University Press.

Skocpol, T. and Amenta, E. (1986) 'States and Social Policies', *Annual Review of Sociology*, 12, 131–57.

Stahlberg, A.-C. (1997) 'Sweden: On the Way from Standard to Basic Security?', in Clasen 1997b, 40–59.

Steinmo, S., Thelen, K. and Longstreth, F. (1992) (eds.) *Structuring Politics: Historical Institutionalism in Comparative Analysis*, Cambridge, Cambridge University Press.

Stephens, J. (1979) *The Transition from Capitalism to Socialism*, Urbana, University of Illinois Press.

(1996) 'The Scandinavian Welfare States: Achievements, Crisis, and Prospects', in Esping-Andersen 1996a, 32–65.

Stone, A. (1992) 'Le néo-institutionalisme: défis conceptuels et méthodologiques', *Politix*, 20, 156–68.

Sturm, P. (1992) 'Population Ageing and Old-Age Income Maintenance: Basic Facts and Problems', in J. Mortensen (ed.) *The Future of Pensions in the European Community*, London, Brassey's, 23–38.

Switzerland, Commission Fédérale pour les Questions Féminines (CFQF) (1988), 'Propositions de la Commission fédérale pour les questions féminines en vue de la 10e révision de l'AVS', *Questions au féminin*, 1, 88.

Switzerland, Conseil National, Groupe de Travail 'Splitting' (1992) *Rapport final du Groupe de travail 'splitting' de la Commission du Conseil national*, 92.149, Berne.

Switzerland, Office Fédéral des Assurances Sociales (OFAS) (1991) *Comparaison entre les modèles de 'splitting'*, 91.656, Berne, OFAS.

(1993) *Rapport concernant les principes et les effets d'une rente unique*, 93.561, Berne, OFAS.

(1995) *Rapport du Département fédéral de l'intérieur concernant la structure actuelle et le développement futur de la conception helvétique des trois piliers de la prévoyance vieillesse, survivants et invalidité*, 318.012.1/ 95 f, Berne, OFAS.

Taylor-Gooby, P. (1996) 'Eurosclerosis in European Welfare States: Regime Theory and the Dynamics of Change', *Policy and Politics*, 24, 2, 109–23.

Télévision Suisse Romande (1995), *AVS 10e, 62 ou 64?*, 10 June.

Thelen, K. and Steinmo, S. (1992) 'Historical Institutionalism in Comparative Politics', in Steinmo et al. 1992, 1–32.

Thurow, L. (1996) *The Future of Capitalism*, London, Nicholas Brealy Publishing.

Trades Union Congress (TUC) (1982) 'Submission of Evidence to the Social Service Committee, Third Report, Age of Retirement', in United Kingdom, Social Services Select Committee 1982, HC 26–2.

(1984a) 'Pensions at the TUC 1984', *Pensions World*, 14, 11, 706–8.

(1984b) 'TUC Submission of Evidence to the Inquiry into Provision for Retirement' (abstract), *Pensions World*, 13, 4, 208.

(1985) 'TUC Response to SERPS Proposals', *Pensions World*, 15, 11, 822.

Tsebelis, G. (1995) 'Decision Making in Political Systems: Veto Players in Presidentialism, Parliamentarism, Multicameralism and Multipartism', *British Journal of Political Science*, 25, 3, 289–325.

United Kingdom, Department of Health and Social Security (DHSS) (1983) *Reply to the Third Report of the Social Services Committee*, London, HMSO, Cmnd 9095.

(1984a) *Personal Pensions: A Consultative Document*, London, HMSO.

(1984b) *Population, Pension Costs and Pensioners' Incomes: A Background Paper for the Inquiry into Provision for Retirement*, London, HMSO.

(1985a) *A Programme for Action, White Paper*, London, HMSO, Cmnd 9691.

(1985b) *Reform of Social Security, Green Paper* (3 vols.), London, HMSO, Cmnd 9517–9.

United Kingdom, Department of Social Security (DSS) (1996) *Social Security Statistics 1996*, London, HMSO.

(1998) *A New Contract for Welfare Partnership in Pensions*, London, HMSO, Cm 4179.

United Kingdom, Government Actuary (1982) *National Insurance Fund Long Term Financial Estimates*, London, HMSO, HC 451.

United Kingdom, Social Services Select Committee (1982), *The Age of Retirement (Third Report)*, 2 vols., London, HMSO, HC 26–1, 2.

United Kingdom, Treasury Department (1984) *The Next Ten Years: Public Expenditure and Taxation into the 1990s*, London, HMSO.

Vinson, N. and Chapell, P. (1983) *Personal and Portable Pensions for All*, London, Centre for Policy Studies.

Vox (1995) *Analyse des votations fédérales du 25 juin 1996*, No. 57, Berne.

Waine, B. (1995) 'A Disaster Foretold?: The Case of Personal Pensions', *Social Policy and Administration*, 29, 4, 317–34.

Walker, A. (1991) 'Thatcherism and the Politics of Old Age', in J. Myles and J. Quadagno (eds.) *States, Labour Markets, and the Future of Old Age Policy*, Philadelphia, Temple University Press, 19–35.

(1993) 'Living Standards and Way of Life', in European Commission, *Older People in Europe: Social and Economic Policies*, Brussels, European Commission, 8–33.

(1994) *My Mother and My Father's Keeper?: The Social and Economic Features of Intergenerational Solidarity*, Helsinki, National Research Centre for Welfare and Health.

Ward, S. (1985) 'Introduction: The Political Background', in S. Ward (ed.), *DHSS in Crisis: Social Security Under Pressure and Under Review*, London, Child Poverty Action Group, 1–12.

Weaver, K. and Rockman, B. (1993a) 'Assessing the Effect of Institutions', in Weaver and Rockman 1993b, 1–41.

(1993b) (eds.) *Do Institutions Matter?: Government Capabilities in the United States and Abroad*, Washington, DC, Brookings Institution.

Whiteford, P. and Kennedy, S. (1995) *Incomes and Living Standards of Older People*, DSS, Research Report 34, London, HMSO.

Wilensky, H. (1975) *The Welfare State and Equality*, Berkeley, University of California Press.

Wilson, F. L. (1987) *Interest-Group Politics in France*, Cambridge, Cambridge University Press.

World Bank (1994a) *Averting the Old Age Crisis*, Oxford, Oxford University Press.

(1994b) *World Population Projections*, Washington, DC, World Bank.

## NEWSPAPERS AND NON-ACADEMIC PERIODICALS

### FRANCE

*Le Monde*, 1988–96.

### SWITZERLAND

*Bulletin Officiel de l'Assemblée Fédérale. Conseil des Etats (BOAF.CdE).*
*Bulletin Officiel de l'Assemblée Fédérale. Conseil National (BOAF.CN).*
*Feuille Fédérale (FF)*, Berne. Various issues.
*L'Hebdo*, 1990–6.
*Le Nouveau Quotidien*, 1992–6.
*Sécurité sociale*, periodical published by the Office Fédéral des Assurances Sociales, various issues.

### UNITED KINGDOM

*Economist*, 1983–7.
*Financial Times*, 1983–7.
*Guardian*, 1983–7.
Hansard, *Parliamentary Debates*, various issues.
*Keesing's Archives of World Events*, various issues.

# Index

185